SHEOL KNOW:

The "Intermediate State"
Between Death and Resurrection

Dirk Waren

Soaring Eagle Press
Youngstown

Sheol Know!

ISBN: 978-0692466971
PUBLISHED BY SOARING EAGLE PRESS
Youngstown

Printed in the United States of America

*"...and death and Hades gave up
the dead that were in them"*

CONTENTS

Introduction

What happens to the soul & spirit of unsaved people when they die? By "unsaved" I'm referring to anyone who has not experienced spiritual regeneration through the gospel (see John 3:3,6 and Titus 3:5), which includes Old Testament saints—holy people who were in covenant with God throughout the Old Testament. The Bible shows that the souls of these people go to (or went to) Sheol at the point of physical decease. Sheol corresponds to Hades in the New Testament. These souls will be resurrected from Sheol/Hades one day (Revelation 20:11-15), which is why Sheol/Hades is described as the "intermediate state" since it refers to the **condition of souls *between* physical death and later resurrection**. So what's the condition of souls in Sheol/Hades? Jesus' story of the rich man and Lazarus, if taken literal, suggests a conscious state where people either hang out in bliss with father Abraham or suffer constant fiery torment begging for less than a drop of water for relief.

Many believers take this story literally rather than figuratively and so they feel the issue's a done deal—Sheol is a place of fiery torment for some souls and a place of bliss with father Abraham for others. However, they're disregarding **the incredible amount of data that God's Word devotes to the topic—vital information of which they are either ignorant or intentionally disregard**.

The purpose of *Sheol Know* is to do an honest, balanced examination of the Scriptures from Genesis to Revelation to determine the precise nature of Sheol/Hades. After all, the rightly-divided Word of God is the blueprint for Christian doctrine and practice, not fallible religious tradition.

Since *Sheol Know* is a thorough study on the nature of the intermediate state we'll address all linking topics, including the believer's intermediate state, the resurrection of the dead, Jesus' Second Coming, the Tribulation, the Millennium and, in the Epilogue, the nature of eternal life.

Why is this book important? Because there's wholesale ignorance in the body of Christ on the nature of Sheol/Hades and, in some cases, intentional misleading. Despite this, the truth about the intermediate state is blatantly revealed in the Scriptures; it's not hidden whatsoever. Once you see what God's Word says on the subject—*completely* and not just a single tale that Jesus told—you'll know the truth and, as the Lord said, **"the truth shall set you free."**

God bless you on this amazing journey of discovery!

<u>Chapter One</u>

What is Sheol:
The "Intermediate State"?

The Great White Throne Judgment is when God will resurrect every un-regenerated soul from Hades *(HAY-deez)* to be judged as shown in this passage:

> **The sea gave up the dead that were in it, and <u>death and Hades gave up the dead that were in them, and each person was judged according to what he had done</u>. Then death and Hades were thrown into the lake of fire. The lake of fire is the second death. If anyone's name was not found written in the book of life, he was thrown into the lake of fire.**
>
> **Revelation 20:13-15**

We see plain evidence here that unredeemed people are held in a place called Hades after their physical death. Hades is called Sheol *(she-OHL)* in the original Hebrew of the Old Testament. These disembodied souls are kept in Hades until Judgment Day when, as you can see, they are resurrected for the purpose of divine judgment. What is the precise nature of these people's condition in Hades during this period between physical death and resurrection? The traditional religious view is that they will be in a state of conscious torment the entire span or, if they're righteous, they'll hang out in bliss with father Abraham. Although this has been the common evangelical position of the "intermediate state," it's rarely mentioned or elaborated on in Christian circles.

Is this what the Bible really teaches? That people who are spiritually dead will suffer hundreds or thousands of years of torment in captivity immediately after they die merely waiting for God to judge them? (As shown in *Hell Know,* the people who believe this also believe the damned will *then* spend all eternity in roasting torture in the lake of fire after they're judged).

Our purpose in this study is to thoroughly search the Holy Scriptures to find out the truth about Sheol/Hades, the intermediate state. If Sheol/Hades is indeed a place and condition of conscious torment, then God's Word will clearly support it from Genesis to Revelation. However, if the Scriptures don't reinforce this then we need to expose it as a false doctrine, eliminate it from our belief system and proclaim what the Bible actually teaches on the subject. This is the only way "the truth will set us free."

Seven Important Facts about Sheol/Hades

Before we turn to the God-breathed Scriptures to discern the nature of the intermediate state of unredeemed people, let's go over seven important facts about Sheol/Hades, some of which are obvious and some not.

1. **Sheol and Hades are synonymous terms, that is, they refer to the same condition or place**. Sheol is the Hebrew term and Hades is the Greek. For proof of this, note the following Psalm passage, which speaks of Sheol, then observe how the Hebrew *sheol* is supplanted by the Greek *hades* when the text is quoted in the New Testament:

> **For Thou wilt not abandon my soul to <u>Sheol</u>; neither wilt Thou allow Thy Holy One to undergo decay.**
>
> **Psalm 16:10** (NASB)

> **"Because Thou wilt not abandon my soul to <u>Hades</u>, nor allow Thy Holy One to undergo decay."**
>
> **Acts 2:27** (NASB)

As you can see, Sheol and Hades are synonymous terms in the Bible.

Since using both words could be overly wordy and confusing we will simply use the term Sheol throughout this book. The main reason for this decision is that the Hebrew *sheol* appears much more often in the Scriptures than the Greek *hades*; the former appears 66 times in the Old Testament and the latter 10 times in the New Testament. A secondary reason is that the word Hades is apt to conjure fantastical images of Greek mythology rather than biblical truth; the Hebrew Sheol, by contrast, offers no such misleading images.

2. Since this is a study on Sheol, what precisely is it? Sheol is defined as **"the world of the dead"** by the popular Hebrew & Greek scholar James Strong, which corresponds to the biblical description of it as "the assembly of the dead," as shown in Proverbs 21:16 (NRSV & NASB). Sheol simply refers to **the place and condition of dead souls after their physical decease and before their resurrection to face God's judgment**. In other words, if people are spiritually dead to God, that is, they've never experienced spiritual regeneration through Jesus Christ, their disembodied souls will go straight to Sheol when they physically die to be held until Judgment Day, at which time they will be resurrected for the purpose of judgment. Since this time period in Sheol is *after* physical death and *before* resurrection it is commonly referred to as the "intermediate state" by theologians.

3. *Where* exactly is Sheol? In our study we shall see clear evidence that **Sheol is located in the heart of the earth, not in the physical realm, but in the dark spiritual realm**. You see, the Bible speaks of three existing realms: **1.** The earth and the physical universe, **2.** the underworld, which is the dark heavenly realm that parallels or underpins the earth and universe, and **3.** God's heaven, called the "third heaven" in Scripture. (For scriptural support of this see the section in <u>Chapter Nine</u> *Understanding the Three Realms— Heaven, Earth and the Underworld)*. It should be understood, however, that Sheol is not the underworld itself; it is a vast compartment or pit *in* the underworld. This will become clear as our study progresses.

4. **Sheol must be distinguished from the grave or tomb where dead bodies are put to rest**. It's necessary to emphasize this because translations often render *sheol* as "the grave;" for example, Psalm 16:10 in the New International Version. Yet scholar W.E. Vine properly points out that *sheol* never refers to the literal grave or tomb where the body is laid to rest (286). There's a separate Hebrew term for the physical grave or tomb, the Hebrew word *qeber (KEH-ber)*.

   Even though this is true, it should be pointed out that since Sheol is "the world of the dead" where souls enter after physical death, Sheol could properly be described as **the graveyard of souls**. In light of this, translations that render *sheol* as "the grave" are not necessarily inaccurate, as long as the reader understands that the text is referring to the soulish grave and not the physical grave/tomb where dead bodies are placed.

5. Another important fact, which I think is obvious, is that **Sheol is a temporary condition, regardless of its nature**. This is important to keep in mind—**Sheol only applies to the intermediate state of the souls of spiritually dead people after their physical death and before their resurrection on Judgment Day**. Why is this significant? Because, regardless of what anyone ultimately believes about Sheol, we can all agree that it's **a temporary state**; it's not something that lasts forever. Because of this, it's obvious that the subject of Sheol is not as important as the subject of the second

death, i.e. damnation in the lake of fire. Why? Because the second death is eternal while Sheol is not. As such, the nature of Sheol is a *secondary* issue on the topic of human damnation.

Consequently, even though the Bible is very clear on the issue of Sheol, no matter what conclusion you draw, it has no bearing on the biblical truths determined in *Hell Know*. This is important to keep in mind.

6. **Sheol is not hell; the lake of fire is hell**. We see in the Scriptures that Sheol and the lake of fire (i.e. Gehenna) are two separate places. Revelation 20:13-15, quoted at the beginning of this chapter, plainly shows this distinction: After people are resurrected from Sheol ("Hades") to face judgment, Sheol itself will then be cast into the lake of fire. Since Sheol and the lake of fire are plainly two separate places in this passage, only one can rightly be designated as "hell"; and since "hell" commonly refers to a fiery, dark netherworld where people suffer eternal damnation then it is the lake of fire (or Gehenna) that should be labeled hell. In light of this, if a person refers to Sheol as hell, they're simply not being scriptural; the lake of fire is the true hell.

However, those of us who understand this should extend grace toward those who mix-up the terms because most of the confusion over this issue is simply the result of bad translating practices; for instance, the King James Version often renders both *sheol/hades* and *gehenna* as "hell," giving the impression to English readers that they're one-and-the-same. They're not. Thankfully, more recent translations have helped correct this mistake.

It's interesting to note, incidentally, that the word "hell" is derived from the Old English 'helan,' which means "to hide or conceal;" hence in Old English literature you may find references to the helling of potatoes—that is, putting them into pits in the ground—and the helling of a house, meaning to cover it with a thatched roof. The term "hell" therefore was originally an accurate description of Sheol because it properly gave the image of souls concealed in a pit in the netherworld until their resurrection on Judgment Day. Of course, "hell" has taken on a radical change in meaning in the centuries since.

An alternative way of looking at the distinction between Sheol and the lake of fire is to simply regard Sheol as temporary hell and the lake of fire as eternal hell. This is good for those who, for whatever reason, insist on referring to both Sheol and the lake of fire as "hell."

7. **Righteous souls went to Sheol before the ascension of Christ**. This significant fact about Sheol is not widely known amongst Christians even though it's obvious in the Scriptures and Christian scholars readily acknowledge it. Before Jesus' death and subsequent resurrection from Sheol (Acts 2:27,31-32) the souls of Old Testament saints had to go to Sheol just as well as the souls of people not in covenant with God. Why? Because spiritual regeneration was not available in Old Testament times since Jesus had not yet spilled his blood for the forgiveness of our sins and was not subsequently raised to life for our justification. The blood of animals shed in Hebrew ceremonies only *temporarily covered* their sins; it was not able to *wash* them from sin. Only the blood of Christ can do this. As it is written: "It is impossible for the blood of bulls and goats to take away sins" (Hebrews 10:4).

In our study we'll observe that **death and Sheol are often spoken of together; they go hand-in-hand and are essentially one-in-the-same: death is Sheol and Sheol is death**. With this in mind, what is the wages of sin? According to the Bible "the wages of sin is death" (Romans 6:23). My point is that the souls of Old Testament saints had to go to Sheol just as heathen people because in order for them to be redeemed from death a person innocent of sin would have to die in their place. The good news is that Jesus Christ did this very thing for all those who believe on him and accept him as Lord.

Some believe that when Jesus Christ was raised from the dead as the "firstfruits" (see 1 Corinthians 15:20-23) and later ascended to heaven the souls of Old Testament saints were raised from Sheol as well. This is the passage they cite to support this:

When he [Jesus] ascended on high, he led captives in his train

Ephesians 4:8

Who were the "captives" who ascended to heaven with Jesus? Some suggest that they were the Old Testament saints who were subject to death and Sheol just as well as heathen people. It is true that Old Testament saints were captives to Sheol—death—until God's ultimate sacrifice for humanity's sins was made. When Jesus died he destroyed "him who holds the power of death—that is, the devil" (Hebrews 2:14) and, by his resurrection, set free those who were captive to death. As such, their souls were either resurrected from Sheol when Christ ascended or they will be at the time of their bodily resurrection, which takes place after the Tribulation and before the Millennium. We'll look at this further in Chapter Eleven.

Whatever the case, now that Jesus Christ has destroyed death and brought eternal life and immortality to light through his death and resurrection (2 Timothy 1:10), no soul that is spiritually born-again and blessed with God's gift of eternal life has to go to Sheol. Now, when a spiritually-regenerated believer physically dies, his or her soul goes straight to heaven, not Sheol. This is plainly evident in such clear passages as Revelation 6:9-11 and 7:9-17, as well as Philippians 1:23 and 2 Corinthians 5:8.

There are, incidentally, many adherents of everlasting destruction who reject this notion that spiritually-rebirthed believers go to heaven when they die; they believe that both heathen and Christian souls alike go to Sheol. I have open-mindedly and thoroughly researched their position but am persuaded by Scripture to embrace the above view. We'll look at this in detail in Chapter Ten and honestly consider arguments for and against. While I think the answer is obvious, you're welcome to draw your own conclusion. Regardless, even though this is an important issue it's a detail matter in the grand scheme of things and actually has no bearing on the nature of Sheol, which is the main subject of this study. Hence, whatever your conclusion after an honest appraisal of the biblical facts, let's strive for unity and loathe division! Amen?

The above notion that death and Sheol are parallel terms and essentially synonymous may sound strange to those of a religiously-indoctrinated mindset; yet, if such a person patiently and honestly seeks the scriptural truth, it will all make sense as we examine the Holy Scriptures on the subject. God's Word is perfectly able to wash our minds of false religious indoctrination.

One last point regarding the seventh fact of Sheol: If Sheol is a condition of conscious torment as religious traditionalists advocate, how do they explain the biblical fact that righteous people went to Sheol in Old Testament times? Their answer is that there was a separate chamber in Sheol for righteous souls with a chasm separating the two sections, which they base on a literal reading of Jesus' story of The Rich Man and Lazarus from Luke 16:19-31. We'll honestly analyze this passage in Chapter Eight to find out if this is true.

Confusion Due to Inconsistent Translating of *Sheol*

Centuries ago many theologians evidently did not believe there was a separate compartment in Sheol for righteous souls during the Old Testament period; they simply believed that Sheol was a place of fiery torment for the damned in the heart of the earth. This caused some obvious problems: If Sheol is a condition of conscious torment, how does one explain the many passages which plainly show that righteous souls as well as heathen souls went to Sheol in Old Testament times?

The solution for the translators of the 1611 King James Version, believe it or not, was to translate *sheol* as "hell" when it applied to unrighteous people and as "the grave" when applied to the righteous. In other words, **they did not uniformly translate *sheol*; in fact, their definition was determined purely by whether the passage referred to the wicked or the righteous**. The translators of the King James Bible—also known as the Authorized Version—embraced this as a general rule. As such, anyone reading this translation would understandably come to the conclusion that heathen people went to a horrible netherworld of torments when they died while righteous people, like Job and David, merely went to "the grave."

Let's observe evidence of this:

> **The wicked shall be turned into <u>hell</u>** *(sheol),*
> **and all the nations that forget God.**
>
> **Psalm 9:17** (KJV)

Since the passage is referring to "the wicked" the King James translators chose to translate *sheol* as "hell;" yet notice how they render *sheol* when the text applies to righteous King Hezekiah:

> **I said in the cutting off of my days, I shall go**
> **to the gates of <u>the grave</u>** *(sheol):* **I am deprived of the**
> **residue of my years.**
>
> **Isaiah 38:10** (KJV)

Hezekiah, a godly king of Judah, is speaking in this passage; he has a fatal illness and clearly doesn't want to die. Unfortunately, the King James rendering isn't very clear to modern readers so let's read the same passage from the New International Version:

> **I said, "In the prime of my life must I go**
> **through the gates of <u>death</u>** *(sheol)* **and be robbed of**
> **the rest of my years?"**
>
> **Isaiah 38:10**

It's obvious that Hezekiah expected to go to Sheol when he died. Since this passage is plainly referring to a righteous man of God, the King James translators decided not to translate *sheol* as "hell" as that would give the impression to readers that godly King Hezekiah went to a place of conscious torment when he died. This contradicted their theology so they simply rendered *sheol* as "the grave."

The Hebrew word *sheol* appears 66 times in the Old Testament and is translated in the King James Version 32 times as "hell," 31 times as "the grave" and 3 times as "the Pit." How the King James translators rendered *sheol* was determined purely by whether the passage referred to the wicked or the righteous. We see evidence of this above and we'll see further evidence as we progress. Scholars agree that there is simply no justification for this lack of uniformity in translating *sheol*.

Before I say anything more, let me stress that I'm not a hater of the King James Bible; I have at least three editions of this fine version in my household and enjoy them greatly. Overall, it's been a great blessing to English speaking people for many centuries (although to most modern readers the language is decidedly archaic and hard-to-understand). Nevertheless, its translation error on this specific issue cannot be condoned.

Needless to say, due to the King James Version's extreme popularity in the English-speaking world in the centuries following its publication in 1611, its lack of uniformity in translating *sheol* has not helped the cause of truth on the nature of the intermediate state.

Today, the King James is no longer the most popular English version of the Bible and more recent translations have, thankfully, corrected this translation error. For instance, the New Revised Standard Version (NRSV) and The New American Standard Bible (NASB) adhere to the policy of not translating either *sheol* or *hades*. It is for this reason that we shall regularly use these translations in this book.

As for the popular New International Version, *sheol* and *hades* are rendered variously as "grave," "death," "depths," and once as "hell." Yet, regardless of how the NIV translates *sheol* and *hades*, it conveniently reveals the original Hebrew or Greek term in the footnotes, which is commendable.

Understanding the Two Views of Sheol

Before we begin our study on the nature of Sheol, let's look at the two possible views. Although there are variations, they all fall within the parameters of the following two definitions:

1. Sheol is a place where unrighteous souls go to immediately after death where they suffer constant flaming torment hoping for less than a drop of water for relief until their resurrection on Judgment Day. Sheol also contains (or contained) a separate compartment for righteous souls from periods preceding the ascension of Christ where they are (or were) comforted and enjoy father Abraham's company. According to this view, the disembodied souls of pagans who died

hundreds or thousands of years ago have been in a constant state of fiery torture ever since even though they haven't even been judged yet. The only legitimate proof text for this position is Jesus' story about the rich man and Lazarus from Luke 16:19-31. This tale is about a wealthy man and poor beggar who die and go to Sheol (Hades) where they experience highly contrasting conscious states— the rich man suffers constant torment while Lazarus enjoys comfort in "Abraham's bosom." Adherents of this position insist that the story should be taken literally and, in some cases, that the rich man and beggar are actual historical figures. In short, they believe it's a literal accounting of what souls experience in Sheol. They further insist that the numerous other references to Sheol in the Bible must be interpreted or ignored in light of this literal interpretation of Jesus' story.

2. Sheol is the graveyard of dead souls, a vast pit in the underworld where dead souls are laid to rest "awaiting" their resurrection to be judged.

Initially I adhered to the first view solely due to Jesus' story of The Rich Man and Lazarus, which was the only passage I ever seriously considered on the topic. This is the case with the majority of believers as well. I have since come to accept the second position after much thorough and honest biblical research—prayerfully analyzing literally hundreds of passages on the subject.

The scriptural evidence for the second position, believe it or not, is overwhelming. Jesus is the *living* Word of God, so it's hardly likely that he would disagree with the *written* Word of God; hence his story of the rich man and Lazarus is likely a parable, a symbolic story intended to convey important truths, not a literal account. This is supported by three facts: **1.** The Bible teaches that Jesus "did not say anything to them without using a parable" (Matthew 13:34), **2.** Jesus' story of the rich man and Lazarus is contained within a string of parables (beginning with *the exact same words as the previous parable*), and **3.** Jesus clearly implemented fantastical elements in the story, such as the roasting rich man crying out for Lazarus to dip the tip of his finger in water and touch his tongue, like that's going to offer any significant amount of relief! And then there's the reference to Lazarus going to "Abraham's bosom," literally his chest cavity, which obviously turned to dust centuries earlier, not to mention there would hardly be enough room in his chest cavity to contain Lazarus. Such fantastical and symbolic imagery points to a fantastical, symbolic story, not a literal accounting of life after death during the Old Testament period.

The fact that the first position remains in the doctrinal books despite the incredible scriptural support for the latter is potent testimony to the formidable force of religious tradition and sectarian bias.

If you find my words hard to believe and doubt the colossal evidence for the second position, judge for yourself as we now journey through the God-breathed Scriptures to discover the truth about the nature of Sheol. God's Word speaks for itself.

"Planting" Requires "Watering"— Repetition

Before beginning, allow me to share a quick word on "planting" and the necessity of "watering."

The material contained in *Sheol Know* will be new to the vast majority of readers and, as such, it's a "planting." This simply means that the scriptural truths contained herein will be new to most readers as it'll be the first time they'll hear them. The Bible shows that the first time someone hears a truth it's like a seed being planted in his or her heart with the potential to grow and bear fruit, which of course requires "watering." For instance, Paul "planted" foundational doctrines in the hearts of the believers in Corinth when he established the Corinthian church. When he eventually left to evangelize other areas Apollos "watered" what Paul planted. This simply means that Apollos taught the same things over again. No doubt he conveyed these doctrines with different words from his unique perspective, but they were essentially the same truths. You can read this in 1 Corinthians 3:5-10.

With this understanding, *Sheol Know* is a "planting" because it will be the first time most readers hear what the Bible **fully says** about Sheol and related issues. Therefore, "watering"—repetition—is necessary in order for these truths to bear fruit in their lives. It is for this reason that you'll encounter some repetition in this book. Certain important passages will be cited repeatedly, as well as various descriptions of Sheol, which I try to convey in different words. This is "watering" and it's necessary for the spiritual growth of the believer. Peter did the same thing, as shown here:

> So **I will always remind you of these things**, even though you know them and are firmly established in the truth you now have. (13) I think it is right to <u>refresh your memory</u> as long as I live in the tent of this body, (14) because I know that I will soon put it aside, as our Lord Jesus Christ has made clear to me. (15) And I will make every effort to see that after my departure <u>you will always be able to remember these things</u>.
>
> **2 Peter 1:12-15**

<u>Chapter Two</u>

SHEOL IN THE BIBLE:
Jacob, Job and Solomon's View

We'll begin our scriptural study by observing how Jacob, Job and Solomon viewed Sheol. All three were godly men of the Old Testament era. Jacob was the grandson of Abraham, the father of faith, and the patriarch of the twelve tribes of Israel. In fact, his name was changed to "Israel." Job was regarded so highly by God that He boasted there was no one on earth as great as him (Job 1:8). As for Solomon, the Bible says "King Solomon was greater in riches and wisdom than all the other kings of the earth. The whole world sought audience with Solomon to hear the wisdom that God had put in his heart" (1 Kings 10:23-24).

These scriptural facts reveal that, although far from perfect, **Jacob, Job and Solomon were great and mighty men of the Old Testament period**. Hence, there's no reason not to assume that their recorded statements about Sheol are sound and particularly so if they're in harmony with what the rest of the Bible teaches.

With this understanding, let's consider the very first passage in the Bible where the Hebrew word *sheol* appears.

What Jacob Said

Sheol first appears in Genesis 37:35. This was the occasion where Jacob's sons treacherously sold their brother Joseph into slavery and then lied to their father by telling him that Joseph was slain by a wild beast. Jacob believed the lie and was understandably heartbroken:

> **All his sons and daughters sought to comfort him** [Jacob]**; but he refused to be comforted, and said, "No, I shall go down to Sheol to my son** [Joseph]**, mourning." Thus his father bewailed him.**
> **Genesis 37:35 (NRSV)**

Two simple facts can be derived from Jacob's brief expression of grief in this passage: **1.** Jacob very much *expected* **to go to Sheol when he died**, and **2.** Jacob **believed that Joseph was already in Sheol, that he would remain there, and that he would himself join him when he eventually died**.

The King James Version translates *sheol* in this passage as "the grave." Why? Obviously because the verse refers to Jacob and Joseph, both righteous men of God (righteous, that is, in the sense that they were in-right-standing with God via their covenant, not that they were unflawed individuals). This is in harmony with the King James translators' policy of rendering *sheol* as "hell" when it applied to unrighteous people and as "the grave" when it applied to the righteous. As pointed out in Chapter One, there's absolutely no justification for this practice; the meaning of the word *sheol* does not change depending on the character of the person going there.

We thus find evidence in the very first appearance of *sheol* in the Bible that religious people have tried to mislead the populace about its nature and who exactly went there.

As for the KJV and other translations rendering *sheol* as "the grave," we observed last chapter that Sheol never denotes the physical grave or tomb where bodies are laid to rest; there's a separate Hebrew word for this. Sheol should only be understood as "the grave" in the sense that it is **the graveyard of souls in the spiritual realm,** where **dead souls are held and "awaiting" resurrection to be judged by God**. This will become more evident as our study progresses.

Another important point concerning Jacob's view of Sheol: Although Jacob doesn't state anything about the nature of Sheol, it's obvious that he didn't regard it as some sort of nether paradise where his son was hanging out with father Abraham, which is what many ministers today advocate. If this were the case, would Jacob be "mourning" and "bewailing" Joseph so grievously? Of course not. It might be argued that Jacob was grieving over his own personal loss and not the destination of his son's disembodied soul. If this were so, wouldn't Jacob likely exclaim something to the effect of, "Praise you LORD that my son is now in the blissful presence of father Abraham, and I will one day go down to this same paradise rejoicing." Yet Jacob says nothing of the kind; in fact, his reaction is completely opposite to this.

"So that We May Live and Not Die"

Further insight concerning Jacob's view of Sheol can be derived from what he later exclaimed to his sons during a widespread famine:

> **"I have heard that there is grain in Egypt. Go down there and buy some for us, <u>so that we may live and not die</u>."**
>
> **Genesis 42:2**

Jacob's son, Judah, made a similar statement in the following chapter of Genesis:

> **Then Judah said to Israel his father, "Send the boy along with me and we will go [to Egypt] at once, <u>so that we and you and our children may live and not die</u>.**
>
> **Genesis 43:8**

Both quotes are in reference to Jacob's sons traveling to Egypt to apprehend food so that their clan "may live and not die." Obviously

Jacob and his family were in no hurry to go to Sheol to commune with father Abraham in some nether-paradise. Please notice that there's mysteriously no accompanying statement like, "...but—thankfully—if we die we'll be in bliss with our forefathers in Sheol." Why? Because this is an unbiblical doctrine.

This same point can be made from similar passages **all over the Bible**. Notice what the Israelites say to Moses when the army of Pharaoh was threatening them:

> **They said to Moses, "Was it because there were no graves in Egypt that you brought us to the desert to <u>die</u>? What have you done to us by bringing us out of Egypt? (12) Didn't we say to you in Egypt, 'Leave us alone; let us serve the Egyptians'? It would have been better for us to serve the Egyptians than to <u>die</u> in the desert!"**
>
> **Exodus 14:11-12**

Just as with Jacob and Judah in the two verses above, the Israelites were obviously in no hurry to die and go to a paradise in the heart of the earth to party with their forefathers. That's because this supposed paradise in Sheol never existed. It's a false doctrine and I find it puzzling that ministers have gotten away with peddling such blatant error for so long, not that they talk about it much, of course.

In all three of these passages the Hebrew word for "die" is *muwth (mooth)*, which simply means "to die" and is used in reference to the death of animals as well as humans (Exodus 7:18). It does not mean "to separate" or, more specifically, "to separate and go to either bliss or torment in Sheol." The Hebrew for 'separate' is *badal (baw-DAL)*, which is used in Genesis 1:4: "God saw that the light was good, and he *separated* the light from the darkness."

Needless to say, statements like "so we may live and not die" and "It would have been better for us to serve the Egyptians than to die in the desert" only make sense if Sheol is **the graveyard of dead souls** in the underworld where souls 'rest' in death until their resurrection.

Job's View of Sheol

Let us now consider Job's view of the intermediate state. Job was the greatest man of his time and God bragged of his integrity, godliness and hatred of evil (Job 1:1,3,8). Furthermore, in the book of Ezekiel God spoke of Job in the same breath as Noah and Daniel, two other great men of God (Ezekiel 14:14-20). The LORD obviously has a very high opinion of Job. We can therefore regard Job's views on Sheol as very reliable.[1]

As we shall see, Job goes into quite a bit of detail on the nature of Sheol. Did he just dream up all this information or did he have divine revelation on the subject? No doubt God revealed these truths to him. We can confidently draw this conclusion because what Job says about Sheol is in complete agreement with what the rest of the Bible teaches on the subject; only if Job's position contradicted the rest of Scripture should we question its validity.

For those unfamiliar with the book of Job, let me briefly explain its contents: Satan argues to God that Job is devoted to Him merely because the LORD blessed him so greatly and contends that Job will curse Him to His face if his blessings were removed. God therefore permits Satan to attack Job to find out. As a result of Satan's attacks, Job loses his ten children, hundreds of his employees (with only four survivors), all his great wealth and even his health as he is afflicted with painful sores from head to toe.

After many months of suffering, three of Job's friends go to "comfort" him, but end up judging & accusing him of some great hidden sin, which they *presume* brought about all his horrible suffering. Most of the book consists of Job, in great anguish, profoundly debating with

---

[1] Some may understandably argue that, since the LORD later accused Job of speaking "words without knowledge" (Job 38:2), his statements concerning the nature of Sheol are unreliable. But which of Job's words did God mean were "without knowledge"? Obviously his erroneous belief that it was God Himself who was afflicting him, not the devil; which naturally provoked Job to rail against the LORD throughout the book, e.g. Job 10:1-3. This is what God understandably took issue with, not his theological insights concerning the intermediate state.

these "friends." It should be noted, however, that much of what Job says is **directed at God Himself**. Such is the case with this passage:

> **"But mortals die, and are laid low; <u>humans expire and where are they</u>? (11) As waters fail from a lake, and a river wastes away and dries up, (12) so <u>mortals lie down</u> and <u>do not rise again</u>; <u>*until* the heavens are no more, they will not awake or be aroused out of their sleep</u>. (13) Oh that you [God] would <u>hide me in Sheol</u>, that you would <u>conceal me until your wrath is past</u>, that you would appoint me a set time, and remember me! (14) If mortals die, will they live again? All of the days of my service I would wait until my release should come. (15) You would call, and I would answer you; you would long for the works of your hands."**
>
> **Job 14:10-15** (NRSV)

Much is said in this passage so let's take it point by point.

Firstly, in verse 10 Job declares that "mortals die" and then asks "where are they?" He partially answers his own question in verse 12 by likening death to "sleep" which humans will not "awake" from until "the heavens are no more," or, we could say, a very long time. What needs to be emphasized from these words is that **Job describes the condition of death as "sleep" from which all human beings will one day "awake" or be resurrected.**

Yet he still hasn't really answered the question of *where* people go after they die. The very next verse answers this (verse 13): In his great anguish he cries out to God to hide him **in Sheol**. Why does Job pray this? Because his suffering was so great he wanted to escape it through death; and obviously when a person died—Job believed—his or her soul would go to Sheol.

One may argue that, in verse 12, Job is perhaps referring to the body "sleeping" in the grave, but the obvious focus of his words is the death condition of the soul in Sheol because in the very same breath he prays to God to go specifically there: "Oh that you would hide me **in Sheol**, that you would conceal me until your wrath is past, that you would appoint a set time and remember me!" (Verse 13).

Job erroneously believed that God Himself was causing his great afflictions because he was unaware of the devil's hand in the situation. In truth, God only permitted Job's afflictions by allowing Satan to attack him. Nevertheless, the fact is that **Job believed that by dying and going to Sheol he would escape his intense suffering**.

Yes, as amazing as it may seem, Job was actually hoping and praying to die and go to Sheol, a place traditionally considered "hell" and viewed as a horrible, devil-ruled torture chamber! Obviously **Job's view of Sheol was quite different from what religious tradition has taught us**. He prayed to go to Sheol because, being one of God's inspired servants, he knew that Sheol was a condition of **unconsciousness**, which he described as **sleep.** Job was understandably weary of his intense suffering and wanted it to end. He knew that **in death, in Sheol, he would find relief from his misery, not an increase of it**.

A vital fact that needs to be stressed from the above passage is that, regardless of the nature of Sheol, **Job definitely believed that everyone would ultimately be resurrected from there**. In verse 12 he makes it clear that all mortals who lie down in the sleep of death will one day awaken, that is, be resurrected when "the heavens are no more." And, while Job prayed to go to Sheol in verse 13, it was not with the expectation that he would remain there forever. Job obviously believed that if God "hid" him in Sheol He would "appoint a set time and remember" him, which is when his "release" would come (verse 14). Release from what? Obviously his release from captivity to Sheol, "the world of the dead" as scholar James Strong defined it. So God "remembering" him and "releasing" him are references to a future resurrection from Sheol, which is in harmony with what the rest of the Bible teaches.

"There the Wicked Cease from Turmoil, and the Weary are at Rest"

Job elaborates greatly on the nature of Sheol in an earlier chapter. In Job 3 he curses the day of his birth because his suffering was so great. In essence, Job was wishing that he were never born because then he would never have had to experience such incredible agony. He then details what it would've been like for him if this were so:

> **"Why did I not <u>perish at birth and die</u> as I came from the womb? (12) Why were there knees to receive me and breasts that I might be nursed? (13) <u>For now I would be lying down in peace</u>; I would be <u>asleep and at rest</u> (14) <u>with kings and counselors of the earth</u> who built for themselves places now lying in ruins, (15) <u>with rulers</u> who had gold, who filled their houses with silver. (16) Or why was I not hidden in the ground like a stillborn child, like an infant who never saw the light of day? (17) <u>There the wicked cease from turmoil, and there the weary are at rest</u>. (18) <u>Captives also enjoy their ease</u>; they no longer hear the slave driver's shout. (19) <u>The small and great are there</u>, and <u>the slave is freed from his master</u>."**
>
> **Job 3:11-19**

Job starts off this passage by asking why he didn't die as an infant. He says that, in that event, he would not be enduring all the great suffering that he was experiencing. He explains in verse 13 that, had he died in infancy he would be peacefully **"lying down... asleep and at rest."**

Job then further explains that he would have **shared this condition of sleep and rest** *with* kings and counselors of the earth, *with* the small and the great, *with* rulers and slaves, *with* captives and weary people and, yes, even *with the wicked!* In this state of death, Job declares in verse 17 that **"there the wicked cease from turmoil**, and there **the weary are at rest**," and in verse 18 he makes it plain that there's no "slave driver's shout" as well.

This coincides with what Job later says concerning the wicked:

"They [the wicked] **spend their days in prosperity and <u>in peace they go down to Sheol</u>."**
Job 21:13 (NRSV)

Notice that Job doesn't say the wicked go down to Sheol in torment; no, they go down to Sheol in peace. This completely contradicts the religious traditional belief that the unredeemed go to some horrible devil-ruled nether realm immediately after physical death to suffer torments as they are goaded on by slave-driving demons in fiery pits with not a single drop of water for relief. Instead Job makes it clear that there is no turmoil or torment for the wicked in Sheol.

If Job's view of Sheol is divinely inspired and therefore coincides with the rest of the God-breathed Scriptures, these are potent facts indeed! They reveal that **at death kings, counselors, rulers, infants, the wicked, the weary, captives, the small, the great and slaves all share the same condition**, a **condition of peaceful "sleep" and "rest," which are obvious references to unconsciousness**. No wonder Job, stripped of all his possessions, forsaken by his wife and friends, tortured by painful sores from head to toe, mocked and made a byword by everyone and mourning for his ten children & hundreds of servants, prayed to go to such a place. Needless to say, Job's understanding of Sheol was quite different from that held by so many misguided religious people today.

Some may wonder if perhaps Job was referring to the literal grave or tomb where the body is laid to rest since there is no specific mention of Sheol in chapter 3. This idea is ruled out because Job makes it clear in verses 13-15 that, if he died, he'd be lying down asleep *with* kings, counselors and rulers. So Job is plainly referring to a common place or condition that all people shared together. Biblically speaking, this would be Sheol, the realm of dead souls, as verified in Ecclesiastes 9:10, a passage we will examine momentarily. In addition, Job would not be referring to the literal grave or tomb for the body because it is not acceptable or usual practice to bury people **together** in mass graves or tombs, then or now.

Before we continue let's remember that, as detailed in <u>Chapter One</u>, this was well before the death and resurrection of Christ, hence spiritual rebirth and the consequent attainment of eternal life were yet to be manifested. For this reason, the souls of Old Testament saints could not be ushered into God's presence when they physically died; the souls of both the righteous and unrighteous went to Sheol at this time because redemption was not yet available.

Amazingly, some righteous captives to Sheol—death—were set free when Jesus was resurrected:

> **And when Jesus had cried out again in a loud voice, he gave up his spirit.**
>
> **(51) At that moment the curtain of the temple was torn in two from top to bottom. The earth shook, the rocks split (52) and the tombs broke open. The bodies of many holy people who had died were raised to life. (53) They came out of the tombs after Jesus' resurrection and went into the holy city and appeared to many people.**
>
> **Matthew 27:50-53**

Notice how verse 52 says that these "holy people who had died were raised to life" and not these "holy people who had died physically, but were still very much alive in the paradise section of Sheol fellowshipping with father Abraham, were raised to life physically." With passages like this it's important to note what the Bible *actually says* and also what it *doesn't say*. Interestingly, there's no account of these resurrected people lamenting that they had to leave paradise with Abraham to come back to this lost world. Why not? Because it's a false doctrine.

What about the rest of the Old Testament saints? They were *possibly* released from Sheol when Jesus ascended (Ephesians 4:7-10); if not, we can be sure that they'll be resurrected at the time of their bodily resurrection when Jesus Christ returns to the earth, which takes place at the end of the Tribulation period and before Jesus' millennial reign (Daniel 12:1-2 & Matthew 19:28-30). We'll look at this in Chapter Eleven.

Solomon's View of Sheol

Solomon was the wisest man on earth in his time (1 Kings 4:29-34) and this explains why God utilized his great knowledge and wisdom in three books of the God-breathed Scriptures.[2] Notice what it says about Solomon when the Queen of Sheba came to visit him:

> **Now when the queen of Sheba heard about the fame of Solomon concerning the name of the LORD, <u>she came to test him with difficult questions</u>... (3) Solomon answered <u>all</u> her questions; <u>nothing</u> was hidden from the king which he did not explain to her.**
> **1 Kings 10:1,3**

The king's wisdom was renowned and so the Queen came to test him with hard questions and verse 3 shows that "*nothing* was hidden from the king which he did not explain to her." Do you think that one of the questions she asked was what happens to people when the die? That is, where they go and what will it be like? Of course she did; after all, it's one of the most common "difficult questions" people ask in life. With this in mind, it says that "Solomon answered *all* her questions" and that there was literally "nothing" he did not explain to her.

Furthermore, we know that Solomon had divine revelation on Sheol, the realm of the dead, because he commented on it quite a bit in the book of Proverbs, as we'll see in <u>Chapter Five</u>. He also elaborates on it in Ecclesiastes, witness:

> **Whatever your hand finds to do, do with your might; for <u>there is no work or thought or knowledge or wisdom in Sheol</u>, to which <u>you are going</u>.**
> **Ecclesiastes 9:10** (NRSV)

---

[2] Although it is traditionally believed that Solomon wrote the book of Ecclesiastes, which I've always felt was fairly obvious, some modern scholars debate this.

The language in this passage describes beyond any question of doubt that Sheol is a condition of **unconsciousness.** Notice that, in Sheol, there's neither good work nor bad work; there's neither positive, hopeful thoughts nor anguished, hopeless thoughts; there's neither knowledge of what's good and holy nor knowledge of what's evil and impure.

This is further verified in verse 5:

> **The living know that they will die, but <u>the dead know nothing</u>.**
>
> **Ecclesiastes 9:5** (NRSV)

The obvious reason the dead "know nothing" is because they're no longer alive and conscious—*they're dead*. This coincides with this passage from the Psalms:

> **His breath goeth forth, he** [his body] **returneth to his earth; <u>in that very day his thoughts perish</u>.**
>
> **Psalm 146:4** (KJV)

The Psalmist makes it clear that when a person physically dies his or her thoughts perish. Note that there is no mention whatsoever of a person's thoughts continuing to live on in some devil-ruled chamber of horrors. This is obviously because a dead person is no longer conscious of anything.

Take another look at Ecclesiastes 9:10 above and notice that Solomon doesn't make a distinction between righteous or unrighteous people. Like Job, he plainly says that **everyone** would go to Sheol during this period of time, whether righteous or wicked, rich or poor, small or great. In fact, Solomon's major point in Ecclesiastes 9 is that **death or Sheol is the common destiny of all people before redemption was made available through Christ's death and resurrection**. He plainly states in verse 3 that "the same destiny overtakes all." What destiny? The destiny of Sheol, the state of death, where—he goes on to say—there is neither work nor thought nor knowledge nor wisdom.

Summary

Jacob, Job and Solomon's views of Sheol can be summarized as follows:

1. Sheol is a condition that every spiritually un-regenerated person will experience immediately following physical decease, which includes godly men and women in Old Testament periods preceding the ascension of Christ. It includes the rich and the poor, the small and the great, the pure and the profane. In other words, **Sheol is the common destiny of anyone who is spiritually dead to God and therefore unredeemed**.

2. Sheol is a condition of **unconsciousness, likened unto sleep**, where there is no work, thought or knowledge of any kind. It is not a place or state of conscious suffering and misery.

3. Sheol is a **temporary condition** and all consigned to Sheol will ultimately be **resurrected.**

Chapter Three

SHEOL IN THE PSALMS, Part I

The book of Psalms consists of 150 songs called psalms. Half of the psalms were written by Solomon's father, King David, and some anonymous ones were likely written by him as well. Other psalmists include Moses, Solomon, Asaph, Ethan and Heman. Regardless of who wrote each psalm, one fact is certain: All the psalms are "God-breathed" (2 Timothy 3:16) since all the psalmists "spoke from God as they were carried along by the Holy Spirit" (2 Peter 1:21). For more proof of this, notice what Jesus said about David in a discussion with the Pharisees:

> [Jesus] **said to them, "How is it then that David, speaking by the Spirit, calls him 'Lord'? For he says,**
> **(44) " 'The Lord said to my Lord: "Sit at my right hand until I put your enemies under your feet." '**
> **Matthew 22:43-44**

Verse 44 is a quote of Psalm 110:1, written by David. Notice how Jesus emphasizes that David was "speaking by the Spirit" when he wrote this verse, which implies all the psalms he wrote. In other words,

David's statements in the Psalms were given by the inspiration of the Holy Spirit and the Holy Spirit is God. As such, David's exposition on the nature of Sheol contained in the Psalms, as well as commentary by other psalmists, shouldn't be considered just "their view" of Sheol. No, it's God's view too because they were "speaking by the Spirit," as Jesus put it.

The book of Psalms contains a wealth of information on the nature of Sheol. Despite the fact that there were several authors, the psalmists are in **complete agreement**. This is unsurprising since they all "spoke from God... by the Holy Spirit." Their many revealing statements about Sheol are also in harmony with the views of Jacob, Job and Solomon, covered last chapter.

Sheol: Where You Cannot Remember or Praise God

Let's examine the very first text in the Psalms where the Hebrew word *sheol* appears:

> **For <u>in death</u> there is no remembrance of you**
> **[God]; <u>in Sheol</u> who can give you praise?**
> **Psalm 6:5** (NRSV)

In this verse David is praying for God to save his life because his enemies were trying to kill him (as indicated in verse 10). Despite his anguish David didn't want to die; he was "a man after God's own heart" (1 Samuel 13:14 & Acts 13:22) and thus wanted to live, serve God and worship Him. **He knew that if he died and went to Sheol he wouldn't be able to do this.**

This simple passage completely contradicts the prominent religious position on Sheol, which suggests that when Old Testament saints died their souls would go to a supposed "paradise" section of Sheol. They would be conscious there and supremely comforted as they fellowshipped with father Abraham. If this were so, wouldn't they be able to remember God? Would they not be praising Him and thanking Him as the righteous are always ever ready to do, that is, as long as it were possible?

However, David makes it clear in this passage that **souls in Sheol do not and cannot remember God and consequently cannot praise Him either**. This suggests that those in Sheol are unconscious—"asleep" in death until their resurrection.

The notion that Sheol is a condition where a person cannot remember or praise God is corroborated by other biblical texts. For instance:

> **The dead do not praise the LORD, nor do any that <u>go down into silence</u>, but we** [the living] **will bless the LORD**
>
> **Psalm 115:17-18** (NRSV)

This passage shows that those who die "go down into **silence.**" Sheol is a place of silence because those who go there are **unconscious,** that is, **dead.** There's no praising and worshipping of God there nor are there horrible screams of torment. It is a condition of silence. It is the living who bless the Lord, the psalmist plainly states, not the dead.

Righteous King Hezekiah's prayer from the book of Isaiah also coincides:

> **"For <u>Sheol</u> cannot thank you, <u>death</u> cannot praise you; those who go down to <u>the Pit</u> cannot hope for your faithfulness. (19) The living, the living, they thank you as I do this day."**
>
> **Isaiah 38:18-19** (NRSV)

First, notice in this passage, as well as Psalm 6:5 above, that **Sheol and death are spoken of synonymously** (we'll look at this in more detail in the next chapter). Secondly, witness how Hezekiah makes it clear that those in Sheol are *unable* to thank or praise God, just as David and the other psalmist did.

The obvious conclusion we must draw is that, if the righteous are unable to remember God and cannot praise or thank Him, **then they must be unable to do so**; that is, they must be either **unconscious** or **dead—no longer alive**. This is supported by Hezekiah's statement in verse 19 where he stresses that only "the living, the living" can thank and praise God, not those who go to Sheol, the world of the dead.

Let's examine one other passage that corresponds to the three just looked at:

> **(3) For my soul is full of trouble and my life draws near the <u>grave</u>** *(sheol).*
> **(10) Do you show your wonders to the dead? Do those who are dead rise up and praise you? (11) Is your love declared in the <u>grave</u>** *(qeber)*, **your faithfulness in destruction. (12) Are your wonders known in the place of darkness, or your righteous deeds in the land of oblivion?**
>
> **Psalm 88:3, 10-12**

Here is further proof that those in Sheol are dead and therefore unable to rise up and praise God. Moreover, Sheol is likened to the **literal grave** *(qeber)* and **destruction,** and is also spoken of as "**the place of darkness**" and "**land of oblivion.**" The psalmist makes it clear that God does not show His wonders to the dead in Sheol; that the dead cannot praise Him there and that God's love, faithfulness and righteous deeds are all unknown there. What unmistakable proof that souls in Sheol are dead and conscious of nothing!

This Psalm, written by Heman the Ezrahite when his life was in mortal danger, is a prayer to God for deliverance from death. Note in verse 3 that Heman clearly expected to go to Sheol when he died just as Jacob, Job, Solomon, David and Hezekiah did. In the King James Version this is kept from the general reader by the use of the word "grave" as a translation of *sheol*, which is likewise the case with the NIV rendering, as shown above, although there's a footnote indicating that the verse is referring to Sheol. Because of this mistranslation the average reader is misled into believing that the psalmist is talking about the condition of the literal grave where the body is buried and not to Sheol where the soul goes. The problem with this is that it obscures the truth about the nature of Sheol to the common person and consequently perpetuates false religious ideas.

Let's recap: The writers of the four passages examined in this section—David, Hezekiah, Heman and the anonymous psalmist—are in perfect agreement that Sheol is not a place of consciousness. According to these inspired biblical writers, **Sheol is synonymous with death and is thus a condition of silence where it is impossible to even remember God, let alone praise and thank Him**.

Sheol: "The Land of Silence"

Let's examine another enlightening Psalm text by David from both the New International Version and the King James:

> let the wicked be put to shame and <u>lie silent in the grave</u> *(sheol)*. **(18)** <u>Let their lying lips be silenced</u>,
> **Psalm 31:17-18**

> let the wicked be ashamed, and <u>let them be silent in the grave</u> *(sheol)*. **(18)** <u>Let their lying lips be put to silence</u>;
> **Psalm 31:17-18** (KJV)

Notice that this passage is solely referring to "the wicked"—people who are in outright rebellion against God, living after the desires of the sin nature. These are David's enemies; they have rejected his God-appointed kingship and are trying to kill him. David is actually praying for their death for **that is the only way their lying lips will be silenced**.

With this understanding, observe how David describes the condition these wicked souls will experience if they die: He plainly says that they will **lie silent in Sheol**.

According to David—the godly king, biblical writer and "man after God's own heart"—the wicked do not constantly scream in torment in Sheol, but rather **lie silent!** This description is in perfect harmony with the view that Sheol is a condition of unconsciousness where souls lie "asleep" in death "awaiting" their resurrection.

This is not the only biblical text that shows that souls lie silent in Sheol. This same thought is expressed in Psalm 115:17, as seen in the previous section. Here's another coinciding verse from the Psalms:

If the LORD had not been my help, <u>my soul</u> would soon have <u>lived in the land of silence</u>.
Psalm 94:17 (NRSV)

The psalmist is simply testifying that, if the Lord had not delivered him from his wicked enemies (referred to in verse 16), they would have killed him and his soul would have gone to "the land of silence." What is "the land of silence"? Since he's addressing the place **his soul** would go to after death we know he's referring to Sheol.

With this in mind, **notice that the psalmist does not describe Sheol as "the land of shrieking in torment" or as "the land of comforts with father Abraham"** (religionists would have us believe Sheol is one or the other, depending on whether the soul is wicked or righteous respectively). That's because **neither of these descriptions is true**; Sheol is, in reality, **the land of dead souls where there's no consciousness of anything and thus only silence**.

Take another look at the King James rendition of Psalm 31:17-18 above and notice that the passage deviates from the King James standard practice of rendering *sheol* as "hell" whenever the text referred to the wicked (and as "the grave" when it referred to righteous people). Why did the translators fail to render *sheol* as "hell" in this particular case since it clearly refers to "the wicked"? Obviously because the passage portrays the wicked in Sheol as lying in silence and **this contradicted their belief that wicked souls in Sheol suffer a constant state of screeching torment**. What hypocrisy!

This reveals the dishonest extents religious people will go to cover up the scriptural truth and perpetuate their false religious beliefs.

Sheol: "The Pit" or "Well of Souls"

The fact that Sheol is a condition of silence is also pointed out in Psalm 30. This psalm shows David expressing thanks because God delivered him from death. He knew that, if he died, his soul would go to Sheol, as indicated in verse 3:

> **O LORD, you brought up my soul from Sheol, restored me to life from among those gone down to the Pit.**
>
> **Psalm 30:3** (NRSV)

The text showcases a form of Hebrew poetry called synonymous parallelism where the second part of the verse simply repeats and reinforces the thought of the first, but in different words. We've already seen examples of this type of poetry (Psalm 6:5 & Isaiah 38:18) and will continue.

With this understanding, notice that Sheol is spoken of as synonymous with "the Pit." Since Sheol is described as "the Pit" we will gain better insight into Sheol by deciphering what "the Pit" means.

The Hebrew word for "the Pit" is *bowr (borr)* which literally refers to a hole or pit in the ground and is used 71 times in the Bible. The setting in which *bowr* is used determines what specific type of hole or pit and, consequently, which English word is used to translate it. For instance, *bowr* is used 26 times in reference to a 'cistern' (e.g. Genesis 37:22,24,28,29), nine times in reference to a 'well' (e.g. 1 Chronicles 11:17-18), five times in reference to a 'dungeon' (e.g. Genesis 40:15; 41:14), once to a 'quarry' (Isaiah 51:1) and once it's even translated as 'death' (Proverbs 28:17).[3]

Why "death"? No doubt because *bowr,* a hole in the ground, is what a grave actually is; and grave, of course, signifies death—the utter absence of life.

What is God trying to tell us in His Word by likening Sheol to *bowr,* a pit? Obviously that **Sheol is like a vast common pit or grave where unregenerated souls are held after physical death and before resurrection**.

Interestingly, since one of the definitions of *bowr* is 'well,' Sheol could be described as "the well of souls."

---

[3] These figures are from the New International Version.

Most of us have probably heard this phrase. "The Well of Souls" is an actual subterranean chamber beneath the Dome of the Rock in the Temple Mount in Jerusalem. Jews believe it is where Abraham almost sacrificed Isaac. The popular 1981 film *Raiders of the Lost Ark* depicts the Well of Souls as the hiding spot of the Ark of the Covenant, but placed it in a lost chamber in Tanis, Egypt, rather than in a cave in the Temple Mount.

From a purely biblical standpoint, however, **the Well of Souls is Sheol**, the pit where unregenerated souls are held between physical death and resurrection. Like the subterranean chamber beneath the Dome of the Rock, Sheol is a dungeon—a dungeon where souls are held **captive to death** after physical decease. This explains why *bowr* is translated as "dungeon" in reference to Sheol in this passage from Isaiah:

> **So it will happen in that day, that the LORD will punish the host of heaven, on high, and the kings of the earth, on earth.**
> **(22) And they will be gathered together <u>like prisoners in the dungeon</u> *(bowr)*, and will be <u>confined in prison</u>; and <u>after many days they will be punished</u>.**
> **Isaiah 24:21-22** (NASB)

The passage is referring to the day when God's cataclysmic wrath will be poured out upon the whole earth; this occurs right before the establishment of the millennial reign of Christ. Because of God's judgments billions of people will die and every unsaved soul will be confined to Sheol "like prisoners in the dungeon." Only "after many days," that is, after the thousand-year reign of Christ, will these souls be resurrected to face judgment and suffer the eternal punishment of the second **death** (see Revelation 20:5,13-15).

Incidentally, observe how verse 22 makes it clear that these unsaved souls will not be punished until *after* they are resurrected from Sheol and judged; this is further evidence disproving the view that unsaved souls are punished with conscious torment while captive in Sheol. The only punishment experienced in Sheol is death itself, the utter absence of life or being. This stands to reason since it is in harmony with the biblical axiom that death is the wages of sin.

The point I want to stress from this passage is that verse 22 likens Sheol to a gloomy dungeon or prison where souls are confined. No wonder David praised and thanked God for delivering him from this death condition. Obviously David didn't share the view of some people today that righteous souls in Sheol are (or were) in some type of "paradise" chummin' around with father Abraham. No, this is a religious myth! Sheol is a dungeon, a prison, a common pit of death where unregenerated souls are confined until their appointed resurrection.

The only soul who can escape this dungeon-like pit of death is the soul that is born-again and thus *possesses* eternal life (John 3:36, 5:24 & 1 John 3:14). This is only possible because "Christ Jesus... has **destroyed death** and has **brought life and immortality to light through the gospel**" (2 Timothy 1:10). The gospel or "good news" refers to all the benefits available to humankind as a result of Jesus' sacrificial death, burial and resurrection (1 Corinthians 15:1-4). Aside from reconciliation with God, the main benefit of this gospel is, of course, eternal life. Until Jesus' death, burial and resurrection, eternal life or immortality was not available and that's why in Old Testament times, before the ascension of Christ, both righteous and unrighteous souls had to go to Sheol after physical decease.

It was necessary to go into detail here about *bowr*—"the Pit"— so now whenever it pops up in our study we'll understand what it means.

Incidentally, I find it interesting that the original definition of the English word 'hell'—"to conceal or cover"—is in harmony with the biblical description of Sheol as "the Pit." This is evidence that the Old English 'hell' was *originally* used as a translation of Sheol because it properly gave the image of souls consigned and concealed in a pit in the netherworld until their resurrection on judgment day. Unfortunately, the definition of 'hell' has taken on a completely different meaning since that time, i.e. perpetually writhing in roasting torment in some devil-ruled torture chamber.

Let's now return our attention to Psalm 30: At the end of this psalm David plainly reveals the state that his soul would have been in if God had not delivered him from death:

> **You have turned my mourning into dancing;**
> **you have taken off my sackcloth and clothed me with**
> **joy, (12) <u>so that my soul may praise you and not be</u>**
> **<u>silent</u>.**
>
>

Psalm 30:11-12 (NRSV)

David is just praising God here because he knew that, had he died, his soul would have been silent in Sheol. He well knew that a person cannot praise God or tell of His faithfulness in Sheol, as indicated in verse 9, because Sheol is a "land of silence."

Sheol: A Condition of the Soul (Mind)

Let's return to Psalm 30:3 to observe another important fact about Sheol:

> **O LORD, you brought up <u>my soul from</u>**
> **<u>Sheol</u>, restored me to life from among those gone**
> **down to the Pit.**
>
>

Psalm 30:3 (NRSV)

David was so close to death that God figuratively "restored" him to life by saving him from Sheol, which is where his soul would have gone had he physically died.

"Soul" in this context refers to his very being or mind, the actual essence or qualities that mark him as an individual human creation of God. This is supported by the second part of the verse, which speaks of "those" who actually died and consequently went to Sheol, the Pit. Notice that he doesn't say "those whose bodies have gone down to the Pit" or "those whose breath of life has gone down to the Pit." That's because a person's body does not go to Sheol when s/he dies; a lifeless body is placed in a grave or tomb. Neither does the breath of life, the spirit, go to Sheol when a person dies; this animating life-force simply returns to God from whence it came, as detailed in the Appendix. No, Sheol is the holding place of a person's very life essence or being, the part of human nature that possesses volition, emotion and intellect. In other words, Sheol is the condition to which the human soul or mind (not brain) enters after physical death.

This is supported by a verse examined in the previous chapter:

Whatever your hand finds to do, do with your might; for there is no work or thought or knowledge in Sheol, to which you are going.
Ecclesiastes 9:10 (NRSV)

Notice how the text plainly states that "you" are going to Sheol; that is, **anyone who has not been spiritually regenerated through Christ**, which included *everyone* in Old Testament times when Ecclesiastes was written. **Sheol is the housing place of people's very being after physical death**, the part that marks them as an individual creation of God, the part of them that thinks, reasons, chooses and feels. Hence, **Sheol is the condition that the mind enters when the body dies**. As shown in the Appendix, "mind" is the Greek word *nous (noos)* and refers to that central part of human nature that decides, thinks and feels. We could put it this way: **Your mind is you and you are your mind**.

The human body separate from mind and spirit is just a slab of flesh that goes to the grave at death. The human spirit separate from mind and body is simply a breath of life, an animating life-force, not a personality. This breath of life comes from the Creator and gives life to our very being, our soul, our mind—our personhood. When a person dies this breath of life, or spirit, merely returns to God who gave it. (I'm not talking about believers who have spiritual regeneration through Christ here, but rather un-regenerated people, which includes Old Testament saints). The unredeemed soul separate from body and spirit goes to Sheol.

Simply put, **Sheol is a condition of the unregenerate human soul, the disembodied mind**.

If any of this is difficult to understand, please see the aforementioned Appendix, which addresses the subject in detail.

Sheol: A Place Where Sheep Go?

Let's now turn to another very enlightening passage from the Psalms written by the sons of Korah:

> **Such is the fate of the foolhardy, the end of those who are pleased with their lot.**
> **(14) <u>Like sheep they are appointed for Sheol;</u> <u>death</u> shall be their shepherd; straight to <u>the grave</u> they descend, and their form shall waste away; <u>Sheol shall be their home.</u>**
> **(15) But <u>God will ransom my soul from the power of Sheol,</u> <u>for he will receive me.</u>**
> Psalm 49:13-15 (NRSV)

The text refers to those who trust in themselves rather than God; verse 13 describes them as the "foolhardy." A 'fool' in the Bible is synonymous with a wicked person since "fool" denotes someone who is morally deficient; that is, someone who rejects God's existence, authority, wisdom & discipline and embraces evil desires (see Proverbs 1:7, 5:22-23 and Psalm 14:1).

Since this passage is definitely referring to ungodly people you would think that the King James translators would have translated *sheol* as "hell," which would be in line with their policy of translating the word as "hell" when the passage referred to wicked people, and as "grave" when it referred to righteous people. Yet, notice how the King James Bible renders verse 14:

> **Like sheep they are laid in <u>the grave</u> *(sheol);* death shall feed on them; and the upright shall have dominion over them in the morning; and their beauty shall consume in the grave from their dwelling.**
> Psalm 49:14 (KJV)

The passage is contextually referring to ungodly people yet the King James translators mysteriously chose not to render *sheol* as "hell," which was their usual practice. Why? Obviously because the verse plainly says that **wicked people are appointed for Sheol LIKE SHEEP!** And everyone knows that sheep don't go to a place of conscious torture when they die; the very idea is absurd. You don't have to be a scholar to realize this. Hence, despite their desire to render *sheol* as "hell" in line with their standard practice they had no choice but to translate it as "the grave" in this case.

This passage coincides with Jeremiah 12:3, which also likens ungodly people to sheep that are to be slaughtered: "Drag them off like sheep to be butchered! Set them apart for the day of slaughter." Note clearly that it says they are to be butchered and slaughtered (which is in harmony with the biblical axiom that "the wages of sin is death"), not tortured in some fiery nether realm until their resurrection thousands of years hence, as some ludicrously teach.

At this point, two questions crop up: Do sheep really go to Sheol as Psalm 49:14 implies? And, if so, does this mean they have souls since, biblically speaking, Sheol is the "world of the dead" where dead souls are specifically laid to rest after physical death?

Do Animals Have Souls? Do They Go to Sheol When They Die?

The answer to both these questions, believe it or not, is yes. Sheep and other animals are described in terms of being "living souls" in the Bible and, when they die, their non-physical essence is indeed laid to rest in Sheol. This may, admittedly, sound odd at first but let's observe what the God-breathed Scriptures have to say on the subject. Some of the following biblical information has already been offered in *Hell Know* and, in detail, in the Appendix, but it's necessary here to brush up on the material in order to answer these questions.

The word "soul" in the Bible is translated from the Hebrew word *nephesh (neh-FESH),* which corresponds to the Greek *psuche (soo-KHAY).*[4]

---

[4] Compare Genesis 2:7 with 1 Corinthians 15:45 for verification.

The creation text, Genesis 2:7, states that God breathed into the body of the first man the **breath of life** and he "became **a living soul**." As such, the passage plainly shows that human beings *are* "living souls." This explains why redeemed people who physically die during the future Tribulation period are described as conscious living "souls" in heaven in Revelation 6:9-11. It's obvious in Genesis 2:7 that **what makes people living souls as opposed to dead souls is God's breath of life**. Without this "breath of life" the human soul is **a dead soul**. This is where the concept of Sheol comes into play: When a person physically dies the Bible teaches that the breath of life (i.e. spirit) returns to God who gave it (Ecclesiastes 12:6-7, Job 34:14-15 & Psalm 146:3-4). What happens to a soul when God's breath of life returns to Him and the soul is no longer a living soul? In other words, **where are dead souls laid to rest? In Sheol, of course!** Remember, as the Bible and James Strong define it, Sheol is "the world of the dead" (Proverbs 21:16). It's *not* the world of the living—the world of conscious beings—no, it's the world of **the dead**. And souls who are no longer animated by God's spiritual breath of life are **dead.** That's why they are placed in Sheol because, again, **Sheol is the world of the dead**.

We know from the Scriptures that every human soul will ultimately be resurrected from Sheol. Old Testament saints will be resurrected at the time of Christ's Second Coming at the end of the Tribulation (although some suggest that their souls were resurrected when Jesus ascended, citing Ephesians 4:8 for support). Everyone else will ultimately be resurrected at the time of the Great White Throne Judgment, which will take place immediately following the millennial reign of Christ on earth; this resurrection includes every unredeemed soul that's ever existed throughout history. Christians don't have to worry about going to Sheol, of course, because they've been spiritually born-again of the imperishable seed of Christ and possess eternal life in their spirits; hence, when authentic Christians physically die they are ushered into the presence of the LORD as shown in the aforementioned Revelation 6:9-11, as well as Philippians 1:20-24 and other passages— death holds no black pall over the blood-washed, spiritually reborn Christian for to "be with Christ… is better by far"! This is fully covered in Chapter Ten.

Why am I emphasizing all this? Because it's important here to understand that Sheol is the holding place of dead souls. It is where God stores the soulish remains of every human being that has ever existed, their immaterial DNA, if you will. This is perhaps necessary so that every person can be resurrected at the appropriate time. Incidentally, this is what makes the "second death" so horrifying: **Everyone will ultimately be resurrected from Sheol, but no one will ever be resurrected from the lake of fire**, which is the **second death** (Revelation 20:14-15). This "second death," as shown in *Hell Know*, is an **"everlasting destruction"** so utterly complete and final that no one will ever be resurrected from it; it is literally a total obliteration of soul and body where one's spiritual DNA is wiped out of existence.

By the way, the fact that everyone will ultimately be resurrected from Sheol, which is the first death, but no one will be resurrected from the second death explains why souls in Sheol are repeatedly described as "sleeping." People who suffer the first death are, in a sense, "sleeping" because they will one day be "awoken," that is, resurrected. By contrast, those who suffer the second death are never described as sleeping because they will never be "awoken" or resurrected. In other words, the first death is temporary, but the second death is everlasting—there's no hope of resurrection from the second death. We'll look at this matter further in the next chapter.

With the above scriptural facts in mind, let's return to the question of whether or not animals have souls and whether or not they go to Sheol when they physically die. The Bible describes animals in terms of being "living souls" just as well as humans. The Hebrew and Greek words for soul—*nephesh* and *psuche*—are repeatedly used in reference to animals in the Bible. For example:

> **So out of the ground the LORD God formed every animal of the field and every bird of the air, and brought them to the man to see what he would call them; and whatever the man called every living <u>creature</u>** *(nephesh)*, **that was its name.**
>
> **Genesis 2:19** (NRSV)

As you can see, land animals and birds are described in the Bible as "living creatures." The word "creature" in this verse is *nephesh*, the Hebrew word for "soul." Water animals are also described in the Bible as "living creatures" (Genesis 1:20-21); this includes Revelation 8:9 where the Greek word for "soul"—*psuche*—is used. My point is that animals are described in the God-breathed Scriptures as "living souls" just as people are. The reason most people don't realize this is because English translations generally don't translate *nephesh* and *psuche* as "soul" when the text refers to animals, as shown above in Genesis 2:19.

Why would Bible translators refuse to translate *nephesh* and *psuche* as "soul" when the terms apply to animals? No doubt because they wanted to draw a distinction between animals and human beings; after all, people are created in the image of God, beasts are not. Yet the original God-breathed Scriptures used the very same Hebrew and Greek word for both, shouldn't we? If God Himself doesn't have a problem with it, why should we?

I suspect the real reason many translators refrain from translating *nephesh* and *psuche* as "soul" when these words apply to animals is that doing so would counterproductive to the doctrine of the "immortal soul." As detailed in Chapter Four of *Hell Know*, this doctrine maintains that souls, once created, can never be de-created—even incorrigibly sinful souls worthy of eternal death. Hence, the immortal soul doctrine is one of the chief pillars for the eternal torture doctrine. This pillar would be severely damaged, of course, if people discovered that animals are described in the Bible as "living souls" just as well as people; after all, even the uneducated public might question the notion that animals possess immortal souls. To solve this dilemma, English Bible translators decided to translate *nephesh* and *psuche* as "creature(s)" or "thing(s)" when the terms applied to beasts. This is another example of religionists attempting to cover-up the scriptural truth in order to perpetuate false beliefs.

The King James translators were so careful in this matter that there's only one passage where *nephesh* is translated as "soul" in reference to animals; and the only reason they did so was because of the curious wording of the passage. Witness for yourself:

> **And levy a tribute unto the LORD of the men**
> **of war which went out to battle: one <u>soul</u>** *(nephesh)* **of**
> **five hundred, both of the persons, and of the**
> **beeves** [oxen]**, and of the asses, and of the sheep."**
>
> **Numbers 31:28** (KJV)

As you can see, "soul" *(nephesh)* in this verse applies equally to people, oxen, donkeys and sheep; the translators couldn't very well render it as "creatures" or "things" since the list includes people as well as animals. They therefore had no other choice but to translate *nephesh* as "soul." (Let's remember that the King James Version is a word-for-word translation so the translators couldn't very well omit the word).

An obvious question crops up at this point: If both humans and animals are described as "living souls" in the Bible, what is the essential difference between them? The difference is that human beings are created in the very image of God whilst animals are not (Genesis 1:27). This not only means that people have the same general *form* of God (head, face, torso, legs, arms[5]), but that human beings possess a spiritual dimension to their make-up that is *aware* of God & the spiritual realm, and Christians even possess the capacity to **know and commune with God because of spiritual rebirth through Christ**.

Animals, of course, lack these characteristics. Yes, they have a spirit but only in the sense of a "breath of life," an animating spiritual life-force from the Almighty. Animals are, of course, awesome creations of God, but they are on a far lower spiritual plane than people. They are instinct-oriented and therefore lack any consciousness of good or evil and have very limited reasoning capabilities. They don't have a God-consciousness (spirit) or a sin-consciousness (flesh). Many animals can be trained to respond to certain words and do various tasks or tricks, but not much more. They cannot build cities, learn languages, understand

---

[5] Don't believe for a second that God is some formless cloud being. Yes, He is spiritual in nature, as Jesus said (John 4:24), but the Bible indicates that He definitely has a central presence that is human-like in form (e.g. Ezekiel 1:25-28 & Revelation 1:14-16). Some may respond: "But isn't He omnipresent?" Yes, He's omnipresent in the sense that he knows what's going on everywhere at the same time and can do innumerable things simultaneously, but this does not mean His being lacks a central presence and form.

algebra, create and appreciate art or worship God. Human beings, on the other hand, are souls of the highest order created in His image and that's why God gave humankind authority over all animals (see Genesis 1:28 and 9:1-3). This is evidenced by the fact that people have zoos for animals and not vice versa.

Okay, so it's clear in the Bible that animals are "souls," but does this mean that their soulish essence goes to Sheol when they die? Evidently, according to Psalm 49:14:

> **<u>Like sheep</u> they** [the foolhardy] **are <u>appointed</u>**
> **<u>for Sheol</u>;**
>
> **Psalm 49:14** (NRSV)

The psalmist is essentially saying that fools under Old Covenant law will prematurely die just as surely as sheep slated to be slaughtered. Note that the Psalmist plainly states that sheep "are appointed for Sheol." There's no reason we shouldn't take this statement literally: When sheep die their souls go to Sheol. Remember, Sheol is simply "the world of the dead" or the "well of souls"—the space in the spiritual realm **where dead souls are stored**. Is there any reason why God wouldn't store the soulish remains of animals there as well as humans? After all, where else would He store them? Especially considering the strong possibility that God will resurrect some or all of them in the age to come. (See the last three sections of the <u>Epilogue</u>). We assume, of course, that there's a separate compartment in Sheol for animal souls, just as pet cemeteries are separate from human cemeteries in the physical world.

Incidentally, the fact the Bible teaches that dead animal souls go to Sheol when they die is further proof that Sheol is not a burial plot in the ground because sheep and other animals are not ordinarily thus buried. The Hebrew word *qeber* denotes the physical grave where bodies are buried; whereas Sheol, again, refers to the 'graveyard' in the spirit realm where dead souls are housed.

"God Will Ransom My Soul from the Power of Sheol"

Let's look again at a verse from Psalm 49:

> **But God will ransom <u>my soul</u> from the power of <u>Sheol</u>, for he will receive me."**
>
> **Psalm 49:15** (NRSV)

Firstly, notice that Sheol is spoken of as a condition of the soul, which was emphasized earlier. A person's body doesn't go to Sheol when s/he dies, nor does the breath of life (spirit), which simply returns to God who gave it; no, **Sheol refers exclusively to the condition of unregenerated souls after physical death**.

Secondly, like Job, the psalmist believed that his non-physical essence would go to Sheol when he died, but, also like Job, he believed God would ultimately ransom his soul from there. 'Ransom' literally means "the redeeming of a captive." When did God eventually redeem the souls of righteous Old Testament saints, including the writer of this psalm, from captivity to Sheol? And with what did He redeem them? The answer to the second question is obvious: God redeemed them by the blood of Jesus Christ when he was crucified for the sins of humanity. The answer to the first question is: Old Testament saints will be resurrected at the time of Jesus' second advent, as shown in Matthew 19:28-30 (although, again, some maintain that captive righteous souls were resurrected when Jesus ascended to heaven, citing Ephesians 4:8). This is when they will be "received" by the Father, as Psalm 49:15 puts it. See Chapter Eleven for details.

Chapter Four

SHEOL IN THE PSALMS,
Part II

Continuing our study of Sheol in the Psalms, let's consider this important question...

Did David Pray for His Ex-Friend to Go to a Hellish Torture Chamber?

Notice David's statement in this passage:

> **Let death seize upon them, and let them go down quick into <u>hell</u>** (*sheol*)**: for wickedness is in their dwellings, and among them.**
>
> **Psalm 55:15** (KJV)

David is obviously referring to his enemies in this verse, yet one of these enemies was once a close friend. This is revealed in the preceding lines, verses 12-14 (as well as verses 20-21). At one time David shared "sweet fellowship" with this person, but by the time of this writing his friend had turned against him.

As you can see, *sheol* is translated as "hell" in the King James Version and most English readers automatically picture "hell" as a devil-ruled torture chamber for wicked human beings. This presents a problem for these readers: How could David, "a man after God's own heart," pray for his enemies—including a former close friend—to go to such a place? The problem is resolved when we realize that Sheol refers to **the graveyard of dead souls** and, hence, **the state of death itself**. As such, David's prayer is in harmony with the law of God, which plainly states that the "wages of sin is **death**" (Romans 6:23).

As a godly king of Judah, David knew that God's Word promised his enemies would be defeated and destroyed (Leviticus 26:8 & Deuteronomy 28:7) and he was merely *praying in accordance with these promises*. True, he was obviously torn-up inside because one of these enemies was once a dear friend, but this ex-friend and his colleagues were trying to assassinate him, the righteous king of Judah. David felt he had no other recourse.

This verse illustrates that a proper, biblical understanding of Sheol clears up passages that present serious problems for those who view Sheol as a nether torture chamber.

"My Life Draws Near to Sheol"

Heman the Ezrahite was facing a grave situation with the possibility of death in this psalm:

> **For my <u>soul</u> is full of troubles, and my life draws near to <u>Sheol</u>.**
> **(4) I am counted among those who <u>go down to the Pit</u>; I am like those who have no help,**
> **Psalm 88:3-4** (NRSV)

While this passage isn't that notable it conveys several things detailed in other areas of *Sheol Know*: **1.** Heman links the destiny of his soul to Sheol, which verifies that (1.) Sheol is a condition of the soul and (2.) that the righteous as well as the unrighteous went there during Old Testament times (because Jesus hadn't yet paid for human redemption and therefore spiritual regeneration wasn't available). **2.** Sheol and "the Pit" are synonymous. **3.** Heman describes the location of Sheol in terms of "**going down** to the pit," which coincides with other passages that show that Sheol is located in the "heart of the earth," not in the physical realm, but in the spiritual realm. We'll address this in Chapter Nine. **4.** Heman says that his life was drawing near to Sheol, the Pit; and since Sheol is essentially synonymous with death (as shown in the next section) his life was drawing near to death.

We'll examine other pertinent verses from Psalm 88 in Chapter Six' *Rapha: "The Dead in Sheol"*

"Who Can Live and Never See Death? Who Can Escape the Power of Sheol?"

Let's observe what Ethan the Ezrahite had to say about Sheol:

> **Who can live and never see <u>death</u>? Who can escape the power of <u>Sheol</u>?**
> **Psalm 89:48** (NRSV)

Here it is as plain as language can communicate that **death and Sheol are essentially synonymous terms**; in other words, the only thing souls going to Sheol will experience is death itself, the utter absence of conscious existence. The obvious implication of both rhetorical questions is that, **apart from Christ's redemption, everyone who lives will ultimately die and go to Sheol, the death state of the soul**. Solomon also declared this:

> **... for death is the destiny of everyman; the living should take this to heart.**
> **Ecclesiastes 7:2b**

Both of these verses were written during the Old Testament era before Jesus' sacrifice for humanity was made; hence, no one living at this time had redemption from sin, regardless of whether or not they had a covenant with God, like the Israelites. **Before Christ's death and**

resurrection no one could escape the power of Sheol, whether moral, immoral or anywhere in between.

The good news is that this is no longer the case ever since Christ died for our sins and was raised to life for our justification (Romans 4:25). Jesus "poured out his soul unto death" (Isaiah 53:12 KJV) so that we don't have to. As it is written: "For God so loved the world that he gave his only Son, so that everyone who believes in him may not perish but may have eternal life" (John 3:16 NRSV). You see, in order for the world—that is, all humankind—to be set free from death, someone innocent of sin and thus not worthy of death had to die in our place. This is exactly what Jesus Christ did. So now when a born-again believer in Christ physically dies, his or her soul does not die, that is, go to Sheol, but rather goes straight to heaven. As it is written: "…to be absent from the body [is] to be present with the Lord" (2 Corinthians 5:8 KJV). Of course, this is only the intermediate state of the Christian soul; ultimately, the believer will receive a new glorified, spiritual, imperishable body at the bodily resurrection of the saints, called the first resurrection (1 Corinthians 15:42-43 & Revelation 20:4-6).

We've already gone over much of this information so why am I re-emphasizing it here? Simply to answer Ethan's question: "Who can live and not see death? Who can escape the power of Sheol?" The answer is *the believer* who has accepted God's sacrifice for humanity's sins, Jesus Christ. Genuine Christians literally possess eternal life in their spirits through spiritual rebirth (John 3:3,6,36), so even when they physically die **Sheol has no power over them**—*Hallelujah!*

"If I Make My Bed in Sheol, You Are There"

Let's examine another Psalm passage by David that comments on Sheol:

> **Where can I go from your Spirit? Or where can I flee from your presence?**
> **(8) If I ascend to heaven, you are there; if I make my bed in Sheol, you are there.**
> **Psalm 139:7-8** (NRSV)

To properly understand what David is saying here we must consider the gist of the entire psalm (remember, "context is king"). In Psalm 139 David is completely awestruck as he contemplates God's omnipresence and omniscience; that is, God being everywhere at the same time and knowing everything. David humbly realizes that he himself is *finite* while God, the Almighty Creator, is *infinite*. This awareness overwhelms him so much that he states, "Such knowledge is too wonderful for me, too lofty for me to attain" (verse 6).

With this understanding, David's words in verses 7-8 above are simply a poetic way of describing God's omnipresence. Where can David go that God isn't? The obvious answer is nowhere. Note how the New International Version renders this passage:

> **Where can I go from your Spirit? Where can I flee from your presence?**
> **(8) If I go up to the heavens, you are there; if I make my bed in the depths** *(sheol)*, **you are there.**
>
> **Psalm 139:7-8**

The NIV is a thought-for-thought translation and, as you can see, Sheol is rendered as "depths." According to the NIV translators the thought of the passage is that, whether David goes far out into the universe or to the lowest depths of the earth, God is there. The translators evidently didn't believe David was being very literal about the usage of *sheol* here; he was just making a point about God's omnipresence in a poetic manner.

However, I don't believe there's any reason we *shouldn't* take Sheol literally in this passage. God *is* everywhere. If David goes to heaven or to "the heavens"—the furthest reaches of the universe—God is there. If he makes his bed in Sheol, the LORD is there as well. God's central presence isn't in Sheol, of course (He's on his throne in heaven), but **He is completely aware at all times of Sheol and of every dead soul housed there**. If you think that might be too difficult for the Almighty, consider that Psalm 147:4 says God "determines the number of the stars and calls them each by name," which is mind blowing when you consider there are roughly 70 billion trillion stars according to current estimates!

David's wording—"make my bed in Sheol"—is important to understanding the nature of the intermediate state for the unredeemed soul. David obviously believed that if he were to go to Sheol he'd essentially be in bed there or, we could say, asleep. This is in harmony with the repeated descriptions of souls in Sheol as "sleeping;" for example, Job's exposition covered in Chapter Two.

Of course, souls in Sheol are not literally slumbering there, *they're dead*. The only "sleep" they experience is the sleep of death. This explains why David said in Psalm 6:5 that souls in Sheol cannot remember or praise the LORD even though God is present there (due to His omnipresent nature):

> **For in death there is no remembrance of you;**
> **in Sheol who can give you praise?**
> **Psalm 6:5** (NRSV)

This is a rhetorical question, meaning the answer is obvious within the question itself. If God is present is Sheol, why are souls held there unable to either remember or praise Him? Obviously because they are unable to do so because **they're dead and lack conscious existence**. In short, they're **"asleep" in death**. This is in complete harmony with the idea that Sheol is "the world of the dead." It's not the world of the living, it's the world of the dead.

"Sleeping" in Sheol

As seen in Chapter Two, Job described the intermediate state in terms of **sleep:**

> **"Why did I not perish at birth and die as I came from the womb? (12) Why were there knees to receive me and breasts that I might be nursed? (13) For now I would be lying down in peace; I would be asleep and at rest (14) *with* kings and counselors of the earth who built for themselves places now lying in ruins,"** **Job 3:11-14**

Let's keep in mind that this passage pertains to the time before redemption was provided for humanity through Jesus Christ's death and resurrection; hence, everyone shared the same fate when they physically died. No one could escape the power of Sheol back then. With this in mind, note how Job describes the condition he would experience if he had died at birth: He says he would be "lying down in peace... asleep and at rest" with other people that died long before him.

Those who advocate that Sheol is a place of conscious existence would argue that Job is referring to his body sleeping in the literal grave and not to the soul sleeping in Sheol. Yet, notice that Job does not say **his body** would be asleep; he plainly states "*I* would be lying down in peace; *I* would be asleep and at rest." Let's remember that, from a purely biblical standpoint, the Judeo-Christian perspective is focused on the inner man, not the body. The apostle Paul even stated that an improper focus on outward appearance rather than the heart is "worldly" (2 Corinthians 5:12-17); in other words, doing such is the carnal perspective or "human point of view" (NRSV), not the godly or divine point of view. Also, consider Jesus' statement that we are not to fear people who can only kill the body, but not the soul; rather, we are to fear God Himself who is able to utterly destroy both body and soul in the lake of fire (Matthew 10:28). You see, a true man or woman of God's outlook is geared toward the inward person, not the body; and, remember, Job was the most righteous man of God on the face of the earth at his time (Job 1: 1,3,8).

But, for the sake of argument, let's consider the possibility that Job was, in fact, referring to his body when he stated that he'd be asleep if he died at birth; and, by contrast, his soul would be fully conscious in Sheol. Let's read the passage as if this were so:

> **"Why did I not perish at birth and die as I came from the womb? Why were there knees to receive me and breasts that I might be nursed? For now I would be lying down in peace; I would be asleep and at rest with kings and counselors of the earth who built for themselves places now lying in ruins.** [I'm, of course, referring to my body here. My

soul—my *real* self—would be fully conscious in Sheol joyously hanging out with father Abraham]."

Job 3:11-14

Is this what Job really meant to say? Of course not. As you can see, altering the passage to fit the beliefs of those who insist that Sheol is a place of conscious existence renders it absurd.

Let's observe a Psalm passage that describes the intermediate state of unredeemed souls in terms of **sleeping:**

> **Consider and answer me, O LORD, my God! Give light to my eyes, or I will sleep the sleep of death.** **Psalm 13:3** (NRSV)

David's life was in mortal danger here; if God didn't save him he was going to die. Notice plainly how he describes the death condition he would experience if the LORD didn't deliver him: "I will sleep the sleep of death." Like Job, above, he wasn't absurdly referring to his body here; he says "*I* will sleep the sleep of death" not "my body will sleep the sleep of death while I go to Sheol and enjoy fellowship with our holy patriarchs."

Let's observe two cases where Jesus Christ himself described the intermediate state in terms of "sleep:"

> **...a ruler came and knelt before him [Jesus] and said, "My daughter has just died. But come and put your hand on her, and she will live." (19) Jesus got up and went with him, and so did his disciples.**
>
> **(23) When Jesus entered the ruler's house and saw the flute players and noisy crowd, (24) he said, "Go away. The girl is not dead but asleep." But they laughed at him. (25) After the crowd had been put outside, he went in and took the girl by the hand, and she got up. (26) News of this spread through all that region.**
>
> **Matthew 9:18-19; 23-26**

Why did the people laugh when Jesus said the girl was "asleep"? Obviously because she was literally dead. She was indeed dead but Christ described her condition as sleeping. Why? Because her soul was in Sheol sleeping the sleep of death and he came to "awaken" her back to life.

This next passage involves the case of Lazarus' death and subsequent resurrection by Jesus. The Lord is speaking:

> **"Our friend Lazarus has <u>fallen asleep</u>; but I am going there to <u>wake him up</u>."**
> **(12) His disciples replied, "Lord, if he sleeps, he will get better." (13) <u>Jesus had been speaking of his death</u>, but his disciples thought he meant natural sleep.**
> **(14) So then he told them plainly, "<u>Lazarus is dead</u>, (15) and for your sake I am glad I was not there, so that you may believe. Let us go to him."**
> **John 11:11-15**

As you can see, Jesus says that Lazarus had "fallen asleep" and that he needs to go to him in order to "wake him up," meaning resurrect him. But his disciples mistook him and thought he was talking about natural sleep. That's when Jesus plainly tells them that Lazarus had actually died. Verse 13 reveals that the Messiah was speaking of Lazarus' death when he said he had "fallen asleep" in verse 11.

What I want to drive home in this section is that the Bible repeatedly describes the intermediate state of the spiritually dead soul in terms of "sleeping." Both the Old and New Testaments do this. Even Jesus Christ himself, the living Word of God, did this.

What can we deduce from this? That when an unredeemed person dies, according to the Bible, his/her soul enters into the sleep of death. Again, this is not literal sleeping; it's "the sleep of death" as David described it above in Psalm 13:3.

Most of us have heard the evangelistic declaration: "If you die today you will wake up in either heaven or hell!" Yet, if unredeemed souls are asleep in death in Sheol until their resurrection to face God's judgment (Revelation 20:11-15), this slogan is only right on the first count. After all, souls can't very well "wake up" in hell (i.e. Sheol) if they're sleeping the 'sleep' of death. Jesus and the apostles never used inaccurate pronouncements like this in their evangelistic efforts, why should we? If you're a Christian, **let's strive to be faithful to biblical truth!**

Why are Souls in Sheol Referred to as "Sleeping"?

If souls in Sheol are dead, why are they repeatedly described as "sleeping" in the Bible? All who go to Sheol are, in fact, dead and have ceased to exist in the sense of conscious existence, but the Bible refers to them as "sleeping" because they will all be awakened or resurrected from death one day. As briefly noted in the last chapter, this is what differentiates Sheol, the first death, from the lake of fire (Gehenna), which is the second death (Revelation 20:6,14, 21:8 & 2:11). **Everyone will be resurrected from the first death, but no one will be resurrected from the second death.** This is why the second death is described as an "*eternal* punishment" (Matthew 25:46) or "*everlasting* destruction" (2 Thessalonians 1:9) because there is no hope of recovery or resurrection from it—it's a fatal destruction of such complete and final magnitude that it lasts forever.

'Soul Sleep'?

Many of you have no doubt heard of "soul sleep" and may be wondering if that's what I'm talking about here. Yes and no. 'Yes' because advocates of soul sleep believe, as noted above, that the soul is simply "sleeping" the sleep of death during the intermediate state between death and resurrection; they don't believe the soul is literally slumbering while awaiting resurrection. 'No' because most adherents of soul sleep believe that the souls of spiritually regenerated people will also experience this condition of soul sleep during the intermediate state. As pointed out repeatedly in our study, this is simply not biblical. If people are born-again of the imperishable seed of Christ and, hence, *possess* eternal life in their spirits, why would they have to suffer death when their bodies perish? This explains why the apostle Paul wrote to the Corinthian believers that being absent from the body is to be present with the Lord (2 Corinthians 5:8). We'll address this issue fully in Chapter Ten.

The doctrinal label "soul sleep" is a good, brief and accurate description of the intermediate state of unregenerated souls but I never use it for two reasons:

1. It gives the impression to the average person that the soul is still alive and merely dozing during the intermediate state.
2. The label is too closely related with cultic or marginally cultic groups with which I don't want to be associated, and understandably so.

Some will inevitably argue: "If cultic or near-cultic organizations adhere in some form to the view that souls in Sheol are asleep in death and therefore not conscious, does this not automatically make it false or, at least, questionable? If nothing else, it doesn't look good."

This argument is addressed in detail in Chapter Six of *Hell Know*,[6] but allow me to briefly address it again here: Christians do not determine the veracity of a doctrine by whether or not an objectionable group adheres to it in one form or another; they determine what is true and not true simply by finding out what the God-breathed Scriptures clearly and consistently teach. If a doctrine is not clearly and consistently taught in the Bible, it's a false doctrine, regardless of what respectable person or group claims otherwise. Likewise, if a doctrine is clearly and consistently taught in the Bible then it's a true doctrine, regardless of what questionable person or group agrees with it. This is in accordance with the theological principle of *sola scripture*, meaning "by Scripture alone," which maintains that the God-breathed Holy Scriptures are the first and final authority regarding every judgment of Christian doctrine and practice.

Let's face it, we all agree with cultic groups on some things; for instance, many cultic or borderline cultic organizations believe that the Bible is the inerrant Word of God. All authentic Christians, of course,

---

[6] In the section *Cults Teach Everlasting Destruction—It doesn't Look Good*

believe this as well. Wouldn't it be ludicrous to reject this belief simply because questionable groups agree with it?

Think about it like this: any person or group that steps outside of the blinding influence of erroneous religious tradition will easily be able to determine what the Bible clearly and consistently teaches on Sheol and the condition of souls held there during the intermediate state, as this study shows. This explains how various cultic or borderline cultic groups are able to discern the truth about the nature of Sheol, at least partially—they weren't blinded by human-made religious tradition.

Chapter Five

SHEOL IN PROVERBS,
The book of Wisdom

Of the 31 chapters of the book of Proverbs, the first 29 were written by Solomon, the wisest person who's ever lived outside of Jesus Christ (1 Kings 3:12). In Chapter Two we saw how Solomon described the nature of Sheol in very clear language. He said that those who die "know nothing" (Ecclesiastes 9:5) because they've gone to Sheol, where "there is no work, or thought, or knowledge or wisdom" (Ecclesiastes 9:10).

Everything Solomon says about Sheol in the book of Proverbs is in harmony with this unmistakable description.

Sheol and Death: Synonymous

The following texts, for instance, reveal that Sheol is essentially synonymous with death because they go hand-in-hand. These first two verses poetically reference the wicked adulteress:

> **Her feet go down to <u>death</u>; her steps follow the path of <u>Sheol</u>.**
>
> **Proverbs 5:5** (NRSV)

> **Her house is the way to <u>Sheol</u>, going down to the chambers of <u>death</u>.**
> **Proverbs 7:27** (NRSV)

These passages apply to those in covenant with God under Old Testament law. They declare a sobering fact: Those who choose to commit sexual immorality with an adulteress "follow the path of Sheol" or are on "the way to Sheol." Proverbs 2:18 teaches the same thing. This is not to suggest that godly people during the Old Testament period didn't go to Sheol when they eventually died because we know from numerous passages that they did; these verses simply reveal that adulterers will **prematurely die**. This was the penalty for adultery and other critical sexual sins under the law of Moses (Leviticus 20:10-16).

Even today, despite the fact that we're living during the New Testament era of grace, those who choose to live sexually immoral lifestyles often suffer serious consequences for their actions, including premature death from AIDS. Other consequences critically hamper the quality of one's life—teenage pregnancy, illegitimate children, abortion, broken relationships, divorce, psychological problems, a multitude of sexual diseases—many of which are incurable—and other negatives, like the wrath of the mate of the person with whom one's cheating. Truly, sexual immorality brings death. Even if it doesn't literally kill you, it will certainly kill the quality of your life.

This next passage personalizes folly as a wicked woman and is referring to the foolish people who choose to follow "her":

> **But they do not know that the <u>dead</u> are there,**
> **that her guests are in the <u>depths of Sheol</u>.**
> **Proverbs 9:18** (NRSV)

The 9th chapter of Proverbs showcases the personal invitations of Wisdom and Folly. Those who prudently enter the house of Wisdom will be rewarded with long lives, as verified by verses 11-12, while those who choose Folly will **prematurely die**.

Premature death is, of course, the gravest consequence of following folly with wild abandon. The graveyard is full of such people, so are our prisons and mental institutions. Those who merely dabble in folly here and there will suffer as well, just not as severely. This is the case even today in the age of grace.

IMPORTANT SIDE NOTE: One may legitimately argue that righteous people who possess godly wisdom sometimes prematurely die. It is true that God occasionally calls people to be martyrs for the advancement of His kingdom, like Stephen (Acts 7). If God calls someone to do this He will reveal it to his or her spirit by the Holy Spirit and give them the grace to handle it. The Bible promises us 70-80 years of life (Psalm 90:10); anything else is a plus. Hence, except for God-ordained martyrdom, any God-fearing person who prematurely dies simply failed to win the "good fight of faith" over the Evil One who desperately desires to bring about the premature death of anyone who is a threat to his kingdom. We must understand that the devil will not appear to those he attacks as a red cartoony figure with a pitchfork. The godly Christian can easily discern an attack of the devil because every satanic attack falls within the spectrum of five general categories: **1.** Enemy attack *and* defeat (not just enemy attack), **2.** financial attack (poverty), **3.** premature death, **4.** physical illness and **5.** mental illness, which includes depression, anxiety, fear, torment and madness. (These five types of attack should be distinguished from temptation to sin and any type of sin bondage; sin and its consequences are simply the result of a Christian falling prey to the weakness of **his or her own flesh** and failing to live by his/her new born-again spirit, which is indwelt by the Holy Spirit). The book of Job powerfully verifies the above data. When God gave permission to Satan to attack righteous Job, the devil attacked him in the five ways listed: (1.) People were stirred up against Job and attacked, (2.) all his wealth was wiped out, (3.) his ten children and hundreds of his employees prematurely died, (4.) Job physically suffered painful boils from head to toe, and, lastly, (5.) Job suffered intense mental ailments—the desire to die, depression, torment and anxiety. Acts 10:38 says that Jesus "went around doing good works and healing all who were under the power of the devil." Those "under the power of the devil" are those who fall prey to one or more of the five satanic attacks above. My point is that premature death is certainly one of the ways in which the enemy attacks those who are a threat to his kingdom, and God's children must be diligent & vigilant and learn to fight "the good fight of faith" to have victory over just such an attack. For a detailed article on effective spiritual warfare read *Spiritual Warfare—The Basics* at the Fountain of Life website (dirkwaren.com).

Getting back to Proverbs 9:18, notice plainly that souls in Sheol are described as "dead," not roasting alive in torment desperate for less than a drop of water for relief. Their sinful lifestyles resulted in their deaths because "the wages of sin is death" (Romans 6:23).

These next two passages equate Sheol with *abaddon*, which is the Hebrew word for destruction:

> **Sheol and <u>abaddon</u>** [destruction] **lie open before the LORD, how much more human hearts!**
> **Proverbs 15:11** (NRSV)

> **Sheol and <u>abaddon</u>** [destruction] **are never satisfied, and human eyes are never satisfied.**
> **Proverbs 27:20** (NRSV)

What I want to emphasize from the five proverbial texts in this section is that **Solomon repeatedly brings up Sheol and repeatedly associates it with death or destruction**. This is not unique to Solomon or the book of Proverbs; here are some passages from past chapters that also equate Sheol with death:

> **For <u>in death</u> there is no remembrance of you; <u>in Sheol</u> who can give you praise?**
> **Psalm 6:5** (NRSV)

"For Sheol cannot thank you, death cannot praise you; those who go down to the Pit cannot hope for your faithfulness.

(19) The living, the living, they thank you as I do this day."

Isaiah 38:18-19 (NRSV)

Who can live and never see death? Who can escape the power of Sheol?

Psalm 89:48 (NRSV)

There are other biblical passages that identify Sheol with death and destruction as well, such as Job 26:6, Psalm 49:14, Hosea 13:14, Habakkuk 2:5, Revelation 6:8 and 20:14. Most of these passages are cases of synonymous parallelism where the second part of the verse simply repeats and enforces the thought of the first in different words.

As you can plainly see, **the God-breathed scriptures repeatedly equate Sheol with death and destruction, not conscious torture**. These passages were written by a variety of godly men separated by many centuries—Job, David, the Korahites, Ethan, Solomon, Hezekiah, Habakuk and John; they all spoke in harmony concerning Sheol because they all "spoke from God as they were carried along by the Holy Spirit" (2 Peter 1:20-21). Do you think the LORD is trying to reveal something to us about the nature of Sheol in these many clear passages? Of course He is! Those who go to Sheol suffer death; their lives are destroyed. Death simply refers to the absence of life because it is, in fact, the opposite of life—the state of non-being or non-existence; it does not refer to a low-quality life separate from God as proven in Chapter Six of *Hell Know*. Living a life of misery in a subterranean torture chamber is still life, after all, but that's not what Sheol is. Biblically speaking, **Sheol is the "world of the dead" where lifeless souls are housed until their resurrection**. They are dead and lack consciousness; they can therefore neither remember nor praise God. How much clearer could the LORD possibly be in his awesome Word?

"To Avoid Sheol Below"

Let's look at another proverbial passage that mentions Sheol:

For the wise the path of life leads upward in order to avoid Sheol below.
Proverbs 15:24 (NRSV)

This verse isn't saying that wise people in Old Testament times (before the ascension of Christ) would go to heaven when they died. We must interpret Scripture in light of Scripture—a hermeneutical rule—and we know that during the Old Testament period both the wise and foolish alike went to Sheol when they died.

The text is simply declaring that, under the law of Moses, living a wise, godly life would guarantee a person a long, blessed life in the "land of the living" and avoid a premature trip to Sheol. As Proverbs 4:18 puts it, "The path of the righteous is like the first gleam of dawn, shining ever brighter till the full light of day." Although death or Sheol was indeed "the destiny of every man" during the Old Testament period (Ecclesiastes 7:2 & Psalm 89:48), those who were wise by living according to godly wisdom would avoid Sheol as long as possible, enjoying a full, productive life.

Observe how the passage makes it clear that Sheol was something to be avoided as long as possible. This doesn't jell with the belief that Sheol had a separate compartment called "paradise" where Old Testament saints enjoyed sweet fellowship with father Abraham far removed from their earthly troubles. If this were so, why would any godly person want to avoid it? Any righteous individual would want to get there as soon as possible if it were true, right? This shows that this belief is unscriptural. Sheol is, in fact, the state of death. Those who go there are dead and therefore no longer exist. Their soulish remains are held there but their conscious life has expired because the animating breath of life has returned to God. Hence, Sheol is to be avoided, not looked forward to.

Sheol: "The Assembly of the Dead"

As noted in <u>Chapter One</u>, Greek & Hebrew scholar James Strong defined Sheol as "the world of the dead." This corresponds to the biblical description as seen in this passage:

> **Whoever wanders from the way of understanding will rest in <u>the assembly of the dead</u>.**
> **Proverbs 21:16** (NRSV)

> **A man who wanders from the way of understanding will rest in <u>the assembly of the dead</u>.**
> **Proverbs 21:16** (NASB)

The International Standard Version translates this passage like so: "Whoever wanders from the path of understanding will end up where the dead are gathered." Where are the dead gathered? In Sheol, "the assembly of the dead."

Someone might argue that "the assembly of the dead" might refer to the physical grave or tomb where bodies are laid to rest, but there are a number of problems with this view: corpses are laid to rest in cemeteries all over the earth and some bodies aren't buried at all, while others are lost at sea or blown to bits, etc. This could hardly be "the assembly of the dead." The phrase, however, perfectly fits the biblical concept of Sheol, which is the graveyard of dead souls in the heart of the earth, truly the "assembly of the dead." And please notice that the souls gathered together in Sheol are dead. They're not living souls or half-living souls. They're **dead** because Sheol is **the realm of the dead**.

"Deliver His Soul from Sheol"

The fact that Sheol is the "assembly of the dead" and, as such, should be avoided as long as possible makes sense of this proverb:

Do not hold back discipline from the child, although you beat him with the rod, <u>he will not die</u>. (14) You shall beat him with the rod and <u>deliver his soul from Sheol</u>,

Proverbs 23:13-14 (NASB)

The passage is simply stressing the importance of godly, loving discipline. It is by no means advocating child abuse; only a wicked heart would entertain such a perverse interpretation. In Old Testament times everyone ultimately went to Sheol when they died, but by properly training a child to live in harmony with the laws of God, and hence acquiring godly wisdom, it would guarantee the child a long, blessed life and keep him or her from the curse of premature death.

Let me use my own life as an example: I grew up in a home where there was almost zero proper parental discipline. I was consequently full of folly as I entered my teenage years because my parents failed to discipline it out of me, that is, beat it out of me.[7]

This folly naturally resulted in a string of critical mishaps throughout my adolescence and young adult years. Some of these misfortunes included overdosing and almost dying on drugs, getting hit by a car and landing on my head resulting in a near-fatal head injury, getting expelled from school for drugs, falling off a 37" cliff during a "party" at a fair and ending up in a body cast for months, not to mention almost committing suicide. The fact that I survived those years is a miracle!

My point is that the folly I walked in was due to lack of parental discipline and it almost resulted in my death on several occasions. So I know from experience how true this proverb is—if parents fail to drive-out folly in their children through proper discipline, folly will either severely hamper their lives or kill them.

By the age of 20 I was understandably starved for godly wisdom, discipline and truth! The LORD revealed Himself to me and I turned to Him in repentance through Christ. I slowly started to acquire wisdom through the study & application of His Word and the relational discipline

---

[7] Proverbs 20:30 includes proper parental discipline when it states: "Blows and wounds cleanse away evil, and beatings purge the inmost being."

of my Heavenly Father by the Holy Spirit. Here's a fact: True love disciplines. Parents who fail to discipline their children are showing that they don't really care nor have the time for them. The truth is, I *longed* for true, loving discipline throughout my teenage years but never received it. Thankfully my Heavenly Father lovingly gave me the discipline I needed when I finally turned to Him.

Observe, incidentally, how the above proverb says that **a child's soul is saved from Sheol**. This is further evidence that Sheol concerns the state of the human soul after physical death. It is not the housing abode of the spirit—i.e. the breath of life—or the physical body. The spirit of life returns to God who gave it and the body simply returns to the dust. The Appendix elaborates on this.

Sheol is Never Satisfied

This next proverb reveals that Sheol is never satisfied:

> **Sheol and abaddon** [destruction] **are never satisfied, nor are the eyes of man ever satisfied.**
> **Proverbs 27:20** (NASB)

Once again, we see that Sheol is associated with **destruction. I** repeat: **Sheol is regularly equated with death and destruction in the Scriptures not conscious torment**.

Secondly, we observe that Sheol is "never satisfied" just as the eyes of man are never satisfied. What's this mean? Concerning the latter, the desires of human nature are never satiated. People always have desires—good, bad, ugly and everything in between—and once these desires are obtained or satiated we desire even more, or something else entirely. It's our nature as human beings; it's how we're wired. This is the nature of Sheol as well.

How is Sheol never satisfied? Well, we've discovered that Sheol refers to the place and condition that all unredeemed souls enter after death; it is the holding place of captive souls, the graveyard of dead souls. Since unredeemed people continue to birth and die year after year, decade after decade, century after century, the "population" of Sheol naturally keeps growing.

For a natural comparison, consider earthly graveyards where bodies are buried. Graveyards remain active for "business" until they become full of bodies. They then become historical in nature. My wife was the office manager of a large burial park for many years. This graveyard has 58 acres of land that are developed for business. It has an additional 60 acres that are undeveloped. As the 58 developed acres become full they will have to expand by developing and utilizing the additional 60 acres. This particular burial park will never be "satisfied" until all 118 acres are full. Sheol, by contrast, has no limits to its "expansion" as unredeemed people continue birthing and dying century after century. It is in this sense that Sheol is never satisfied.

This next passage addresses the same point:

> **There are three things that will not be satisfied. Four that will not say, "Enough": Sheol, and the barren womb, earth that is never satisfied with water, and fire that never says, "Enough."**
> **Proverbs 30:15-16 (NASB)**

Four things are listed that are "never satisfied": Sheol is never satisfied with its increasing population of dead souls, the barren womb is always ready to produce another child, the earth will always drink up more water, particularly dryer landscapes like Israel, and fire always keeps devouring combustible matter. Yet, **none of these four items are insatiable in an absolute sense**: A womb can only produce so many babies in a lifetime; the earth can only take so much water before flooding begins; fire only destroys until it is extinguished one way or another. Just so, Sheol will one day stop receiving dead souls, and every lifeless soul resident there will be resurrected to face judgment; in fact, Sheol itself—i.e. "Hades"—will ultimately be thrown into the lake of fire, as shown in Revelation 20:11-15.

Chapter Six

THE PROPHETS
and the Intermediate State

Let's now observe what the Old Testament prophets had to say about the nature of Sheol.

"Sheol has Enlarged its Appetite"

We'll start with the book of Isaiah:

Ah, you who rise early in the morning in pursuit of strong drink, who linger in the evening to be inflamed by wine,

(12) whose feasts consist of lyre and harp, tambourine and flute and wine, but who do not regard the deeds of the LORD, or see the work of his hands!

(13) Therefore my people go into exile without knowledge; their nobles are dying of hunger and their multitude is parched with thirst.

(14) Therefore Sheol has enlarged its appetite and opened its mouth beyond measure; the nobility

of Jerusalem and her multitude go down, her throng
and all who exult in her.

Isaiah 5:11-14 (NRSV)

This passage is referring to the wicked nobles of Judah and the numerous people corrupted by their leadership. According to verses 11-12 these people had completely forsaken the LORD, plunging into a flood of "partying" and dissipation. In fact, earlier in chapter 3 the LORD remarked that they had become as brazenly shameless as Sodom (3:9)—that's pretty bad! As a result of their evil deeds, God had to justly pronounce judgment on them as shown in verses 13-14 above. Many were to be taken into captivity, no longer blessed with the knowledge of God. Ohers would die of hunger and thirst or be slain by the sword (1:20).

Clearly, multitudes would die because of God's righteous judgment. This explains why verse 14 proclaims, "…Sheol has enlarged its appetite and opened its mouth beyond measure."

This is obviously not a literal statement. Sheol is not some living entity that possesses a colossal maw and appetite, but God uses this metaphor to effectively illustrate that numerous people would die because of His just judgment. "The wages of sin is death" and these rebels were going to eat the fruit of their actions (after much merciful patience on the LORD's part, I might add).

In verse 24 God uses clear metaphors to illustrate the nature of Sheol and eternal damnation:

Therefore, as the tongue of fire devours the
straw and as dry grass sinks down in the flame, so
their root will become rotten [i.e. decay] **and their**
blossom go up like dust; for they have rejected the
instruction of the LORD of hosts, and have despised
the word of the Holy One of Israel.

Isaiah 5:24 (NRSV)

We know this text is referring to the death of these people because the very next verse says so (verse 25). The root that decays is probably referring to their bodies in light of verse 25: "their corpses were like refuse in the streets." But their immaterial being, their soul that goes to Sheol, is likened to straw devoured by fire and dry grass that goes up in flame. The example is unmistakable: straw and grass that are set ablaze go up in smoke and cease to exist; likewise blossoms that "go up like dust" no longer exist as well. This corresponds to the nature of Sheol because Sheol is a condition of non-existence where dead souls are held until their resurrection on judgment day. These metaphors are applicable to both Sheol, which is the temporary hell or **the first death**, and the lake of fire (Gehenna), which is the eternal hell or **the "second death."**

Since Isaiah 5:14 blatantly refers to wicked people, the King James translators rendered *sheol* as "hell." They obviously did this to give the impression that wicked people go to a nether realm of conscious torment when they die. This is in contrast to Isaiah 38:10 where they rendered *sheol* as "the grave" because the text refers to godly king Hezekiah. Needless to say, this schizophrenic practice is a translation error of the greatest magnitude. It grieves my heart to see how the truth about Sheol was purposefully covered up in order to support the religious myth that Sheol ("hell") is a nether torture chamber where undying souls suffer conscious torture without respite until their resurrection on judgment day.

Let's observe what Hezekiah said in this particular passage:

> **A writing of Hezekiah king of Judah, after his illness and recovery:**
> **(10) I said "In the middle of my life <u>I am to enter the gates of Sheol</u>; I am to be <u>deprived of the rest of my years</u>."**
> **(11) I said, "<u>I shall not see the LORD, the LORD in the land of the living; I shall look on man no more</u> among the inhabitants of the world.**
> **(12) Like a shepherd's tent my dwelling is pulled up and removed from me; as a weaver I rolled up my life. He cuts me off from the loom; from day until night Thou dost make <u>an end of me</u>."**
> **Isaiah 38:9-12** (NASB)

In this passage Hezekiah is praying for deliverance from a fatal illness that would cause him to die prematurely. Note that Hezekiah clearly expected to go to Sheol when he died—just like Jacob, Job, David, Solomon and other people of God in the Old Testament era. The rest of his statements are revealing. In verse 10 he says that, if he dies and goes to Sheol, he will "be deprived of the rest of his years." The rest of his years of what? The rest of his years of *life!* Hezekiah knew that if he died and went to Sheol, the spiritual graveyard of souls, he would be **dead**—he would not have life anymore; he would cease to have consciousness or feeling. That's why, in verse 11, he speaks of life in this world as "the land of *the living*." This is in contrast to the land of Sheol, which is the land of the dead where lifeless souls are held until their resurrection on judgment day. Notice also, in verse 11, he makes it clear that he "shall not see the LORD" in Sheol. This is further proof that souls held in Sheol are dead and conscious of nothing. After all, the Bible reveals God to be omnipresent. Consequently, a righteous man like Hezekiah would certainly be able to sense God's presence even in the nether abode of Sheol; that is, as long as he were alive, conscious and able. We saw in Chapter Four that, although the LORD has a central presence and throne, he's everywhere all the time, including heaven and Sheol (Psalm 139:7-8). However, since souls held in Sheol are dead they are unable to experience God in any sense. Because they lack conscious existence the only thing they can "experience" is death itself, utter non-being. This is why Hezekiah would "not see the LORD" in Sheol.

In addition, notice Hezekiah's statement that he "shall look upon man no more" in Sheol. How can this be if Sheol was, in part, a paradise where righteous people hanged out with father Abraham and other saints, as religionists claim? If this teaching were true then Hezekiah would be looking upon many people in Sheol. Furthermore, if this doctrine were true, why would Hezekiah pray so earnestly *not* to go there? You would think he'd want to go to a pleasant paradise, the sooner the better. This shows that this belief is unbiblical and therefore false. Hezekiah knew that he wouldn't be seeing the LORD or anyone else in Sheol because he understood that Sheol was and is a condition where people only "experience" death itself. Although he knew he'd eventually go there, as every righteous (and unrighteous) person did when they died in Old

Testament times, he wanted to avoid it as long as possible and enjoy a long, productive life in "the land of the living."

Regarding this last point, some may argue that Hezekiah technically stated, "I shall look on man no more among the inhabitants of the world" (verse 11). The argument being that, although Hezekiah will not see people in the physical world any longer, he will definitely see multitudes of people in the paradise compartment of Sheol, as well as others being tormented in the fiery compartment across the (supposed) great chasm. Momentarily accepting this argument, let's read Hezekiah's statement as if this contention were true: "I shall look on man no more among the inhabitants of the world, but—Praise God—I shall look upon many people in Sheol while communing with Abraham and friends." Let's face it, this belief makes an absurdity of passages like this. Hezekiah was simply saying that, because he was about to die and go to the graveyard of dead souls, he would no longer see and commune with his fellow human beings anymore. You see? With a proper understanding of the nature of Sheol, scriptural statements like this make perfect sense.

Let's now address an important question that is naturally raised in light of the fact that Hezekiah and other righteous people were destined to go to Sheol: What benefit was there to serving God in Old Testament times if both the righteous and the unrighteous went to Sheol when they died? For one, those who served God were promised a full, blessed life on earth (Deuteronomy 8:1 & Ezekiel 18:5-9, 14-17, 27-28), whereas those who forsook Him were risking the judgment of premature death unless, of course, they repented (Deuteronomy 8:19-20 & Ezekiel 18:10-13, 18, 20, 26). Secondly, although both the righteous and the wicked went to Sheol when they died, the righteous were promised a resurrection unto eternal life (Daniel 12:2-3), whereas the wicked would only be resurrected to face divine judgment and suffer the destruction of the second death (Daniel 12:2, Revelation 20:11-15, Matthew 10:28 & 2 Peter 3:7).

Before the ascension of Christ every soul had to die because no ransom of innocent blood had yet been paid; thus no soul could obtain intrinsic immortality and, consequently, go to heaven at the time of physical death. In our present era redeemed men and women go to heaven when they physically die to bask in the presence of the LORD while awaiting their glorious bodily resurrection—death and Sheol have zero power over blood-bought spiritually-regenerated children of the Most High God!

The Proud King of Babylon Brought Down to Sheol

Isaiah 14:1-23 addresses the LORD's just judgment on the king of Babylon. "The wages of sin is death" and this was the Almighty's sentence for the notorious king. Consequently, he died and his body was not given a proper burial. The passage also shows the king's soul going to Sheol.

Out of the multitude of passages in the Old Testament that describe the nature of Sheol, this is one of only two that advocates of eternal torture occasionally cite to support their belief (we'll examine the other one at the end of this chapter). They're not overly gung ho about either of them, however, since nothing is said about souls writhing in fiery torment pleading for less than a drop of water, but they do occasionally cite this one in a weak attempt to support the idea that souls in Sheol are conscious and can talk. Let's examine the passage piece by piece to see if this is so.

Verses 1-3 show that the LORD will deliver the Israelites from their Babylonian captivity and bring them back to their homeland. Starting in verse 4 we see the Israelites taunting the fallen, dead king of Babylon:

> **you will take up this taunt against the king of Babylon: How the oppressor has ceased! How his insolence has ceased!**
>
> **(5) The LORD has broken the staff of the wicked, the scepter of rulers,**
>
> **(6) that struck down the peoples in wrath with unceasing blows, that ruled the nations in anger with unrelenting persecution.**
>
> **(7) The whole earth is at rest and quiet; they break forth into singing.**

(8) The cypresses exult over you, the cedars of Lebanon, saying "Since you were laid low, no one comes to cut us down."

Isaiah 14:4-8 (NRSV)

These verses reveal how oppressive, insolent and wicked the king of Babylon was to all the peoples and nations surrounding him. Verses 5-6 show that the LORD Himself had broken the king's staff and scepter; in other words, God's sentence of death brought an end to his tyrannical reign. Hence, all the peoples of the earth who were either oppressed by him or feared his threat were now at peace and even celebrating in song (verse 7). Verse 8 even says that the trees the king would regularly cut down for his numerous building projects would break out in exultation. Did these trees literally break out in triumphant jubilation? Of course not, this is **figurative language**. God is a master communicator and he uses figurative language here to make a point—the king of Babylon was so wicked that even inanimate objects would rejoice over his death (!); not literally, of course, but in essence.

Continuing with the passage:

Sheol beneath is stirred up to meet you when you come; it rouses the shades [the dead] to greet you, all who were leaders of the earth; it raises from their thrones all who were kings of the nations.

(10) All of them will speak and say to you: "You too have become as weak as we! You have become like us!"

(11) Your pomp is brought down to Sheol, and the sound of your harps; maggots are the bed beneath you and worms are your covering.

Isaiah 14:9-11 (NRSV)

Sheol is preparing to receive soul of the Babylonian king. The dead are "roused" to greet the king, including those who were once mighty kings of various nations. The Hebrew word for the dead in verse 9 is *rapha (raw-FAW)* which the NRSV translates as "shades," as shown above. This word refers to **the dead** and can also mean "ghost." Both the

KJV and the NKJV translate *rapha* as **"the dead"** while the NASB renders it "the spirits of the dead" and the NIV as "the spirits of the departed." Although these latter two translations use "spirits" in their multi-word definition of *rapha,* the Hebrew word for 'spirit'—*ruach*—does not appear in the text. Why do I point this out? Because when an unredeemed person dies their spirit (or breath of life) returns to God from whence it came; their dead soul goes to rest in Sheol until their resurrection.

With this understanding, verse 10 shows these **dead souls** greeting the Babylonian king by informing him that, despite all his former glory and infamous power, he has now become weak like they are, signifying that human distinctions of greatness are meaningless in Sheol, the world of the dead.

Should we take verses 9-10 literally? Did the dead souls in Sheol really rise up to greet and mock the king of Babylon? Absolutely not. We confidently conclude this for three reasons: **1.** These people who are greeting the king are described as "dead" in verse 9. The dead are dead. Dead people are not conscious and cannot talk. **2.** The passage switches from literal language to figurative language in verse 8, which is obvious because trees don't talk and celebrate. Verses 9-11 continue in this figurative mode. Why should we assume this? Because, once again, the dead souls housed in Sheol are dead. Anything that is soulishly dead is not alive or conscious and therefore cannot very well think, speak or greet; hence, the language must be figurative. **3.** We've examined a multitude of clear passages in our study that plainly reveal Sheol as the nether realm of the dead, the "land of silence" where the dead know nothing and therefore cannot think or even remember God. This is verified by numerous respected men of God throughout the Old Testament and even by the LORD Himself, as we shall see later this chapter. Scripture is not open to isolated interpretations based on personal bias (2 Peter 1:20-21). How is Scripture interpreted? Simple: Scripture interprets Scripture; it's an interpretational law. Consequently, verses 9-10 must be interpreted as figurative language. And please notice that, figurative or literal, nowhere is anyone shown writhing in fiery torment begging for less than a drop of water for relief.

Verse 11 continues, showing that the Babylonian king's "pomp" has brought him the sentence of premature death. Surely "Pride goeth before destruction, a haughty spirit before a fall" (Proverbs 16:18 KJV). It goes on to say that **maggots will be the king's bed** and **worms his covering**. This is insightful in multiple ways: The verse specifically refers to Sheol, which is backed up by its mention in verse 9, so we know the text is specifically talking about the world of the dead where the soul goes after death and not to the physical grave or tomb. It is said that maggots are his bed and worms his blanket. Is this literal language? Are there literal maggots in Sheol feeding upon dead souls? Not likely. This is more figurative language drawing a parallel to the physical grave to produce a powerful image (in the next chapter we'll examine how Sheol and the physical grave are distinct yet parallel concepts in Scripture). What's the picture we get from this image? Since maggots consume only carcasses, the imagery is that of death. It's not a pretty picture, but it's not supposed to be. Death was God's judgment on the pompous Babylonian king for that is the wages of sin. Also consider the imagery of maggots being his bed and worms his covering.[8] The picture is clearly that of **'sleeping' in death, not roasting and wailing in conscious torment**, which is why they had to be "roused" (verse 9).

Paralleling Sheol to the physical grave offers further insight. The Babylonian king was not given a proper burial like other rulers placed in personal tombs; the king's body was discarded in a big hole with other Babylonian corpses and devoured by maggots. This is corroborated by verses 18-20:

> **All the kings of the nations lie in glory, each in his own tomb;**
>
> **(19) but you are cast out, away from your grave, like loathsome carrion, clothed with the dead, those pierced by the sword, who go down to the stones of <u>the Pit</u>, like a corpse trampled underfoot.**
>
> **(20) You will not be joined with them in burial because you have destroyed your land, you have killed your people.**
>
> **Isaiah 14:18-20** (NRSV)

---

[8] Even though "bed" isn't in the original Hebrew text, the obvious implication of the verse is that maggots would be what he would lie on, like a mattress, which explains why the NRSV and NASB add the word "bed."

Not being given a proper burial was a deep degradation to the ancients of biblical lands. Ecclesiastes 6:3-6 shows that dying without mourners or honors was considered worse than being born dead, even if the person lived a full life and had numerous children (!). Such was the pompous Babylonian king's dishonorable and humiliating demise. Verses 18-19 show that other kings were honorably placed in tombs and "lie in glory" whereas the Babylonian king is merely tossed into a mass grave with other dead Babylonians, a meaningless, unmarked grave that people walk over with no regard.

As noted, the passage parallels the soulish grave with the physical grave. The text is clearly talking about the physical tomb and suddenly mentions that the king will be "clothed with the dead, those pierced by the sword, who go down to the stones of **the Pit**, like a corpse trampled underfoot" (verse 19). We discovered in Chapter Three that "the Pit" is another biblical term for Sheol. Obviously the physical grave and Sheol are distinct yet parallel concepts: Just as a body lays dead in a grave or tomb, so the soul lies dead in Sheol. Please note the language that is repeatedly used to describe the people in either the physical grave or Sheol—**"carrion," "the dead"** and **"corpse."** What's God trying to communicate to us by the usage of this language? **Just as a physical grave or tomb is meant only for that which is dead, so it is with Sheol. Souls in Sheol are carrion, not living, thinking, talking people**.

How much plainer could God be in His Word? Isaiah 14 in no way supports the idea that souls are conscious in Sheol.

The Fall of the King of Babylon Parallels the Fall of Lucifer

There's one section of Isaiah 14 that we skipped above, the section that prophesies the fall of the king of Babylon, Sennacherib, and parallels it with the earlier fall of Lucifer, one of the LORD's top archangels who fell from his lofty position in heaven due to the infection of pride:

> **How you have <u>fallen from heaven</u>, <u>morning star</u>** [Lucifer], **son of the dawn! You have been <u>cast down to the earth</u>, you who once laid low the nations!**

(13) You said in your heart, "I will ascend to the heavens; I will raise my throne above the stars of God; I will sit enthroned on the mount of assembly, on the utmost heights of Mount Zaphon.

(14) I will ascend above the tops of the clouds; I will make myself like the Most High."

(15) But you are brought down to <u>the realm of the dead</u>, to the depths of <u>the pit</u>.

(16) Those who see you stare at you, they ponder your fate: "Is this the man who shook the earth and made kingdoms tremble,

(17) <u>the man</u> who made the world a wilderness, who overthrew its cities and would not let his captives go home?"

Isaiah 14:12-17

This passage is a good example of **the law of double reference**, which is a tendency of Old Testament prophets to prophesy two things simultaneously—one being relevant to the general time of the prophecy and the other relating to the distant past or far-flung future. In this case, Isaiah prophesies Sennacherib's doom and parallels it with the much earlier fall of Lucifer, who became Satan. Verse 12, for instance, is an obvious reference to Lucifer and could only be applied to the king of Babylon in a figurative sense. After all, did Sennacherib literally fall from heaven down to the earth, like the devil? Was he nicknamed "morning star," aka "Lucifer" (which is how the King James and New King James translate the Hebrew word for "morning star")? Furthermore, Jesus partially cites verse 12 as a reference to the devil in Luke 10:18, which is reinforced by Revelation 12:7-10.

The question must be asked: Why would the LORD draw a parallel between the king of Babylon and Satan? The answer: The same reason Jesus rebuked Peter as "Satan" in Matthew 16:23 for being a mouthpiece for the devil's ungodly agenda. Just as Satan was the spiritual force *behind* Peter's rash words, so he was the diabolic authority *behind* Sennacherib's oppressive reign.

Whereas verses 12-14 obviously refer to the devil and only figuratively to Sennacherib, verses 15-17 solely relate to the earthly king (although verses 16-17 *may* refer to the devil by extension). Verse 15 shows Sennacherib's soul being housed in "the pit" after his death, which is Sheol, the "realm of the dead" located in the heart of the earth.[9]

Verses 16-17 relate to the ensuing verses 18-20, covered in the previous section, which detail Sennacherib's disgrace as an **unburied corpse**. As such, verse 16 is not a reference to dead souls in Sheol speaking to the king's similarly dead soul. This is in line with the hermeneutical rules: "Context is king" and "Scripture interprets Scripture." Even advocates of the immortal soul apart from Christ acknowledge this, like John MacArthur.

The Fall of the King of Tyre Parallels the Fall of Lucifer

We observe a similar parallel between the fall of Lucifer and another pompous king in Ezekiel 28.

The opening ten verses of the chapter are a denouncement of the king of Tyre, Ithobaal II, where the LORD rebukes his arrogance. Tyre was a city just north of Israel along the coast of the Mediterranean. The great wealth that Ithobaal II had amassed resulted in pride to the point that he perceived himself as god (verse 2). Such pomposity brought righteous judgment as the LORD said he would send foreign nations to humble the king by drawing "their swords against his beauty and wisdom" bringing him "down to **the pit**" through a "violent death" (verses 7-8). God's judgment ends with this humbling pronouncement:

> **Will you then say, "I am a god," in the presence of those who kill you? You will be but a mortal, not a god, in the hands of those who slay you.**
>
> **(10) You will die the death of the uncircumcised at the hands of foreigners.**
>
> **Ezekiel 28:9-10**

---

[9] See the sections in Chapter Nine: *Understanding the Three Realms— Heaven, Earth and the Underworld* and *Sheol: "The Heart of the Earth" and "the Earth Below"*).

As you can see, the LORD's judgment on Ithobaal II was to die prematurely, which is in line with the biblical axiom "the wages of sin is death" (Romans 6:23). The passage clearly says that Ithobaal II was mortal, not immortal, and that he would die and his soul would go to "the pit," which is a reference to Sheol, as shown in <u>Chapter Three</u>'s *Sheol: "The Pit" or "Well of Souls."* In fact, a literal reading of verses 8-10 declares that the king was going to be slain *seven times* (see, for instance, the KJV and the NASB, both word-for-word translations). God is speaking in this passage and he's getting something across loud and clear: Ithobaal II was going to be put to death for his gross arrogance and wickedness!

The next nine verses of Ezekiel 28 are *another* prophecy against the same king, but this time it clearly parallels the fall of Satan and his banishment from heaven to the underworld:

> **'This is what the Sovereign Lord says:**
>
> **"'You were the seal of perfection, full of wisdom and perfect in beauty.**
>
> **(13) You were in Eden, the garden of God; every precious stone adorned you: carnelian, chrysolite and emerald, topaz, onyx and jasper, lapis lazuli, turquoise and beryl. Your settings and mountings were made of gold; on the day you were created they were prepared.**
>
> **(14) You were anointed as a guardian cherub, for so I ordained you. You were on the holy mount of God; you walked among the fiery stones.**
>
> **(15) You were blameless in your ways from the day you were created till wickedness was found in you.**
>
> **(16) Through your widespread trade you were filled with violence, and you sinned. So I drove you in disgrace from the mount of God, and I expelled you, guardian cherub, from among the fiery stones.**
>
> **(17) Your heart became proud on account of your beauty and you corrupted your wisdom because**

of your splendor. So I threw you to the earth; I made a spectacle of you before kings.

(18) By your many sins and dishonest trade you have desecrated your sanctuaries. So I made a fire come out from you, and it consumed you, and I reduced you to ashes on the ground in the sight of all who were watching.

(19) All the nations who knew you are appalled at you; you have come to <u>a horrible end</u> and will be <u>no more</u>.' "

Ezekiel 28:12-19

Just as Isaiah 14 parallels the fall of Satan with the demise of the king of Babylon, so this passage parallels Lucifer's fall with the king of Tyre's doom. Why? Because the devil was the evil spiritual authority who pulled the strings of these pagan kings. With this understanding, Ezekiel 28:12-19 is speaking of either Satan or the king of Tyre, and sometimes both, depending on the verse.

Verses 12-17 refer to Lucifer and could only be applied to the king of Tyre in a figurative sense. After all, the person addressed is described as "the seal of perfection, full of wisdom and perfect in beauty" (verse 12) who dwelled in "Eden, the garden of God" and is plainly called a "guardian cherub"—an angel—in verses 14 and 16. The LORD then throws this archangel to the earth in disgrace after he's corrupted by pride due to its beauty.

Verses 18-19, however, more clearly apply to the earthly king of Tyre because they show his body being "reduced to ashes" in the sight of spectators as he comes to "a horrible end" and is "no more." Since we know from numerous other passages that Lucifer wasn't reduced to ashes when he fell to the earth and didn't become "no more," these statements obviously refer to Sennacherib and not Satan. The latter's alive and not-well on planet earth to this day. As Chapter Nine details, he dwells in the underworld, the dark spiritual realm that parallels or underpins the earth and universe.

While this information about Lucifer and his fall in Ezekiel 28:12-19 is fascinating, it's ambiguous enough to spur speculation, which isn't necessary to get into here. Besides, the main point about

Lucifer rings loud and clear: This blessed archangel foolishly allowed himself to be corrupted by pride due to his incredible beauty and other blessings, which resulted in his ousting from glory.

What *is* relevant to this book is that verses 7-8 show the king of Tyre being judged with premature death by the LORD and his soul going to "the pit"—sheol—which verse 19 describes as being "no more." Take note that **God Himself describes the condition of wicked souls in Sheol as being "no more,"** not suffering roasting conscious torment for hundreds or thousands of years before their resurrection to be divinely judged. We'll examine this insightful description of souls in Sheol in the next chapter.

"Until They are Destroyed from the Land"

Let's now consider a minor point from the book of Jeremiah:

> " 'But like the bad figs, which are so bad they cannot be eaten,' says the Lord, 'so will I deal with Zedekiah king of Judah, his officials and the survivors from Jerusalem, whether they remain in this land or live in Egypt. (9) I will make them abhorrent and an offense to all the kingdoms of the earth, a reproach and a byword, a curse and an object of ridicule, wherever I banish them. (10) <u>I will send the sword, famine and plague against them until they are destroyed from the land I gave to them and their ancestors</u>.' "
>
> **Jeremiah 24:8-10**

The passage details God's stern punishment on wicked Zedekiah—the puppet king of Judah—his corrupt officials and the Jews under them, as well as those who escaped God's discipline (the Babylonian invasion) by fleeing to Egypt. The LORD was going to "destroy them from the land" by means of sword, famine and plague.

If wicked people suffer roasting torture in Sheol until their resurrection hundreds or thousands of years later, isn't it curious that

God didn't add something to the effect of: "I will destroy them from the land I gave to them and their ancestors and they will subsequently suffer fiery torment in Sheol until their resurrection." This is the case with numerous other passages that address God's earthly judgment on wicked people as well. The point? If Sheol is a place of conscious existence where the unrighteous experience constant roasting agony until their resurrection in the distant future why would God omit such important information? It's not like it's an insignificant detail. The reason He "omits" it is because it's simply not true. Sheol isn't a torture chamber in the heart of the earth for conscious wicked souls (and neither is it a blissful paradise for righteous souls), it's the graveyard of *dead* souls where people 'sleep' in death until their resurrection.

"The Soul who Sins will Die"

In Ezekiel 18 the LORD Himself makes an enlightening statement that indirectly addresses the nature of Sheol:

> **(4) "Behold, all souls are mine; the soul of the father as well as the soul of the son is mine. <u>The soul who sins shall die</u>...**
> **(20) <u>The soul who sins shall die</u>. The son shall not bear the guilt of the father, nor the father bear the guilt of the son. The righteousness of the righteous shall be upon himself, and the wickedness of the wicked shall be upon himself."**
> **Ezekiel 18:4,20** (NKJV)

The LORD is getting across to the Israelites that each person is to die for his or her *own* sins. Sons should not bear the guilt of their fathers and vice versa. Notice clearly what God says will happen to those who engage in sin as a lifestyle without care of repentance: "The *soul* who sins shall **die**."

Keep in mind that this is YaHWeH Himself speaking here. The LORD of course knows everything there is to know about Sheol and yet he doesn't say anything about the wicked soul going to Sheol to experience constant roasting torment when the body physically dies. Why? Because souls—people—who unrepentantly sin will die; and Sheol is the "world of the dead" where dead souls 'rest' in death till their resurrection on judgment day (Revelation 20:11-15).

The Longest and Most Detailed Passage on Sheol

Ezekiel 32 features the longest passage on Sheol in the Bible. Chapters 31-32 of Ezekiel address God's judgment on the nation of Egypt where Egypt is likened to a great cedar of Lebanon that is about to be felled by the nation of Babylon and, consequently, descend into Sheol where other nations condemned by God had descended, like Assyria, Elam and Edom. This passage powerfully drives home the image of Sheol as the common soulish grave of humankind where dead souls are housed until their resurrection on judgment day. God Himself is speaking in this passage from verse 18 onward:

> **In the twelfth year, in the first month, on the fifteenth day of the month, the word of the LORD came to me:**
>
> **(18) Mortal, wail over the hordes of Egypt, and send them down, with Egypt and the daughters of majestic nations to <u>the world below</u>, with those who go down to <u>the Pit</u>, (19) "Whom do you surpass in beauty? <u>Go down</u>! Be <u>laid to rest</u> with the <u>uncircumcised!</u>"**
>
> **(20) They shall <u>fall</u> among those who are <u>killed by the sword</u>. Egypt has been handed over to <u>the sword</u>; carry away both it and its hordes. (21) The mighty chiefs shall speak of them, with their helpers, out of the midst of <u>Sheol</u>: They have come down, <u>they lie still</u>, the uncircumcised killed by the sword."**
>
> **(22) Assyria <u>is there</u>, and all its company, <u>their graves all around it</u>, all of them <u>killed, fallen by the sword</u>. (23) <u>Their graves are set in the</u>**

uttermost parts of the Pit. Its company is all around its grave, all of them killed, fallen by the sword, who spread terror in the land of the living.

(24) Elam is there, and all its hordes around its grave; all of them killed, fallen by the sword, who went down uncircumcised into the world below who spread terror in the land of the living. They bear their shame with those who go down to the Pit. (25) They have made Elam a bed among the slain with all its hordes, their graves all around it, all of them uncircumcised killed by the sword; for terror of them was spread in the land of the living, and they bear their shame with those who go down to the Pit; they are placed among the slain.

(26) Meshech and Tubal are there, and all their multitude, their graves all around them, all of them uncircumcised, killed by the sword; for they spread terror in the land of the living. (27) And they do not lie with the fallen warriors of long ago who went down to Sheol with their weapons of war,[10] whose swords were laid under their heads, and whose shields are upon their bones; for the terror of the warriors was in the land of the living. (28) So you shall be broken and lie among the uncircumcised, with those who are killed by the sword.

(29) Edom is there, its kings and all its princes, who for all their might are laid with those who are killed by the sword; they lie with the uncircumcised, with those who go down to the Pit. (30) The princes of the north are there, all of them, and the Sidonians, who have gone down in shame

---

[10] Verse 27 (of the NRSV) is an obvious improper translation: The statement made in the negative—"And they do not lie"—makes no sense in light of its context. The New International Version properly translates this verse in the form of a rhetorical question as such: "Do they not **lie with the other uncircumcised warriors who have fallen**, who went down to **the grave** with their weapons of war, whose swords were placed under their heads?"

with the slain, for all the terror that they caused by their might; they lie uncircumcised with those who are killed by the sword and bear their shame with those who go down to the Pit.

(31) When Pharaoh sees them, he will be consoled for all his horde—Pharaoh and all his army killed by the sword, says the Lord GOD. (32) For he spread terror in the land of the living; therefore he shall be laid to rest among the uncircumcised, with those who are slain by the sword—Pharaoh and all his multitude, says the Lord GOD.

Ezekiel 32:17-32 (NRSV)

As you can see, the Pharaoh of Egypt and his army have been judged and condemned by God. What is the LORD's sentence? God states in verse 20 that "Egypt has been handed over to **the sword**" and, in verse 31, "Pharaoh and all his army **killed by the sword**." So God's sentence is death. Is this a just sentence? Absolutely. It's in line with the biblical axiom "the wages of sin is death."

Since Egypt's sentence is death, verse 18 says that the Egyptians shall be sent down "to **the world below**, with those who **go down** to **the Pit**." "The Pit" is *bowr* in the Hebrew and is another term for Sheol, as detailed in Chapter Three; this synonym for Sheol appears 4 more times in the passage (verses 24, 25, 29 & 30) while Sheol itself appears twice (verses 21 & 27). As such, there's no doubt that this section of Scripture is addressing the subject of Sheol, the intermediate state of un-regenerated souls between physical decease and resurrection.

With this understanding, let's work our way through the long passage point by point.

Verse 18 describes Sheol as "the world below." Sheol is described this way because it is part of the underworld. We'll look at this in detail in Chapter Nine but, briefly put, the Bible speaks of three realms or universes: **1.** heaven, which is described as "the third heaven" in Scripture and is where God's throne is located, **2.** the earth & physical universe, and **3.** the underworld (see Philippians 2:10 for verification). You'll note that verse 18 above describes this "world below" as "the

Pit." Why? Because **Sheol is a pit or dungeon in the underworld where dead souls are housed until their resurrection**. Sheol has levels and chambers where dead souls are "laid to rest" in an orderly fashion according to nation and so on.

We know souls housed in Sheol are dead because the Bible repeatedly says so in numerous ways as detailed throughout this study. For instance, Ecclesiastes 9:5 & 10 explicitly state that "there is no work or thought or knowledge or wisdom in Sheol" and that the people housed there are "dead" and "know nothing."

The fact that souls in Sheol are dead is verified in verse 19 where it says that the Egyptians will be "**laid to rest** with the uncircumcised." Notice they will be "**laid to rest**," not writhe in screaming torment for over a thousand years without a break, as some ludicrously teach. No, they are simply laid to rest; this phrase is repeated in verse 32 in reference to the Pharaoh being "laid to rest" in Sheol. The two words "laid" and "rest" used in conjunction evoke the image of sleep. In addition, verse 21 says that people in Sheol "**lie still**," verse 25 that Elam will be in "**bed**," and verses 27, 28 and 30 that those in Sheol "**lie**" there. All these images clearly suggest **sleep**, not conscious suffering in fiery torment. Of course, these descriptions aren't suggesting literal physical sleep, but rather the 'sleep' of death itself, from which all unrighteous souls will be "awakened" to undergo the Great White Throne Judgment (Revelation 20:11-15).

Verse 25 flat out states that souls in Sheol are dead: "they bear their shame with those who go down to the Pit; they are placed among **the slain**." In other words, the newest group of souls entering Sheol will be "placed among **the slain**." You see? Souls in Sheol are dead; they are not alive and are therefore conscious of nothing. How much clearer could God be?

Note also how verse 19 says that the Egyptians will be laid to rest *"with* the uncircumcised." Who are the "uncircumcised"? In the Bible circumcision was a sign that a person was in covenant with God under the law of Moses. The Scriptures always distinguish between those who are in right-standing with God and those who are not. The "uncircumcised" in this text did not have a contract with God and therefore were not right with Him. This would include the numerous peoples cited throughout the passage—the Assyrians, Edomites,

Sidonians, etc. In other words, verse 19 is simply pointing out that the Egyptians will be laid to rest in the very same section of Sheol that housed other uncircumcised godless people from that era.

As noted throughout our study, souls in right-standing with God also went to Sheol at the time of death during the Old Testament period but were not laid to rest with the uncircumcised. There was obviously a separate section in Sheol for those in covenant with God. If this sounds strange to you, consider the fact that bodies are buried in earthly graveyards in an orderly fashion according to family, purchaser and sometimes even religious faith (for instance, there are Catholic cemeteries and church cemeteries where only those of that specific faith can be buried), why would we think it would be any different for dead souls in Sheol? These righteous souls will be resurrected at the time of their bodily resurrection when the Lord returns to earth to establish his millennial reign (Daniel 12:1-2 & Matthew 19:28-30), although I leave room for the *possibility* that their souls were raised to life when Jesus ascended to heaven (Ephesians 4:7-10). In any case, righteous souls no longer go to Sheol when believers die because they possess eternal life through spiritual regeneration via the imperishable seed of Christ (1 Peter 1:23).

Verse 20 states that those in Sheol have been "killed by the sword" and that the Egyptians will suffer this same fate. This phrase (or similar phrasing) is used for every group mentioned in the passage. In other words, the text **repeatedly emphasizes that these people are dead.** Also notice that it says they were killed "by the sword." If taken in a strictly literal sense we would have to conclude that each of these thousands upon thousands of people from varying nations perished by the stroke of a sword. Is this what happened? Of course not. Many obviously died from other methods—arrow, spear, club, fire, etc. "The sword" simply refers to the God-ordained right of a government to inflict the penalty of death on those who have committed capital crimes or those judged and condemned by God (see Romans 13:4). For instance, Ezekiel 31-32 show that Egypt had been judged and condemned to death. Whom does God commission to carry out this sentence? Babylon, as verified in Ezekiel 32:11: " 'For this is what the Sovereign LORD says: 'The sword of the king of Babylon will come against you [Pharaoh and his army]'." It's unlikely that the Pharaoh carried a sword and, even if he did, it was merely for show; so "the sword" that the king of Babylon carried was actually the authority from God to carry out His just sentence of death.

Verses 22-23 introduce a revealing concept:

> **Assyria is there, and all its company, <u>their graves all around it</u>, all of them killed, fallen by the sword. (23) <u>Their graves are set in the uttermost parts of the Pit</u>. Its company is all around <u>its grave</u>, all of them killed, fallen by the sword, who spread terror in the land of the living.**
>
> **Ezekiel 32:22-23** (NRSV)

These verses reveal that the Assyrians are in Sheol and that they are killed, fallen by "the sword" of the LORD's judgment. In addition, three times the passage emphasizes that **the graves of the Assyrians are in Sheol**. The words "graves" and "grave" are respectively translated from the Hebrew words *qibrah (kib-RAW)* and *qeburwrah (keb-oo-RAW)*, which refer to literal graves or tombs. What's this mean? Simply what we've been discovering throughout this study—**Sheol is a graveyard in the underworld where dead souls are laid to rest until their resurrection**. Just as dead bodies are laid to rest in grave plots on earth, so dead souls are laid in grave plots in Sheol.

Is a grave ever intended for anything other than that which is dead? Of course not. This is further proof that souls in Sheol are dead and that Sheol itself is a **soulish graveyard in the underworld, not a diabolical torture chamber**.

Verses 24-26 likewise point out that there are **"graves"** in Sheol for the people of Elam, Meshech and Tubal. Tell me: Are people **placed in graves** for the purpose of conscious torture or simply to lie in the 'sleep' of death?

Notice in verse 23 that the Assyrians' graves are set "in the **uttermost** parts of the Pit." This is evidence that there are **levels** in Sheol and **distinct sections**. The dead souls of the Assyrians were, evidently, placed in one of the **lowest levels**.

Verse 23 ends by pointing out that the Assyrians once "spread terror in the land of the living." The "land of the living" obviously refers to life on earth where the Assyrians warred, conquered and ruled. This is in contrast to Sheol, the land of the dead, where they would spread terror no more. How is it that they won't spread terror anymore? Because *they're dead*. Sheol is the land of the dead where "there is no work or thought or knowledge or wisdom."

The very same point is made in reference to Elam, Meshech, Tubal and Egypt in verses 24, 25, 26, 27 and 32. We'll look at this further in the following chapter.

As you can see, throughout this long passage God repeatedly uses unmistakable and vivid language to show that souls in Sheol are dead. God is without doubt a master communicator. With this understanding, verse 31 must be taken in a non-literal sense because it states that, after Pharaoh dies, he will "see" the other groups laid to rest in Sheol and be "consoled." This is obviously not to be taken literally. Pharaoh and his men will be dead at this point and will not be able to see anyone or anything; they'll be laid to rest in the sleep of death just like the other groups in Sheol. In fact, the very next verse—verse 32—emphasizes that Pharaoh is "laid to rest" in Sheol, not alive and making observations; and please notice that he's "laid to rest" not suffering in fiery torture. However, even if we were to view verse 31 literally it still wouldn't support the religious view that pagan souls are in a state of constant torment until the Day of Judgment. After all, how would Pharaoh possibly be consoled by the fact that he and his army are going to join thousands upon thousands of writhing, screaming souls in roasting agony? Do you see how unscriptural this mythical belief is?

"Progressive Revelation" on the Nature of Sheol?

The above passage from Ezekiel 32 and other texts disprove the theory that humanity had a "progressive revelation" concerning the nature of Sheol. This theory suggests that the Hebrew understanding of Sheol evolved over time and, of course, is embraced by those who advocate that Sheol is a place of conscious torture. The reason they are forced to adopt this odd theory is obvious: The many Old Testament passages on Sheol that we've examined in this study clearly reveal that Sheol is a "Pit" in the underworld where dead souls are laid to rest in the sleep of death—a vast soulish graveyard where there is consciousness of nothing. Since they are unable to reconcile these numerous passages with their belief that Sheol is a place of constant conscious torment they have no recourse but to completely 'write them off ' with this theory. This is a blatant case of "taking away" from God's Word, a practice severely condemned in Scripture (see Deuteronomy 4:2, Proverbs 30:5-6 and Revelation 22:18-19).

The reason these people are compelled to such error is because they've been indoctrinated that Jesus' story of the Rich Man and Lazarus from Luke 16:19-31 is a literal account of life after death for un-regenerated souls. Yet, if we take this tale literally the entire rest of the Bible is in error on the nature of Sheol. Hence, they had no recourse but to concoct the idea of "progressive revelation." Aside from the obvious fact that this reasoning conflicts with the weight of scriptural testimony, there are two problems with this position: **1.** Jesus' story of the Rich Man and Lazarus is clearly a fantastical story that was never meant to be taken literally. We'll examine it in detail in <u>Chapter Eight</u> where you'll see that it would be absurd to take it literally. And **2.** the idea of "progressive revelation" suggests that humanity's awareness of the nature of Sheol slowly evolved over time. The problem with this is that there is clearly no *progressive* revelation on Sheol in the Bible. The testimony of Scripture goes from the concept of Sheol as a nether graveyard where dead souls are conscious of nothing as they "sleep" in death, to the abrupt and completely opposite notion (based *solely* on a literal interpretation of Jesus' parable) that Sheol is a nether realm where souls are fully alive and conscious, either in a state of constant fiery torment or hanging out with Abraham in communal bliss, depending upon whether the soul is wicked or righteous.

So how does Ezekiel 32:18-32 disprove this theory of "progressive revelation"? Simply because **God Himself is speaking throughout this long passage.** Throughout this study we've examined numerous passages on Sheol that reflect what various Old Testament characters believed about the nature of the intermediate state. We've looked at Job's view, Solomon's view, David's view, Hezekiah's view and many others. All of their views coincide that Sheol is a "Pit" in the underworld where dead souls are laid to rest in the unconscious sleep of death 'awaiting' their resurrection. One may argue that their views are the result of a limited understanding of the subject and are therefore inaccurate. Yet, one cannot make this argument concerning Ezekiel 32:18-32 because **God himself is speaking**. It's the same thing with Ezekiel 18:4,20 and 28:7-8,19, which we looked at earlier this chapter. Not to mention Ezekiel 26:19-21, which we'll examine next chapter. The LORD Himself is speaking in all these passages. Does anyone ludicrously think that God had a "limited understanding" of the nature of Sheol? Does anyone absurdly think that the LORD had to have "progressive revelation" on Sheol? Or has He always known precisely and completely everything there is to know about it? The answers are obvious.

The vast majority of people who believe that Sheol is a place of conscious torment (or bliss for Old Testament saints) have never researched the subject of Sheol beyond Jesus' story of The Rich Man and Lazarus. I know because I was once one of them. As such, I understand their reasoning: The story of the Rich Man and Lazarus, if taken literally, reveals that people are in a conscious state in Sheol; and since Jesus Christ himself is speaking it's not necessary to look into the subject any further. In other words, Jesus' tale tells us everything we need to know about Sheol; after all, who would know more about Sheol than Jesus Christ himself?

Well, according to the Bible there's only one higher than the Son, and that's God the Father, and He is the One speaking in Ezekiel 32:18-32 wherein He repeatedly and explicitly reveals that souls in Sheol are "slain," "laid to rest," "lie still," in "bed" in "graves," etc. There's mysteriously no hint of souls suffering in roasting anguish crying out for less than a drop of water that won't be given. Why is it that advocates of conscious torture fail to bring up this long commentary on Sheol by God the Father Himself in Ezekiel 32? Because it contradicts their false religious belief, that's why.

Am I suggesting that that the Father and Son contradict each other? Absolutely not; that's an impossibility. What I am saying is that the Scriptures very clearly show that the Father is the head over the Son and this is explicitly stated (1 Corinthians 11:3 & 15:27-28). (We could say that the Father and Son are equal in being, but the Son is subordinate to the Father in function or relationship). Hence, Jesus would never contradict the Father; in fact, he *can't* contradict the Father because, as he said, "I and the Father are one" (John 10:30). Consequently, Jesus' story of the Rich Man and Lazarus must be interpreted in light of what the entire rest of the Bible teaches on the subject of Sheol, including what the Father, who is the head, plainly taught, not to mention the Spirit, which brings us to one more crushing point...

Another reason this "progressive revelation of Sheol" argument holds no water is because the psalms are "God-breathed" (2 Timothy 3:16) and, as such, all the psalmists "spoke from God as they were carried along by the Holy Spirit" (2 Peter 1:21). This is why Jesus said David was "speaking by the Spirit" when he quoted Psalm 110:1 (Matthew 22:43-44). This, of course, implies that David was "speaking by the Spirit" in all his psalms (and he wrote at least half of them). In other words, David's statements in the Psalms were spoken by the inspiration of the Holy Spirit and the Holy Spirit is God. In light of this, David's exposition on Sheol contained in the psalms, as well as statements by other psalmists, shouldn't be considered just "their view" of Sheol. No, it's God's view too because they were "speaking by the Spirit," as Jesus put it, and the Holy Spirit is God; and God had no "progressive revelation of Sheol." He's *always* known the truth about its nature.

"Where, O Sheol, Is Your Destruction?"

The Hebrew word Sheol appears twice in the book of Hosea, both in the same verse:

> **I will ransom them from the power of the grave** *(sheol);* **I will redeem them from death.**
> **Where, O death, are your plagues? Where, O grave** *(sheol)* **is your destruction?**
> **Hosea 13:14**

This passage is simply God's promise that all his children shall be ransomed from Sheol and redeemed from death. This was accomplished, of course, through the death and resurrection of Jesus Christ "who became a ransom for all men" (1 Timothy 2:6). Jesus took our place and died for our sins so we don't have to. Christians who are spiritually born-again of the imperishable seed of Christ have eternal life in their spirits. Consequently, the only death they'll undergo is physical death. The simple reason for this is that "flesh and blood cannot inherit the kingdom of God" (1 Corinthians 15:50). Which is fine because those redeemed through Christ are going to ultimately receive a much better body—an imperishable, glorified, powerful, spiritual body (see 1 Corinthians 15:42-44)! The awesome thing about this new body, unlike the old one, is that it can inherit the kingdom of God!

You'll observe that Sheol is mentioned synonymously with death and destruction in Hosea 13:14. In other words, Sheol is death and death is Sheol. The condition of souls in Sheol is destruction, not flaming torture. That's why the LORD raises the question: "Where, O Sheol, is your destruction?" and not, "Where, O Sheol, is your continuous fiery torment?" The Bible is so easy to understand once you're freed up from erroneous religious indoctrination!

Samuel, Saul & the Witch of Endor (and Elijah & Enoch)

Let's now venture back to the Old Testament historical books and observe a fascinating incident that concerns Sheol. Samuel was the last of the judges and the first of the major prophets (1 Samuel 3:19-21). After Samuel died, ungodly King Saul was desperate for counsel and so went to a medium to get word from the dead prophet, which was a wicked act strictly forbidden by the LORD (Deuteronomy 18:10-13). The appearance of the dead prophet to the witch of Endor provokes questions on the nature of Sheol because Samuel went to Sheol when he died.

Let's read the passage in question:

> Now **Samuel was dead**, and all Israel had mourned for him and **buried him** in his own town of Ramah. **Saul had expelled the mediums and spiritists from the land.**
>
> **(4) The Philistines assembled and came and set up camp at Shunem, while Saul gathered all Israel**

and set up camp at Gilboa. (5) When Saul saw the Philistine army, he was afraid; terror filled his heart. (6) He inquired of the Lord, but the Lord did not answer him by dreams or Urim or prophets. (7) Saul then said to his attendants, "<u>Find me a woman who is a medium, so I may go and inquire of her</u>."

"There is one in Endor," they said.

(8) So Saul disguised himself, putting on other clothes, and at night he and two men went to the woman. "Consult a spirit for me," he said, "and <u>bring up</u> for me the one I name."

(9) But the woman said to him, "Surely you know what Saul has done. He has cut off the mediums and spiritists from the land. Why have you set a trap for my life to bring about my death?"

(10) Saul swore to her by the Lord, "As surely as the Lord lives, you will not be punished for this."

(11) Then the woman asked, "Whom shall I bring up for you?"

"Bring up Samuel," he said.

(12) <u>When the woman saw Samuel, she cried out at the top of her voice</u> and said to Saul, "Why have you deceived me? You are Saul!"

(13) The king said to her, "Don't be afraid. What do you see?"

The woman said, "I see a <u>ghostly figure</u> [a "spirit" or "god" in the Hebrew] <u>coming up out of the earth</u>."

(14) "What does he look like?" he asked.

"An old man wearing a robe is coming up," she said.

<u>Then Saul knew it was Samuel</u>, and he bowed down and prostrated himself with his face to the ground.

(15) <u>Samuel said to Saul</u>, "Why have you <u>disturbed me</u> by bringing me up?"

"I am in great distress," Saul said. "The Philistines are fighting against me, and God has departed from me. He no longer answers me, either by prophets or by dreams. So I have called on you to tell me what to do."

(16) <u>Samuel said</u>, "Why do you consult me, now that the Lord has departed from you and become your enemy? (17) The Lord has done what he predicted <u>through me</u>. The Lord has torn the kingdom out of your hands and given it to one of your neighbors—to David. (18) Because you did not obey the Lord or carry out his fierce wrath against the Amalekites, the Lord has done this to you today. (19) The Lord will deliver both Israel and you into the hands of the Philistines, and tomorrow you and your sons will be with me. The Lord will also give the army of Israel into the hands of the Philistines."

(20) Immediately Saul fell full length on the ground, filled with fear <u>because of Samuel's words</u>. His strength was gone, for he had eaten nothing all that day and all that night.

1 Samuel 28:3-20

Was Samuel's appearance after his death an illusion, an evil spirit masquerading as Samuel or Samuel himself coming back from the dead; that is, coming back from Sheol? Scholars may be divided on the issue, but the evidence shows that it was indeed Samuel in disembodied form. Verses 12, 14, 15, 16, 17 and 20 prove this and a couple verses **state point blank** that it was Samuel; for example, verse 15 says "*Samuel said* to Saul" and verse 16 that "*Samuel said*." Notice that these verses don't say "A spirit masquerading as Samuel said." No, "*Samuel said*."

As we've seen in this study, souls in Sheol are dead because the spiritual breath of God that animates them—that is, gives them life—has returned to the Creator. People become *living* souls when God animates them with a breath of life, as the 'creation text' shows (Genesis 2:7). Just as a *physical* breath of life is required for a body to live, so a *spiritual* breath of life is necessary for a soul to exist in a conscious sense. In the Old Testament period people's souls went to Sheol at the point of physical death and the breath of life returned to the Almighty; this included both the righteous and the unrighteous. Elijah and (apparently) Enoch were exceptions (2 Kings 2:11 & Genesis 5:24). They bypassed death—Sheol—and went straight to heaven. God is the all-knowing, all-powerful Sovereign Creator of the universe and he occasionally chooses to treat some differently for his own purposes. God chose to spare them from death—Sheol—as examples of future resurrections, as detailed in Chapter Nine. Again, these are *exceptions*.

The case of Samuel is a *temporary* exception where God, in His divine wisdom, chose to allow Samuel to be resurrected to 'witness' to the witch and prophesy to King Saul. Further proof that this was actually Samuel can be observed in that the witch cries out in fear when she sees the prophet coming up out of the earth; in other words, she wasn't used to such real manifestations! Secondly, notice that what Samuel says is in line with God's Word, and what he predicted came to pass—Saul and his sons were dead the next day (1 Samuel 31).

The passage says nothing about the nature of Sheol so we must turn to the rest of Scripture for answers on that question, but it fits the Sheol-as-the-sleep-of-**death** model in that Samuel says, "Why have you *disturbed* me by *bringing me up*?" This implies, of course, that he was disturbed from his 'rest' in Sheol. Numerous other Scriptures reveal what this 'rest' is—the 'sleep' of death where the soul is not conscious of anything because it's **dead**.

How did God work this miraculous temporary resurrection? He simply breathed a spiritual breath of life into Samuel's dead soul, which was housed in Sheol, and Samuel became conscious—i.e. a *living* soul—and came up. Speaking of coming up, note that Samuel came up from down in the earth, which is where Sheol—the world of the dead—is located: in the heart of the earth, albeit in the spiritual realm, not the physical, since Sheol and disembodied souls are not physical in nature (Matthew 12:40). Also, Samuel states that when Saul and his sons perish the next day they "will be *with* him." My point? Both the righteous and wicked went to Sheol upon physical death in the Old Testament era. In our era, however, death has no power over those of us who've been born again of the imperishable seed of Christ, the second Adam—*Praise God!*

If my comments on human nature seem hard to understand (e.g. "spiritual breath of life", etc.) please read the <u>Appendix</u>: *Human Nature: Spirit, Mind & Body.*

Rapha: "The Dead in Sheol"

NOTE: This section gets rather technical and is therefore only recommended for detail-oriented readers; all others are encouraged to jump to the next chapter.

A Hebrew word was brought up earlier this chapter that we need to look at in more detail, so let's go back to the book of Isaiah:

> **<u>Your dead</u>** *(muwth)* **shall live, their <u>corpses</u> shall rise.**
> **O dwellers in the <u>dust</u>, awake and sing for**
> **joy!**
> **For your dew is a radiant dew,**
> **and the earth will <u>give birth to those long</u>**
> **<u>dead</u>** *(rapha).*
> **Isaiah 26:19** (NRSV)

The verse appears in the context of Isaiah 25-27, which addresses events after the Tribulation and at the beginning of the Millennium. The "Millennium" refers to the thousand-year reign of Christ on earth before the eternal age of the new heavens and new earth manifests (see Revelation 20-21).

The passage details the resurrection of Old Testament saints, as well as the bodily resurrection of Tribulation martyrs. This is the *third stage* of what the Bible calls the "first resurrection," which concerns the resurrection of the righteous (Revelation 20:4-6). We'll examine these stages in <u>Chapter Eleven</u>. Let's focus here on this verse and a couple of the Hebrew words in the text.

Firstly, the language of the passage explicitly speaks of a resurrection: It says "Your **dead** shall live" and "their **corpses** shall rise" and those who **dwell in the dust** shall "awake and sing for joy." The word for "dead" in the opening phrase is the Hebrew word *muwth (mooth)*, which means "to die" or that which is "dead" or has "died." It is used in reference to the death of animals, as seen in Exodus 7:18. It's also the word God used when he instructed Adam & Eve to *not* eat of the tree of the knowledge of good and evil in Eden: "for when you eat of it you will surely **die**" (Genesis 2:17). Hence, the word refers to the wages of sin (Romans 6:23). Actually, *muwth* is used twice in this text and, as such, the LORD was saying "in **dying** you will **die**." In other words, the moment they ate of the forbidden fruit part of them would die, leading to their eventual demise. This is covered in Chapter Four of *Hell Know*.

With this understanding, the final statement of Isaiah 26:19 declares that "the earth will give birth to those long dead." The phrase "those long dead" is one word in the Hebrew, *rapha (raw-FAW)*, noted earlier this chapter, which the *Brown-Driver-Briggs Lexicon* defines as "the dead in Sheol." It's sometimes translated as "shades." The King James renders *rapha* as "the dead" in this verse and the NIV as the earth's "dead," while the NASB translates it as "the departed spirits."

There are a few things I'd like to point out about *rapha*. In Isaiah 26:19 (above) it refers to the same "dead" mentioned at the beginning of the verse, which is *muwth*. In other words, *muwth* and *rapha* are synonymous in this passage since it's a case of synonymous parallelism wherein the second part of the verse repeats the first with different words and minor variation.

The variation here is that the first part addresses the bodily resurrection of these people, which is obvious in light of the terminology of "corpses" and "dwellers in the dust," and the second part addresses their soulish resurrection from Sheol: "the earth will give birth to those long dead." We conclude this because the Hebrew word *rapha* refers to "the dead in Sheol," as shown above. For further evidence, *rapha* is used in reference to dead souls in Sheol in these passages from Proverbs, previously noted in Chapter Five:

> **Whoever wanders from the way of understanding will rest in the assembly of the <u>dead</u>** *(rapha)*.
>
> **Proverbs 21:16** (NRSV)

> **But they do not know that the <u>dead</u> *(rapha)***
> **are there, that her guests are in the depths of Sheol.**
> **Proverbs 9:18** (NRSV)

The Hebrew words *muwth* and *rapha* are used interchangeably in another verse in Isaiah 26:

> **The <u>dead</u> *(muwth)* do not live;**
>   **<u>shades</u> *(rapha)* do not rise—**
> **because you have punished and destroyed them,**
>   **and wiped out all memory of them.**
> **Isaiah 26:14** (NRSV)

The "dead" and "shades" here refer not to the Israelites, but to the "other lords" noted in the previous verse; that is, foreign overlords who subjugated Israel, like Assyria, Egypt, Midian, Philistia, Babylon, and so on. During the Millennium no pagan power will dominate God's people because they'll all be dead in Sheol, which is confirmed in the second part where it says that God "punished and destroyed them." What was their punishment? Death, for that's the wages of sin. Notice that people in Sheol are "destroyed." They're not consciously roasting in torment crying out for less than a drop of water that won't be granted. They're *dead* because Sheol is the "assembly of **the dead**" not the living. They'll be resurrected to face judgment at the White Throne Judgment. This resurrection is the second resurrection, which concerns all unredeemed souls throughout history (Revelation 20:11-15). We'll address this in <u>Chapter Eleven</u>, but it's covered in detail in *Hell Know*.

    Muwth and *rapha* are also used interchangeably in the following Psalm by Heman the Ezrahite:

> **Do you work wonders for the <u>dead</u> *(muwth)*?**
>   **Do the <u>shades</u> *(rapha)* rise up to praise you?**
> **(11) Is your steadfast love declared in <u>the grave</u>,**
>   **or your faithfulness in <u>Abaddon</u> [destruction]?**
> **Psalm 88:10-11** (NRSV)

Verses 3-4 of this Psalm verify that Heman is describing the nature of Sheol. Furthermore, Heman's commentary on Sheol is in the context of his being on the verge of death and therefore Sheol. For instance, in verse 3 he points out that his "life draws near to Sheol." This shows, again, that both righteous and unrighteous souls went to Sheol in periods preceding the death and resurrection of Christ, which is when Jesus paid for human redemption and justified the repentant.

With this understanding, notice how Heman describes Sheol: He plainly says that those in Sheol are *dead*, not living. This is the Hebrew word *muwth*, which he equates with *rapha* in the second part of the verse. Heman says that God doesn't work his wonders for the dead in Sheol and that these dead are unable to rise up and praise Him. This mirrors David's exposition on Sheol in Psalm 6:5 (see the beginning of Chapter Three). Remember, Heman is talking about a righteous soul going to Sheol—himself—and he makes it clear that God doesn't work his wonders for such souls and neither can these souls rise up and praise the LORD. Why? Because they're dead. This completely contradicts the unbiblical position that righteous souls are conscious in Sheol and housed in a supposed paradise compartment where they commune with Abraham.

The passage is another example of synonymous parallelism where statements are repeated in different words with minor variation. With this in mind, notice how verse 11 equates the dead in Sheol with the literal grave and also "Abaddon," which is the Hebrew word for destruction. Is anything other than that which is dead placed in a grave or tomb? It's the same thing with souls in Sheol. They're dead, not alive; and they can only become alive again when the Creator resuscitates them via the breath of life, as covered in the Appendix.

The reason I'm spending so much time on *rapha* is because I want to establish beyond any shadow of doubt that this word, which appears eight times in the Old Testament, clearly refers to dead souls in Sheol and not to half-conscious ghosts that are partially alive and are either suffering constant roasting agony without a drop of water for relief or having a good ol' time in paradise with father Abraham. Both concepts are foreign to the Scriptures beyond Jesus' fantastical parable (see Chapter Eight).

Another reason I'm taking time for this is because *rapha* is used in the following passage by Job, which some try to argue supports Sheol as a place of conscious torment for unrighteous souls:

The <u>dead</u> *(rapha)* **tremble**
    under the waters and their inhabitants.
(6) Sheol is naked before God,
    and Abaddon has no covering.

                         Job 26:5-6 (ESV)

These verses are indeed referring to the dead in Sheol because **1.** the usage of *rapha* in verse 5, which—again—refers to the "dead in Sheol" and **2.** the usage of "Sheol" in verse 6.

The second part of verse 5 has confused some translators. For instance, the New Revised Standard Version renders verse 5 like so: "The shades below tremble, the waters and their inhabitants." This makes it sound like the first part of the verse refers to the dead in Sheol while the second part refers to sea creatures in the oceans. Yet this isn't accurate when considering verse 6, which refers solely to Sheol and says nothing about sea creatures in the seas. It simply doesn't fit to have both verses addressing Sheol with the second part of verse 5 curiously digressing to creatures in the sea.

The English Standard Version (above) is the correct wording along with other English versions, like the NIV. Job says in the first part of the verse that the dead in Sheol tremble and is still referring to them in the second part. In other words, "under the waters and their inhabitants" is a poetic reference to the dead in Sheol. How so? Because Sheol is a "pit' in the underworld located in the heart of the earth, in the spiritual realm, not in the physical realm.[11] As such, the dead in Sheol inhabit the realm of the dead, which—from Job's perspective—is somewhere beneath the deep oceans of the earth.

What does Job mean by declaring that the dead in Sheol—the *rapha*—"tremble"? Is he saying that they suffer in roasting conscious

---

[11] See the sections in <u>Chapter Nine</u>: *Understanding the Three Realms— Heaven, Earth and the Underworld* and *Sheol: "The Heart of the Earth" and "the Earth Below"*.

torment until their resurrection on judgment day (Revelation 20:11-15)? No. How do we know this? Because of two hermeneutical rules **1. Scripture interprets Scripture** and **2. context is king**.[12]

Concerning "Scripture interprets Scripture," we examined Job's view of Sheol in <u>Chapter Two</u> wherein we saw how Job viewed Sheol as the graveyard of dead souls where souls "sleep" in death until their resurrection. He even said that "the wicked cease from turmoil" and "the weary are at rest" (Job 3:17). This rules out that Job is describing conscious souls trembling in fiery anguish in 26:5-6.

As for "context is king," it is through this principle that we discover what Job meant. Although Job was severely suffering, he still offered the sacrifice of praise by boldly declaring God's greatness, which can be observed in Job 9 and 12. This is what he's doing in Job 26 in response to Bildad's exaltation of God in the previous chapter. He was in effect saying that Bildad didn't go far enough in describing the LORD's awesome power. See for yourself:

> **The <u>dead</u>** *(rapha)* **tremble**
> **under the waters and their inhabitants.**
> **(6) Sheol is naked before God,**
> **and Abaddon has no covering.**
> **(7) He stretches out the north over the void**
> **and hangs the earth on nothing.**
> **(8) He binds up the waters in his thick clouds,**
> **and the cloud is not split open under them.**
> **(9) He covers the face of the full moon**
> **and spreads over it his cloud.**
> **(10) He has inscribed a circle on the face of the**
> **waters**
> **at the boundary between light and darkness.**
> **(11) <u>The pillars of heaven tremble</u>**
> **and are <u>astounded at his rebuke</u>.**
> **(12) By his power he stilled the sea;**
> **by his understanding he shattered Rahab.**

---

[12] See *Hell Know* <u>Chapter Nine</u> for details on the four common sense hermeneutical laws.

(13) <u>By his wind the heavens were made fair;</u>
<u>his hand pierced the fleeing serpent</u>.
(14) Behold, these are but the outskirts of his ways,
and how small a whisper do we hear of him!
But the thunder of his power who can understand?"
Job 26:5-14 (ESV)

Despite his great suffering, Job testifies to God's greatness over all creation in this passage. He either raves about the LORD doing something awesome or reveals how everything figuratively trembles in awe of the Creator: Verses 5-6 address the dead in Sheol; verse 7 addresses the earth and space; verses 8-9 cite the waters above, i.e. clouds and the precipitation in them; verse 11 notes the "pillars of heaven"; verse 12 the waters below on earth; and, lastly, verse 13 the stars.

Job is obviously using hyperbole and symbolism to accentuate God's magnificence. Hyperbole is exaggeration for effect. For instance, are the "pillars of heaven" in verse 11 literal or figurative? Do they actually tremble before God? Are they literally astounded at his rebuke? No, because they're not even living things. What about God piercing the "fleeing serpent" in verse 13? The first part of the verse shows that this is linked to the LORD making the heavens fair by his "wind" (other versions translate this as "breath," giving the image of the Creator blowing air from his mouth). I've heard a couple of good interpretations of this reference to God piercing the "fleeing serpent" but, whatever it means, it's clearly figurative language and not literal.

In verse 7, Job says that God "hangs the earth upon nothing." This is a poetic way of declaring the literal truth, which didn't become known until thousands of years later, thus verifying the Divine authorship of Scripture.

With all this information about the context of Job 25:5-6, let's read it again:

> The <u>dead</u> *(rapha)* tremble
>> under the waters and their inhabitants.
> (6) Sheol is naked before God,
>> and Abaddon has no covering.
>
> **Job 26:5-6** (ESV)

Verse 5 declares that the dead *(rapha)* in Sheol tremble before God. Do the dead *(rapha)* in Sheol really tremble before God? No, because they're not even alive; in fact, the passage plainly says they're *dead*. They no more tremble before the Almighty than the "pillars of heaven" tremble at His rebuke (verse 11). Again, this is simply hyperbolic language whose purpose is to rave and boast about the Creator.

In this section we've looked at five of the eight biblical passages where the Hebrew word *rapha* appears. The other three times are Proverbs 2:18, Proverbs 9:18 and Isaiah 14:9, all addressed elsewhere in this book.

Chapter Seven

VARIOUS DESCRIPTIONS
of Sheol in the Bible

Let's now look at various biblical descriptions and insights about Sheol not yet addressed or, at least, not addressed in detail.

Sheol is Contrasted with "the Land of the Living"

The reality that Sheol is the realm where dead souls are held 'awaiting' their resurrection can be derived from the fact that **Sheol is often spoken of in contrast to "the land of the living."** In the previous chapter we witnessed evidence of this in Hezekiah's statements from Isaiah 38:9-12. Let's look at some other biblical examples:

> **For thou hast rescued <u>my soul from death</u>, my eyes from tears, my feet from stumbling.**
> **(9) I shall walk before the LORD in <u>the land of the living</u>.**
>
> **Psalm 116:8-9** (NASB)

We see here that the LORD delivered the psalmist from a life-threatening situation. Verse 3 reveals that the psalmist was distressed and sorrowful because, as he puts it, "The cords of death encompassed me and the terrors of **Sheol** came upon me." (Notice, once again, that death and Sheol are essentially synonymous terms in the Bible). The psalmist was seriously concerned that he'd lose his life in this situation, but the LORD ultimately delivered him and that's why he exclaims in verse 8: "thou hast rescued my soul from death." The psalmist knew that, if he died, his soul would go to Sheol, the world of the dead where lifeless souls experience only death (naturally). Note that God saved his soul from **death**. He did not save him from fellowship with father Abraham in the paradise compartment of Sheol; he saved him from death. Because the LORD delivered him, he states in verse 9: "I shall walk before the LORD **in the land of the living**." Why does he say this? Obviously because you *can't* walk before the LORD in Sheol.

If life in this world is "the land of the living" then it follows that Sheol is the land of the dead or "the world of the dead," as James Strong and Proverbs 21:16 define it, where souls suffer death itself—the state of non-existence.

David speaks of "the land of the living" in these two passages:

> **I would have despaired unless I had believed that I would see the goodness of the LORD <u>in the land of the living</u>.**
>
> **Psalm 27:13** (NASB)

> **I cried out to Thee, O LORD; I said, "Thou art my refuge. My portion <u>in the land of the living</u>."**
>
> **Psalm 142:5** (NASB)

In each case David was in a life-threatening situation. If the LORD failed to come through he would have died and gone to Sheol. As you can see, David speaks of life in this world as "the land of the living" as opposed to the alternative—dying and going to Sheol. Allow me to repeat: If life in this world is "the land of the living" then Sheol is obviously the land of not-living—the land of the dead, the realm of non-existence.

When his life was in danger, Jeremiah likewise used the phrase "land of the living" in this prayer:

Because the LORD revealed their plot to me, I knew it, for at the time he showed me what they were doing. (19) I had been <u>like a gentle lamb led to the slaughter</u>; I did not realize that they had plotted against me, saying,

"Let us <u>destroy</u> the tree and its fruit; <u>let us cut him off from the land of the living</u>, that his name be remembered no more."

(20) But, O LORD Almighty, you who judge righteously and test the heart and mind, let me see your vengeance upon them, for to you I have committed my cause.

Jeremiah 11:18-20

There were people out to kill Jeremiah; their intent was to "slaughter" him and "destroy" his very life, thus cutting him off from "the land of the living." These evil plotters rightly knew that if they successfully murdered Jeremiah his soul would go to Sheol. Since souls in Sheol are literally dead, Jeremiah would be completely cut off from those who are alive in "the land of the living."

But let's suppose for a moment that Sheol is a place where souls are alive and conscious as religionists contend—the wicked suffer continuous torment without a drop of water for relief while the righteous blissfully enjoy paradise. Let's reword the evil plotters words in verse 19 as if this belief were true:

> "Let us physically destroy Jeremiah and cut him off from the land of the living on earth. Unfortunately his soul will immediately go to the paradise compartment of Sheol where he'll enjoy blissful communion with father Abraham and other righteous saints who have passed on."

Once again, we see that adjusting the Scriptures to fit the religious belief that souls are alive in Sheol, whether tormented or comforted, makes an absurdity of God's Word. If souls in Sheol are alive and conscious then Sheol is just as much "the land of the living" as life on earth is "the land of the living." Yet, this would make nonsense of the Scriptures.

If life on earth is "the land of the living" then we naturally conclude that Sheol must be the land of *not-living*, **the land of the dead**.

Sheol: The Soulish Grave of "All the Living"

Notice what David exclaims to God after having been rescued from a life-threatening situation:

> **For you have <u>delivered my soul from death</u> and my feet from falling so that I may walk before God <u>in the light of life</u>.**
> **Psalm 56:13** (NRSV)

Obviously David knew that Sheol was the state of death where "the dead know nothing" and where "there's no work or thought or knowledge or wisdom" (Ecclesiastes 9:5,10). The only reason he could "walk before God in the light of life" was because God rescued his "soul from death." He knew, as we've looked at before, that Sheol is a state where you cannot remember or praise God (Psalm 6:5). God used David himself to reveal this in Scripture. Thus, if the LORD hadn't delivered him on this occasion, his soul would have dwelt in the silent darkness of non-existence.

This is the common spiritual grave of all humankind where the souls of non-born-again people go at physical death. No one had the opportunity to be reborn spiritually and receive immortality until Jesus died and was raised. Before that, all humanity went to Sheol, the soulish grave. This is why, when Joshua was nearing his time of death, he said he was "about to go the way of all the earth" (Joshua 23:14). What is "the way of all the earth"? Sheol, the graveyard of souls.

In complete agreement with Joshua, Job made the statement:

> **"I know that you [God] will <u>bring me to death</u>, and <u>to the house appointed for all the living</u>"**
> **Job 30:23** (NRSV)

What is "the house appointed for all the living"? Sheol, of course. Notice that Job makes it very clear that "all the living" would go there. That's why Ethan the psalmist asked the rhetorical question: "Who can live and never see **death**? Who can escape the power of **Sheol?**" (Psalm 89:48 NRSV).

Thus Sheol can be described as the common grave of humankind. People's bodies may, in fact, be housed in separate, individual graves, tombs, mausoleums or whatever all over the earth, but throughout history all people's souls have shared the common spiritual grave, Sheol. We see this evident in Job 3:13-19 where Job says that, if he died, he would experience the sleep of death *"with* kings and counselors of the earth... *with* princes... *There* the wicked cease from troubling and *there* the weary are at rest. *There* the prisoners are at ease together... The small and great *are there* and the slaves are free from their master" (NRSV).

Job makes it clear that kings, counselors, princes, wicked people, weary people, prisoners, people of small and great social stature, and slaves will all be housed in the same condition together. Indeed, Sheol is the common grave of every soul throughout human history, "the house appointed for all the living," as Job describes it above. The only people who can escape the power of Sheol are those who have obtained immortality by being spiritually reborn of the imperishable seed of Christ (1 Peter 1:23 & 1 John 3:9).

W.E. Vine, the Hebrew and Greek scholar, points out in his lexicon that Sheol/Hades "never denotes the grave" (286) and he's technically right if, in fact, "grave" is referring to the physical hole, tomb or mausoleum where corpses are housed. As pointed out earlier in our study, the Hebrew word *qeber (KEH-ber)* is the biblical word used to specify this. However, although Sheol doesn't refer to the literal physical grave where the body is buried, it can accurately be described as the grave of the soul—the common spiritual graveyard where all dead souls are housed.

We see this in Ezekiel 31:14-18 where it says that whole nations (which are likened to trees, e.g. "trees of Eden," "cedars of Lebanon") will go to "Sheol, to those **slain** by the sword... to the earth beneath; you will **lie** in the midst of the uncircumcised **with** those who were **slain** by the sword" (verses 17-18 NASB). Sheol is specifically mentioned three times in this passage (verses 15, 16 & 17) and the context clearly states that Sheol is death: "For they have all been given over to **death**, to the earth beneath" (verse 14 NASB). "The earth beneath" or "world below" (NRSV) is a descriptive phrase for Sheol, which we'll analyze in Chapter Nine. Note, incidentally that this passage describes souls as *lying* in Sheol with other dead people (verse 18). "Lie" is *shakab (shaw-KAB)* in the Hebrew, meaning "to lie down" or "sleep," which indicates being in a horizontal or prostrate position as on a bed or the ground. The image is that of resting or sleeping, not writhing and wailing in constant roasting torment begging for less than a drop of water. The latter notion simply isn't biblical. A belief that's not biblical is false and, as such, is a false doctrine. It may be religious, it may be traditional in the sense that it goes back to the time of Augustine and the Pharisees, but it's false nevertheless. A lie 1600-2000 years ago is still a lie today; the mere passage of time does not give credence to error.

My main point here is that, because of God's judgment, whole nations of people will go to Sheol and lie together "in the midst of the uncircumcised." This clearly shows that Sheol is indeed the common grave of all spiritually un-regenerated souls.

In the New International Version, which is the most popular modern translation of the Bible, Sheol is consistently translated as "the grave" in the Old Testament. At first, I considered this an improper translation of the word since Sheol does not technically refer to the physical grave where bodies are housed. However, as I studied the subject and discovered that Sheol clearly refers to the common graveyard of unregenerated souls, I've concluded that "the grave" is indeed a sound translation. (Unfortunately, some modern translations sometimes translate Hades as "hell," which is erroneous because it gives the impression that Hades and the lake of fire—hell—are one-and-the-same, which they're not, as seen in Revelation 20:11-15).

Lastly, by describing Sheol as the "common grave" of dead souls I don't want to give the impression that the remains of souls are thrown into Sheol and placed haphazardly like a mass grave during wartime or what have you. We saw evidence last chapter, in the section on Ezekiel 32:17-32, that there are compartments and levels to Sheol. Whole nations of dead souls are kept in one section on a certain level and others elsewhere. Solomon mentioned the "chambers" of Sheol in Proverbs

7:27. Bodies are buried in earthly graveyards in an orderly fashion according to family, purchaser and sometimes even religious faith; for instance, there are Catholic cemeteries and church cemeteries where only those of that specific faith can be buried. Why would we think it would be any different for dead souls in Sheol?

Sheol and the Physical Grave: Distinct Yet Parallel

Although the physical grave *(qeber)* and the soulish grave *(Sheol)* are indeed separate terms in the Bible they are often mentioned in the same breath. Why? Obviously because the two go hand in hand—if an unredeemed person physically dies his or her soul goes to Sheol; if his/her soul is in Sheol it's because s/he physically died. Simple, right? Let's look at a few examples:

In Psalm 30:3 David says, "O LORD, you brought up **my soul from Sheol**, restored me to life from among those gone down to **the Pit**" (NRSV). Here, again, David is praising God for deliverance from a life-threatening situation. On this occasion David was so close to death that he considered himself as good as dead; that's why he symbolically exclaims, "you brought up my soul from Sheol [and] restored me to life." David obviously didn't literally die, but he came so close that he spoke as if he did. Also notice that David makes it clear that Sheol is the condition and place that souls specifically go to upon physical death; this is, of course, in contrast to the physical grave where bodies are housed. Take note as well that David describes Sheol as "the Pit," a synonym for Sheol.

With this understanding, consider what David goes on to say in verse 9: "What profit is there in my **death,** if I go down to **the Pit**? **Will the dust praise you? Will it tell of your faithfulness?**" (NRSV). Observe how David mentions "the Pit," which is a reference to Sheol, and then in the very next breath asks, "Will the dust praise you?" "Dust" is definitely a reference to the physical grave *(qeber)* or tomb *(qeburah)* where the body is housed because dust is what (unpreserved) bodies revert to after death. The reason David refers to Sheol and the physical grave interchangeably is simply because the two, although distinct, go together.

We also see this in Psalm 88 where Heman prays for deliverance from a serious life-threatening situation. In verse 3 Heman says, "For my soul is full of troubles and **my life draws near to Sheol**. (4) I am counted among those who **go down to the Pit**; I am like those who have no help, (5) like those forsaken among **the dead** like the **slain** that **lie in the grave** *(qeber)*" (NRSV). By saying his "life draws near to Sheol," Heman is simply expressing how close he was to losing his life in this situation. Now observe what Heman declares in verses 10-12:

> **"Do you** [God] **work wonders for <u>the dead</u>? Do the <u>shades</u> rise up to praise you?**
>
> **(11) Is your steadfast love declared in <u>the grave</u>** *(qeber)*, **or your faithfulness in <u>abaddon</u>** [destruction]?
>
> **(12) Are your wonders known <u>in darkness</u>, or your saving help in <u>the land of forgetfulness</u>?"**
> **Psalm 88:10-12** (NRSV)

Heman specifically mentions Sheol in verse 3 and refers to it as "the Pit" in verse 4. His reference to "darkness" and "the land of forgetfulness" in verse 12 are also references to Sheol, although they could arguably apply to the physical grave as well. In addition, he refers to Sheol as "regions dark and deep" in verse 6. He also mentions the literal grave, *qeber,* in verses 5 and 11.

Why is this important to our subject? I just want to show how Sheol and the physical grave are sometimes noted in the very same breath. Although Sheol refers to the soulish grave—"gravedom"—where un-regenerated souls go and *qeber* refers to the physical grave where bodies are laid to rest, both terms are parallel and signify the same condition: DEATH, the cessation of life. *Qeber* **signifies the utter absence of life in the physical realm and Sheol denotes the utter absence of conscious life period**.

Because Sheol and *qeber* are sometimes spoken of in the same breath some theologians have mistakenly theorized that Sheol refers to the physical grave, at least in the context in question. Yet, Sheol is repeatedly described in the Scriptures as a place and condition where immaterial souls go, not bodies. This has been firmly established in our study. As such, the idea that Sheol refers to the physical grave must be rejected.

Our conclusion is that Sheol and *qeber* are distinct yet parallel terms in the Bible; they have separate definitions but naturally go together. Being parallel terms, they signify the same thing—death, the absence of life. Is there any life in a physical grave? No. Neither is there life in Sheol, the soulish grave. **Is a grave meant for anything other than that which is dead**? **No. The same goes for Sheol**. Both terms, though distinct, denote the utter absence of life.

This presents a problem for the religious view which teaches that Sheol/Hades is a nether realm where unrighteous souls exist in a state of conscious torment desperately hoping for less than a drop of water for relief while Old Testament saints hang out in paradise with father Abraham. If this were so, Sheol and *qeber* couldn't possibly be sister terms. Why? Because *qeber* would signify the utter absence of life whereas Sheol would refer to the express opposite—conscious life in a spiritual dimension, whether in misery or bliss. They wouldn't be parallel terms at all if they represent two opposite conditions.

Job Spoke of "Sheol" and "Dust" in a Parallel Sense

The above explains why Job spoke of Sheol and "the dust" as parallel concepts:

> **"If I look for <u>Sheol</u> as my home, <u>I make my bed in the darkness</u>;**
> **(14) If I call to <u>the pit</u>, 'You are my father';**
> **To <u>the worm</u>, 'my mother and my sister';**
> **(15) Where now is my hope? And who regards my hope?**
> **(16) Will it go down with me to <u>Sheol</u>? Shall we together go down into the <u>dust</u>?"**
> **Job 17:13-16** (NASB)

Job's suffering was so great that he considered himself on the verge of death, which is why he says he's looking for Sheol as his home in verse 13 and equates it with making his "bed in the darkness."

This is synthetic parallelism where related thoughts are brought together to show similarities or some other correlation, including contrast. In this case, Job says that if he makes Sheol his home he will "make his bed in darkness." Does this sound like Job will be conscious and active in Sheol, chummin' around with father Abraham in some nether-paradise? No, he'll "make his bed in darkness," which perfectly coincides with his earlier statement that, if he died and went to Sheol, he'd be **"lying down... asleep** and **at rest."** (Job 3:13). He'd be 'sleeping' the 'sleep' of death in his "bed in darkness."

Verse 16 is another example of parallelism where the second part of the verse essentially restates the first part in different words: "Will it [hope] go down with me to **Sheol**? Shall we together go down into the **dust**?"

Job is obviously likening the soulish grave—Sheol—to the physical grave or tomb where the body returns to dust. Why? Because, as noted in the previous section, Sheol and the physical grave/tomb are distinct yet parallel concepts; they are different but go together. Being parallel, they signify the same thing—death, the absence of life. Is there any life in a physical grave? Neither is there life in Sheol, the soulish grave. **The physical grave or tomb isn't meant for anything other than that which is dead. The same goes for Sheol.** Both terms, although distinct, denote the absence of life.

People Who Go to Sheol are "No More"

David says something interesting in Psalm 39 while lamenting about God's severe discipline and the brevity of life:

> **Look away from me, that I may enjoy life again before I depart and am <u>no more</u>."**
> **Psalm 39:13**

We don't know what David's sin was or the nature of God's discipline, but the psalm shows David's suffering and his forlorn reflections on the transient nature of life. God's hand of discipline was so heavy that David no longer even enjoyed living and was concerned for his very life, which is why he asks the LORD to look away from him before he departs—*dies*—and is "**no more.**"

Please notice what David does *not* say. He doesn't say, "Look away from me… before I depart and share fellowship with Abraham in the paradise compartment of Sheol." This belief makes utter nonsense of the passage because it's not true. David knew that if he died he'd go to Sheol and be "no more," meaning he'd be **dead**—his conscious life would expire as the breath of life returned to the LORD and his soulish remains would go to Sheol to 'rest' **in death**.

This is not an isolated example as there are many other passages revealing that those who die and go to Sheol are "no more." We observed this last chapter with the king of Tyre in Ezekiel 28:7-8,18-19. Another example is Psalm 59 where David prays that the LORD would hold his adversaries accountable for their sins:

> **For the sins of their mouths, for the words of their lips, let them be caught in their pride. For the curses and lies they utter**
>
> **(13) consume them in your wrath, consume them till they are <u>no more</u>. Then it will be known to the ends of the earth that God rules over Jacob.**
>
> **Psalm 59:12-13**

Notice that David doesn't say, "Consume them until they physically die and their souls go to Sheol where they'll suffer constant fiery torment." Why doesn't he phrase it like this? Because—again—it's simply not true. It's a false doctrine; a religious myth. When God's wrath fell, David's enemies would die and be "no more" because their soul would go to Sheol, which is the "world of the dead," not the world of fiery conscious torture or the world of chummin' with father Abraham in bliss.

Here's an example from the LORD Himself against the city of Tyre:

> "This is what the Sovereign LORD says: 'When I make you a desolate city, like cities no longer inhabited, and when I bring the ocean depths over you and its vast waters cover you, (20) then I will bring you down with those who go down to <u>the pit</u>, to the people of long ago. I will make you dwell in <u>the earth below</u>, as in ancient ruins, with those who go down to <u>the pit</u>, and you will not return or take your place <u>in the land of the living</u>. (21) I will bring you to <u>a horrible end</u> and <u>you will be no more</u>. You will be sought, but you will never again be found, declares the Sovereign LORD'."

Ezekiel 26:19-21

When God's judgment falls on Tyre it will become a desolate city as the inhabitants will be wiped off the face of this earth. Verse 20 shows that they will go to the "the pit" and "the earth below," which are synonyms for Sheol; verse 21 elaborates that this is a "horrible end" where they will be "no more." Please notice that going to Sheol is spoken by God as a horrible **END** and not the beginning of a life of roasting torture until their resurrection on judgment day. When these people go to Sheol they will be "no more" because Sheol is the "world of the *dead*," which is in contrast to life on earth, the "land of the living" (verse 20). In other words, if life on earth is the "land of **the living**" then Sheol must be the land of **the dead** where souls rest in the 'sleep' of **death** until their resurrection. Take note: **God Himself describes their condition in Sheol as being "no more,"** which mirrors His description in Ezekiel 28:7-8,18-19.

For more examples see Genesis 42:13,32,36, Job 7:21, Psalm 104:35 and Isaiah 26:14.

The Fire of God's Wrath "Burns Down to Sheol Below"

Sheol and death are synonymous terms in the sense that unredeemed people who die go to Sheol and are "no more." As such, they only 'experience' the condition of death, which makes sense of something the LORD says in the Song of Moses:

> **(21) "They made me jealous by what is no god**
>   **and angered me with their <u>worthless idols</u>.**
> **I will make them envious by those who are not a**
>   **people;**
> **I will make them angry by a nation that has no**
>   **understanding.**
> **(22) For <u>a fire will be kindled by my wrath</u>,**
>   **<u>one that burns down to the realm of the dead</u>**
>   *(sheol)* **<u>below</u>.**
> **It will devour the earth and its harvests**
>   **and set afire the foundations of the**
>   **mountains.**
> **(23) <u>I will heap calamities on them</u>**
>   **and spend my arrows against them.**
> **(24) I will send wasting famine against them,**
>   **consuming pestilence and <u>deadly plague</u>;**
> **I will send against them the fangs of wild beasts,**
>   **the venom of vipers that glide in the dust.**
> **(25) In the street <u>the sword</u> will make them childless;**
>   **in their homes terror will reign.**
> **The young men and young women <u>will perish</u>,**
>   **the infants and those with gray hair."**
>   **Deuteronomy 32:21-25**

Those who claim that Sheol is a torture chamber in the heart of the earth where unrighteous souls suffer constant roasting torment until their resurrection on Judgment Day sometimes cite verse 22 to support their view, but they're not too enthusiastic about it because it lacks the diabolical details inherent to their position. Thankfully, the meaning of the verse is clear within the context.

The LORD Himself is speaking and His verbiage shows Him to be quite angry. Verse 21 reveals why: the Israelites engaged in unrepentant idolatry and therefore a "fire" was kindled by God's wrath that "burns down to the **realm of the dead** below" (verse 22). The "realm of the dead below" refers to Sheol while the "fire" is figurative of the punishment that will be inflicted on the unrepentant due to God's wrath, provoked by their stubborn idolatrous spirit. Their precise punishment is detailed in the rest of the passage:

- The Israelites' crops will fail (verse 22).
- The LORD will "heap calamities" on them and many will perish as God spends his "arrows against them" (verse 23).
- The failure of their crops will result in famine (verse 24).
- God will send a "deadly plague" (verse 24).
- They will be struck down by the "fangs of wild beasts" and the "venom of vipers" (verse 24).
- On the streets and in their homes "the sword" will take them out, which is figurative of any deadly weapon of evildoers or foreign invaders (verse 25).
- God's sentence for the community of idolaters—young and old—is death, for that is the wages of sin (verse 25).

While this might seem like a harsh punishment it's in line with the terms of the Old Covenant that the LORD had with the Hebrews. The terms were simple: blessings for obedience to God's law and curses for disobedience (see Deuteronomy 28). If the Israelites were willing to humbly repent of their idolatry it would've resulted in God's mercy and forgiveness, but this obviously wasn't the case. They were obstinate about their sin.

As you can see from the passage itself, the LORD's wrath against the idolatrous Israelites would result in the sentence of **death** through various means. This explains why verse 22 says that the fire of God's wrath burns down to the realm of the dead below—because the outcome of God's wrath is death for "the wages of sin is death" (Romans 6:23). The souls of those who die would be housed in the realm of the dead in the heart of the earth below, i.e. Sheol.

You see? The passage is simple to understand when you grasp both the nature of Sheol and the biblical penalty for sin—death, not constant fiery torture.

With this understanding, notice that absolutely nothing is said about souls in Sheol suffering roasting torment without a tiny bit of water for relief; neither is anything said about a "paradise" compartment that also supposedly exists in Sheol. Why not? Because they're false doctrines foreign to the Scriptures.

"Gathered to His People"

Let's now consider an interesting phrase that is often used in the Old Testament to describe the perishing of an Israelite. Notice what the LORD tells Moses at the end of his life:

> **"There on the mountain that you have climbed <u>you will die and be gathered to your people</u>, just as your brother <u>Aaron died</u> on Mount Hor <u>and was gathered to his people</u>."**
>
> **Deuteronomy 32:50**

What does "gathered to your people" mean? We know it's linked to the death of a person, but does it refer to the body being placed in a tomb amongst others from one's people? No, this phrase refers to the soul going to Sheol. For proof consider a similar statement in the previous chapter of Deuteronomy:

> **The LORD said to Moses, "Soon you will <u>lie down with your ancestors</u>. Then this people will begin to prostitute themselves to the foreign gods in their midst, the gods of the land into which they are going; they will forsake me, breaking my covenant that I have made with them."**
>
> **Deuteronomy 31:16** (NRSV)

God informs Moses that he was soon going to die and describes it in terms of "lying down with his ancestors," which—like "gathered to his people"—refers to his soul going to Sheol, the graveyard of dead souls. We know that God wasn't referring to Moses' *body* "lying down with his ancestors" because Moses' body was not buried with his forefathers, but in an unknown grave in Moab, as shown in Deuteronomy 34:6. With this understanding, notice that God Himself describes the condition of the soul in Sheol in terms of **lying down**, which corresponds to Sheol as the condition of death where dead souls 'sleep' in death until their resurrection.

Let's observe further proof that being "gathered to his people" refers to the soul "lying down" in Sheol and not to the dead body resting in a tomb:

> **When Jacob had finished giving instructions to his sons, he drew his feet up into the bed, <u>breathed his last and was gathered to his people</u>.**
>
> **Genesis 49:33**

And the following verses of the next chapter:

> **Joseph threw himself on his father and wept over him and kissed him. (2) Then Joseph directed the physicians in his service to embalm his father Israel. So the physicians embalmed him,**
>
> **Genesis 50:1-2**

The instant Jacob breathed his last breath he was "gathered to his people." He of course left behind his physical shell and that's what Joseph throws himself on in grief.

Additional proof can be observed in an earlier statement that Jacob made to Joseph:

> **When the time drew near for Israel [Jacob] to die, he called for his son Joseph and said to him, "If I have found favor in your eyes, put your hand under my thigh and promise that you will show me kindness and faithfulness. <u>Do not bury me in Egypt</u>, (30) <u>but when I rest with my fathers, carry me out of Egypt and bury me where they are buried</u>."**
>
> **Genesis 47:29-30**

Whether Jacob's *body* was buried in Canaan or not he acknowledged that *he* would "rest with his fathers." Where? In Sheol, the graveyard of dead souls.

These verses show that being "gathered to his people" is not a reference to the body, but rather to the soul going to Sheol and being laid to rest with the deceased's countrymen: Jacob died and his *soul*—his immaterial being—was "gathered to his people" and Joseph subsequently gave directions about the embalming of Jacob's *body*.

We discovered in the previous chapter that dead souls in Sheol are laid to rest according to nation, family and so on (see *The Longest and Most Detailed Passage on Sheol*). In Chapter Three we saw that the Hebrew word *bowr (borr)* is used as a synonym for Sheol, meaning "pit," "well" or "dungeon." Moreover, Proverbs 7:27 suggests that there are "chambers" or orderly sections to Sheol. As such, **Sheol is a colossal pit or dungeon in the underworld where dead souls are housed until their resurrection**. Sheol has levels and chambers where dead souls are "laid to rest" in an orderly fashion, according to nation, clan and family, much the way that bodies are buried in earthly graveyards or put in tombs or mausoleums in an orderly fashion according to citizenship, family, purchaser and sometimes even religious faith.

So when the Bible talks about Aaron, Moses, Jacob and others dying and being "gathered to their people" it means that their dead souls went to Sheol—the graveyard of souls—where they were laid to rest with their countrymen, tribe and family in an orderly fashion, just as the warriors of Egypt and other pagan nations were laid to rest with their countrymen, as seen in Ezekiel 32:17-32. It doesn't mean that they went to Sheol and consciously hanged out with their dead loved ones and enjoyed sweet communion in a supposed paradise compartment of Sheol, as some teach. This is a false doctrine that's incompatible with the Scriptures. After all, when the phrase "gathered to his people" is used, as well as any reference to a person dying and going to Sheol, does the passage say anything anywhere about them being conscious and buddying around with their countrymen in Sheol? No. On the contrary, the language is always that of lying down, "sleeping" in death, being silent, not being able to remember or praise God, resting, being "no more," and so on. It's the language of **the condition of death, the state of utter non-being**, which means **the absence of consciousness**.

In Genesis 50:1 above we observe Joseph mourning greatly for his father, as does the entire family and others nine verses later:

> **When they reached the threshing floor of Atad, near the Jordan, they lamented loudly and bitterly; and there Joseph observed a seven-day period of mourning for his father.**
>
> Genesis 50:10

Why all the loud, bitter lamentations if Jacob went down to a nether-paradise to fellowship with father Abraham? Jacob reacted the same way when he was informed that Joseph was dead, as shown in Chapter Two (Genesis 37:34-35). Such a reaction makes no sense if Old Testament saints went to a conscious life of bliss where they communed with their countrymen. If this were the case, would he be "mourning" and "bewailing" him so grievously? Of course not. Someone might argue that Joseph and the other family members were grieving over their own personal loss and not the destination of Jacob's disembodied soul. If this were so, wouldn't they likely exclaim something to the effect of, "Praise you LORD that our father is now in the comforting presence of Abraham, and we will one day go to this same paradise to reunite with them." Yet they say nothing of the kind; in fact, their reaction is completely opposite to this. Why? Because the idea that Sheol is a place where souls are conscious and holy people of the Old Testament went to paradise with father Abraham is a false doctrine.

Wicked Kings "Rested with their Fathers"

As noted in Genesis 47:30 above, Jacob spoke of dying in terms of "resting with his fathers." Interestingly, this same phrase is used in reference to wicked kings in the Old Testament. For instance, these first two references refer to two of the *worst* kings of Judah:

> **So Joram** [aka Jehoram] **<u>rested with his fathers</u>, and was buried with his fathers in the City of David.**
>
> **2 Kings 8:24** (NKJV)

> **So Ahaz <u>rested with his fathers</u>, and was buried with his fathers in the City of David.**
> **2 Kings 16:20** (NKJV)

Please notice that, in both cases, "rested with his fathers" is differentiated from their bodies being buried. In other words, "resting with their fathers" is a reference to their souls going to Sheol where they were "gathered to their people," as detailed in the previous section.

These next two verses refer to the *wickedest* kings of the northern kingdom of Israel:

> **So Omri <u>rested with his fathers</u> and was buried in Samaria. Then Ahab his son reigned in his place.**
>
> **1 Kings 16:28** (NKJV)

> **So Ahab <u>rested with his fathers</u>. Then Ahaziah his son reigned in his place.**
> **1 Kings 22:40** (NKJV)

Like righteous Jacob, these wicked kings and many others are said to have "rested with their fathers" when they physically perished. The Hebrew for "rested" is *shakab (shaw-KAB)*, which literally means "to lie down," "sleep" or "slept." They obviously "lied down" or "slept" in the figurative sense of 'sleeping' in death in Sheol, the graveyard of dead souls, until their resurrection to be judged.

While these kings were all Israelites they were *wicked* leaders who turned the Hebrews away from the LORD. In fact, Ahaz was the *worst* king of Judah; and Omri and Ahab were the *evilest* kings of the northern kingdom. If the doctrine that Sheol is a place of conscious existence where wicked souls suffer constant fiery torment and righteous souls are comforted in paradise, then these four kings would've certainly gone to the torments section, right? Yet there's no indication of this in these passages because it's a false doctrine. These evil kings died and they "*rested* with their fathers" in Sheol. That's what the Bible plainly teaches.

<u>Chapter Eight</u>

RICH MAN & LAZARUS:
Fantastical Parable or Literal?

Let's now look at the sole reason why Christians have traditionally believed that Sheol is a state of conscious existence where bad people suffer constant fiery torment hoping for a tiny bit of water for relief and Old Testament saints are comforted in paradise at Abraham's side. I'm, of course, referring to Jesus' story of the rich man and Lazarus:

> **"There was a rich man who was <u>dressed in purple and fine linen</u> and <u>lived in luxury every day</u>. (20) At his gate was laid a beggar named Lazarus, covered with sores (21) and longing to eat what fell from the rich man's table. Even <u>the dogs</u> came and licked his sores.**
>
> **(22) "The time came when the beggar died and the angels carried him to Abraham's side. The rich man also died and was buried. (23) <u>In Hades</u>, where he was in torment, he looked up and saw Abraham far away, with Lazarus by his side. (24) So he called to him, 'Father Abraham, have pity on me and send Lazarus to dip the tip of his finger in water**

and cool my tongue, because I am in agony in this fire.'

(25) "But Abraham replied, 'Son, remember that in your lifetime you received your good things, while Lazarus received bad things, but now he is comforted here and you are in agony. (26) And besides all this, between us and you a great chasm has been set in place, so that those who want to go from here to you cannot, nor can anyone cross over from there to us.'

(27) "He answered, 'Then I beg you, father, send Lazarus to my family, (28) for <u>I have five brothers</u>. Let him warn them, so that they will not also come to this place of torment.'

(29) "Abraham replied, '<u>They have Moses and the Prophets</u>; let them listen to them.'

(30) " 'No, father Abraham,' he said, 'but if someone from the dead goes to them, they will repent.'

(31) "He said to him, 'If they do not listen to Moses and the Prophets, they will not be convinced even if someone rises from the dead.' "

Luke 16:19-31

The first thing that needs to be stressed about this story is that, whether a person takes it literally or figuratively, **it does not refer to the eternal fate of damned people**; that is, the "second death." In the story, the rich man and beggar are said to be in **Hades**, which refers to the intermediate state of un-regenerated souls between physical death and resurrection to stand before God and be judged. The Greek Hades corresponds to the Hebrew Sheol, as established in Chapter One. Once everyone is resurrected from Hades (Sheol) and judged, Hades will itself be thrown into the lake of fire.

See for yourself:

> **The sea gave up the dead that were in it, and
> <u>death and Hades gave up the dead that were in them</u>,
> and each person was judged according to what he
> had done. Then <u>death and Hades were thrown into
> the lake of fire</u>. The lake of fire is the second death.
> Anyone whose name was not found written in the
> book of life was thrown into the lake of fire.**
>
> Revelation 20:13-15

So regardless of how a reader views Jesus' imaginative story, **it's not applicable to the eternal fate of unredeemed people**. It amazes me how often this tale is brought up when discussing the topic of human damnation with others. Anyone who cites this story to support eternal conscious torture hasn't studied the subject of damnation to any great length.

With that understanding, let's now consider Jesus' story—it's meaning and importance.

Someone wrote me:

> "There's got to be something more to this tale as I've found that every time there's a seeming contradiction in Scripture, a deeper truth is waiting to be discovered. The story of the rich man and Lazarus bothers me. If this was a common story of the time, why did it make it into Scripture? Jesus did so much stuff that didn't get written down and since God knew this tale would get confused in future generations, why was it included for us to scratch our heads over? There's something there."

I agree, so we'll focus on mining insights from Jesus' story, but—at the same time—we shouldn't overstate its importance. Unlike the Parable of the Sower, which appears in 3 of the 4 gospel accounts, the Parable of the Rich Man and Lazarus only appears once. I'm not saying it's not important, but it's no more important than, say, the Parable of the Shrewd Manager that also appears only once in Scripture, also in Luke 16, and is of comparative length. How often do we hear anything about that parable? Almost never, right? But *everyone* seems to know about the tale of the rich man and Lazarus and ask questions about it ad nauseam (don't take me wrong as the tale naturally provokes important questions; I'm just making a point).

Now, someone might object that I just referred to Jesus' story as a "parable"—a figurative tale—but be patient because I'm going to prove beyond any shadow of doubt that the story of the rich man and Lazarus is just that—a symbolic tale that makes many potent points.

E.W. Bullinger's View

Greek scholar E.W. Bullinger maintained that Jesus was using **the Pharisees own teachings** and **own words** to convict them. This makes sense for two reasons: **1.** The story, if taken literally, blatantly contradicts what the rest of Scripture teaches about Sheol, including the LORD's own descriptions, as detailed in Chapter Six' *The Longest and Most Detailed Passage on Sheol.* And **2.** the Pharisees embraced the unbiblical Hellenistic concept of the immortal soul apart from Christ and, consequently, eternal roasting of damned souls. As such, Jesus' parabolic tale mimicked their beliefs with the twofold purpose of rebuking them and conveying one of the most important themes of the Bible, both of which we'll extract from the story in this chapter.

You can read Bullinger's take on the story on the internet.[13] I should warn you though that he has an archaic and convoluted style of writing that'll likely turn-off most modern readers. Let me also add that I don't embrace everything Bullinger advocates, but who agrees with anyone about everything? As they say, "Eat the meat and spit out the bones."

The Living Word of God Would NOT Contradict the Written Word of God

Here's my take on Jesus' story of the rich man and Lazarus:

---

[13] Just Google "E.W. Bullinger rich man and Lazarus" and it will come up.

Jesus Himself is the living "Word of God," so he's not going to contradict the written Word of God. This is another key that the story is not to be taken literally. After all, *anyone*—regardless of sectarian mindset—who simply does an honest, systematic study on Sheol in the Bible will admit that a literal reading of Jesus' tale contradicts what the entire rest of the Bible teaches about Sheol. As the previous seven chapters of this study have shown, many of the most important men of God in the Old Testament, and even the LORD Himself, describe Sheol as **the world of the DEAD** where souls 'sleep' in death until their resurrection & judgment (and by 'sleep' I don't mean literal snoozing, but rather **the condition of death itself**—i.e. **non-existence as far as conscious life goes**; please read the previous seven chapters *before* automatically assuming that this is erroneous[14]). No one's roasting in conscious torture crying out for tiny bit of water; and neither are (or were) Old Testament saints chummin' around with father Abraham in paradise. Jesus said the TRUTH will set us free, which is **God's Word** (John 8:31-32 & 17:17). By contrast, that which is false cannot set us free, because it's *not* **true**.

With this understanding, God didn't place the Parable of the Rich Man and Lazarus in the Bible to "confuse anyone in future generations" because he knew (and knows) that **anyone who is diligent and simply studies the subject from Genesis to Revelation will be set free by the truth**. Only those who are unwilling to search for the truth or are too proud to admit they might be wrong and insist on following uninformed leaders will be misled by it (see Matthew 15:14). Most of these are sincere God-fearing brothers and sisters in the Lord who've simply been misled about Jesus' tale and only casually view it as a literal teaching; in other words, they're simply ignorant on the subject. However, some of their leaders are rigid, unthinking sectarians poisoned by legalism, like the Pharisees. To them Jesus' story is **a stumbling block**.

Believe it or not, the LORD and godly characters in the Bible have been known to set out "stumbling blocks" to intentionally discombobulate proud fools, whether legalists or libertines; see, for example, Ezekiel 3:20, Romans 11:9 and Psalm 69:22. I'm not saying

---

[14] I only say this because, with a book like this, many people will be tempted to jump ahead to this chapter without reading the previous seven.

there's no hope for these people. I'm very patient and merciful; in fact, my ministry is all about *setting the captives free*, including those who are figuratively blind. I want to stress that I'm not suggesting that *everyone* who regards the story of the rich man and Lazarus as a literal description of life after death is a modern-day Pharisee, not at all. Again, most are simply ignorant on the subject. I wrote *Sheol Know* for just such people.

"Scripture Interprets Scripture" is a Hermeneutical Law

I said above that the tale of the rich man and beggar "if taken literally, doesn't gel with what the rest of Scripture teaches on the nature of Sheol, including the LORDs own descriptions;" I also said "Jesus Himself is the *living* 'Word of God,' so he's not going to contradict the *written* Word of God." Both statements are rooted in the hermeneutical rule that **Scripture interprets Scripture**, which is a common sense guideline for proper biblical interpretation. Without this rule, people could take any passage in the Bible and declare that it means whatever they say it means, which Peter condemned when he said, "no prophecy of Scripture is a matter of one's *own* interpretation" (2 Peter 1:20[15]). In other words, the way you interpret a passage is **1.** According to its immediate context where the surrounding texts usually indicate the meaning of the passage; and **2.** According to the context of the whole of Scripture whereupon you ask: What does the rest of the Bible say about this particular subject? The clearer or more detailed passages obviously take precedence over the more ambiguous and sketchy ones.

Here's an excellent example of Jesus utilizing this rule when the devil attempted to mislead him by quoting a passage:

> **Then the devil took him to the holy city and had him stand on the highest point of the temple. (6) "If you are the Son of God," he said, "throw yourself down. For it is written:**

---

[15] Revised NIV (2011).

> **'He will command his angels concerning you,**
> **and they will lift you up in their hands, so that you**
> **will not strike your foot against a stone.' "**
>
> **(7) Jesus answered him, "<u>It is also written</u>:**
> **'Do not put the Lord your God to the test.' "**
>
> **Matthew 4:5-7**

As you can see, the devil—who knows the Bible verbatim—was trying to use a biblical passage to spur Jesus to do something wrong, but Jesus didn't fall for it because he followed the principle of interpreting Scripture with Scripture. So He responds, "It is *also* written…" In other words, the verse the devil quoted must be viewed in light of what *other* passages say. When a person fails to do this they inevitably get off track and fall into error. The problem with error is that it's not true; even partial error is not wholly true; and it's only the truth that can set people free, as the Lord taught (John 8:31-32).

With this understanding, Jesus' tale of the rich man and beggar is not open to *private* interpretation because doing so is condemned in the Bible. The parable must be interpreted in light of what the **whole of Scripture** teaches on the subject of Sheol, as well as the other topics that the tale addresses. This is the approach we'll take.

A Literal Interpretation Doesn't Mesh with either Old Testament or New Testament Theology

If taken literally the Parable of the Rich Man and Lazarus does not support either Old Testament or New Testament theology, which is another indication that the tale's not to be taken literally.

For instance, notice that nothing is said of the rich man being immoral or evil, nothing. In fact, it's implied that he gave handouts to the beggar. Also, according to Old Testament theology, the Mosaic covenant Israel had with YHWH (the LORD), being consistently financially blessed indicated God's blessing—generally speaking—whereas **poverty indicated being cursed** (see Deuteronomy 28).

Let's honestly consider what this story says if we embrace it as a literal accounting of life after death in Sheol. In other words, what does this tale *literally say*? Please disregard any sectarian bias and what you *think* it says, just focus on what it actually says:

1. If one is prosperous, gives to the poor,[16] respects authority and is concerned about his loved ones, he will go to Sheol at the point of death and suffer constant roasting torment desperately hoping for less than a drop of water for relief, but it won't be given.
2. If one is poverty-stricken, diseased, has no faith to be healed, is not physically blessed of God and has a life of bad things, he will go to the paradise compartment of Sheol to hang out with father Abraham and be perpetually consoled and comforted.

Let's face it: This literal data from the story totally butchers Old and New Testament theology concerning eternal salvation. The fact that it's diametrically opposed to Old Testament theology has already been stated while the latter is obvious: Nowhere in the story does it indicate that Lazarus expressed repentance and faith for salvation (Acts 20:21). Nowhere does Lazarus indicate or imply that "Jesus is Lord" (Romans 10:9-10). If we take the facts of the story as literal history we must conclude that being a diseased bum equals paradisal bliss at Abraham's side. Is this the case? Does the rest of Scripture back up such a conclusion, such a warped theology? If so, we're damned and so are 99.9% of the people we know!

The Story of the Rich Man and Lazarus is a Parable—a Symbolic Tale

This is just further evidence that the story was never meant to be taken as a literal account of the nature of Sheol. It's *symbolic*, meaning it's **a parable**—a **figurative story**. This is in line with the generality that Jesus "did not say anything to them without using a parable" (Matthew 13:34) and that Jesus' story of the rich man and Lazarus **comes in a long line of parables**: The whole first half of Luke 16 is a parable that starts

---

[16] For those who argue that the rich man didn't give anything to Lazarus, why else would the beggar be laid at his gate (verse 20) if he wasn't receiving *anything* from him? It would be pointless.

with the **same exact words** as Jesus' tale of the rich man and Lazarus; and Luke 15 consists of three other parables. It simply makes no sense that Jesus would suddenly switch to giving a supposedly historical account that contradicts what the Word of God has plainly established about Sheol up to this point.

Add to this the fact that the story clearly contains **fantastical elements**. For instance, the rich man is in literal agony in the fire and so he asks Abraham to have Lazarus dip the tip of his finger in water so he can cool his tongue—not even his hand or finger, the *tip* of his finger! Like that's going to help his roasting condition one iota. It's as if Jesus was getting a megaphone and declaring, *"This is a fantastical tale that is not meant to be taken literally!"* How much more evidence do people need that this is not a literal accounting of life after death?

With the understanding that this is a fantastical symbolic story, Jesus knew that unspiritual people would wrongly interpret it as a literal account in centuries to come, just as a religionist misinterpreted Jesus' statement about being born-again to refer to literal physical rebirth (John 3:3-4). Please understand that Jesus didn't tell parables to reveal truth to the masses, but rather to *hide it* for those with spiritual discernment (Matthew 13:10-15 & 1 Corinthians 2:14). As such, the Parable of the Rich Man and Lazarus is **a stumbling block to the carnal person**—those who are spiritually blind—including religious people with a Pharisaical spirit.

The Surface Meaning of the Parable

The surface meaning of The Parable of the Rich Man and Lazarus is obvious: Jesus had just finished rebuking the Pharisees' greed:

> **"No one can serve two masters. Either you will hate the one and love the other, or you will be devoted to the one and despise the other. You cannot serve both God and money."**
>
> **The Pharisees, who loved money, heard all this and were sneering at Jesus. He said to them, "You are the ones who justify yourselves in the eyes**

of others, but God knows your hearts. What people value highly is detestable in God's sight.

Luke 16:13-15

As you can see, the Pharisees worshipped Mammon (money) and therefore scoffed at Jesus' correction. The Lord's wise response was to reprimand them further via a **classic tale of reversal of fortune**. This was possibly Jesus' unique take on a common story of the time, perhaps a favorite of the Pharisees. In any case, the tale mimics the Pharisees' Hellenistic belief in the immortal soul apart from Christ with the dual purpose of rebuking them and conveying one of the most important themes of Scripture.

The rich man in the parable obviously represented the Pharisees (and Hebraic leaders in general) whereas Lazarus symbolized the Gentiles. We'll look at this further in the next section, but allow me to point out the obvious: We live in a world of lies where the devil is the "god of this world" (2 Corinthians 4:4) and not everything is as it might appear. In this case the Pharisees claimed to be Abraham's offspring (John 8:38-44) and prided themselves on being rich in God's truth—not to mention they were physically rich due to their greedy manipulations— but Jesus' parable reveals them be greatly impoverished in reality and that it is the Gentile beggar who's actually Abraham's "bosom" buddy, not the Pharisees.

Needless to say, if the Pharisees sneered with contempt *before* Jesus gave the parable they were absolutely livid now!

Jesus' punchline in verse 31 is that, if the Pharisees did not listen to Moses and the Prophets, they will not be convinced even if someone rises from the dead. Christ was potently proclaiming two things by this statement:

1. Although the Pharisees claimed to strictly follow the Torah—God's Law—they really didn't. The reference to "Moses" is a reference to the Law; and "the Prophets" refers to all the prophets who rebuked Judah & Israel's wickedness in times past and were rejected. In other words, Jesus was saying that the Pharisees and other religious leaders of Israel were not who they claimed to be—devout men of God who strictly followed the Law. No, they were *hypocrites*, which literally

means **actors**. In fact, Jesus blatantly told them this to their faces on other occasions, as shown in Luke 11:37-54 and Matthew 23:13-35. In short, the Pharisees were *fakes*.

2. Since the Pharisees and other Judaic leaders weren't really listening to Moses and the Prophets—even though they put on *airs* that they did—they wouldn't likely believe even if someone rose from the dead, which is not only a reference to Jesus' later resurrection, but also to Martha & Mary's brother, Lazarus, whom Jesus raised from the dead, as seen in John 11:1-44. This is one of the reasons Jesus utilized the name 'Lazarus' for his parable. You see, many people *believed* in Jesus because of Lazarus' resurrection, but not the proud, stubborn religious leaders of Israel; in fact, they proceeded to plot to kill Lazarus—as well as Jesus—because so many people believed on account of Lazarus' awesome resurrection (John 12:9-11)! Unbelievable, isn't it? This shows why Jesus shared the parable in an effort to rebuke these disingenuous religious authorities. As far as them not having faith even after Jesus later rose from the dead, this is precisely how history panned out: When Jesus was resurrected, the Pharisees and other stuffy Judaic rulers refused to believe it and tried to stamp out those who *did* believe in Christ and his resurrection. The few Pharisees who humbly repented were the exception, like Nicodemus and Saul (Paul).

Now, notice the key words in Jesus' punchline in verse 31: The Pharisees and other hypocritical Judaic rulers wouldn't believe even when the Lord rose from **the dead**. You see, Jesus died and his soul went to Sheol (Hades) when he was crucified. In other words, Jesus himself described the condition he was soon going to experience in explicit terms of being **dead**. If Jesus' story of the rich man and Lazarus was a literal account of life after death and not a fantastical tale Jesus would have said something like, "If they do not listen to Moses and the Prophets, they will not be convinced even if someone rises from blissful communion with father Abraham in the paradise compartment of Hades." Sounds absurd, doesn't it? Yet this would be what Jesus really meant if his story of the rich man and Lazarus is taken literally rather than symbolically. Of course, Jesus said nothing of the kind. He indirectly declared that he was going to rise from **the dead**, which perfectly coincides with the Bible's clear descriptions of Sheol/Hades as "the world of **the dead**," as scholar James Strong defined it, or "the company of **the dead**," as Proverbs 21:16 defines it, or "the realm of **the dead**," as the New International Version translates it on a number of occasions (e.g. Isaiah 14:9,15, Ezekiel 31:15,17 and 32:21,27; the verses from Ezekiel, incidentally, are the LORD Himself speaking).

Of course, there are some ministers who teach that Jesus didn't go to be with Abraham in Sheol; instead they maintain that he was tormented in fire for three days & three nights, like the rich man in the story. If this were so, Jesus' punchline would've been something akin to this: "If they do not listen to Moses and the Prophets, they will not be convinced even if someone rises from three days & nights of fiery torment in Hades." Whether a person holds to this interpretation or the other one it doesn't matter because Jesus said nothing of the kind. He plainly said that he was going to rise from **the dead**, not rise from comforts in paradise with Abraham or rise from horrible roasting agony. Neither belief washes with the Scriptures because they're false doctrines based on an erroneous interpretation of a tale Jesus told that is clearly parabolic and fantastical in nature, not literal.

Getting back to the reason Jesus used the name 'Lazarus' in his parable, we observed one notable reason above and we'll see another below, but Jesus didn't give a name for the rich man in his story. Why? Because the rich man is not a real person but rather is symbolic of group of people, which we'll look at momentarily. This shatters the argument that Jesus' story is a historical account on the grounds that he uses the proper name of 'Lazarus,' which Jesus didn't do in any of his other parables. Bear in mind, however, that the rich man is the sole character in proving the conscious roasting of the damned in Sheol and yet he's not given a name!

Chew on that.

Interpreting the Symbolism—the Bigger Picture

With the understanding that Jesus' tale of the rich man and Lazarus is a parable, how are we to interpret it? Believe it or not, the symbolism of the parable is obvious for anyone who's adequately familiar with the Scriptures and isn't blinded by religious sectarian mumbo jumbo:

The rich man represents the **Pharisees or Judaic rulers—and the Hebrews in general**—who had the truth and who were therefore **spiritually rich**. His purple linen represents the priesthood (Exodus 39:1) and the abundant food on his table represents the blessings of truth and the oracles of God that were entrusted to the Israelites (Romans 3:1-2). The beggar at the gates refers to **the gentiles** who didn't have a covenant with YHWH and were therefore **spiritually poor** (Ephesians 2:11-12). Lazarus in the story wanted even crumbs that fell from the table of the rich man, which corresponds to the Syro-Phoenician woman who begged Jesus to heal her daughter of the evil spirit in Mark 7:24-30. To further support this, dogs lick Lazarus' sores in the story and Hebrews contemptuously called *gentiles* "dogs."

Another indication is Lazarus' name, which means "One in whom **God helps or saves**." In the New Testament, who is God's salvation focused on? Paul said, "because of [Israel's] transgression, salvation has come to **the Gentiles**" (Romans 11:11). He goes on to point out: "But if their transgression means **riches for the world**, and their loss means **riches for the Gentiles**, how much greater riches will their fullness bring?" (verse 12).

In the Bible, the Word of God is likened to spiritual food and compared to bread (Matthew 4:4 & Deuteronomy 8:3). In verses 20-21 we see Lazarus being laid at the rich man's gate and hoping for crumbs from his table. This was the way it was for Gentiles during the Old Testament period: The Israelites were blessed with the Word of God—spiritual bread—while Gentiles rarely heard God's word and essentially settled for "crumbs" from the Israelite's table, which perfectly coincides with the Gentile woman's response to Jesus in Matthew 15:27 after he told her that it wouldn't be right to take the children's bread—the Israelite's bread—and toss it to "dogs," i.e. the Gentiles. Her response was brilliant and showed great faith & persistence: "Yes, Lord, yet even the dogs eat the crumbs that fall from their masters' table" (NRSV).

In short, the rich man and poor man refer to **spiritual riches** and **spiritual poverty**. If you have a covenant with God you're spiritually rich; if not, you're poor, no matter how much material wealth you might possess. The rich man refers to the Hebrews who had a covenant with

God, which is verified by the statement concerning his brothers having "Moses and the Prophets" (verse 29) while Lazarus is figurative of the Gentiles who through faith in Christ **become "Abraham's offspring"** (Galatians 3:29), spiritually born of Abraham's "bosom." Lazarus being carried into Abraham's bosom symbolizes the "grafting in" of believing Gentiles to a place once possessed by Israel (Romans 11:11-24).[17]

Death for the rich man represents the **end of their covenant** with God (Hebrews 8:13 & Romans 11:15, 21) while death for Lazarus represents a believer's death to the old nature when they're spiritually regenerated through Christ (Galatians 2:20 & Titus 3:5) and **the beginning of their new covenant** with the Almighty. Think of it this way: The rich man was blessed and Lazarus was impoverished at the beginning of the parable, but these conditions are **reversed** when they die. Their deaths represent the end of the old covenant and the beginning of the new: Now the Gentiles have spiritual riches through the gospel while the Hebrews languish in unbelief. This was prophesied by Amos:

> **"The days are coming," declares the Sovereign Lord, "when I will send a famine through the land—not a famine of food or a thirst for water, but a famine of hearing the words of the Lord.**
> **(12) People will stagger from sea to sea and wander from north to east, searching for the word of the Lord, but they will not find it."**
> **Amos 8:11-12**

The rich man's torment likely refers to the humbling torment of seeing God's favor—His grace—shift to all the world who genuinely believe (Matthew 21:43), and possibly to the Jews' extraordinary persecution and trouble throughout the last 2000 years.

Finally, if there was any question as to whom the Lord was referring to by the rich man, the parable reveals that he had five brothers.

---

[17] The King James Version and the New American Standard Bible, which are both literal word-for-word translations, say that Lazarus was "In" Abraham's "bosom" in verse 23.

The significance of this is that Jesus shared this parable in Jerusalem, which was part of the southern kingdom of Israel, Judah. Genesis 35:23 shows that Judah—the person—had five brothers just as the rich man in the story. So the Lord was condemning the southern kingdom of Israel whose capital, Jerusalem, he described as "the city that kills the prophets and stones those sent to her" (Luke 13:34), the same city where Jesus— *The* Prophet (Deuteronomy 18:15)—was soon to be put to death. Through the parable Jesus rebukes the Judaic leaders for not genuinely following the law and the prophets (Luke 16:31) because they, in fact, pointed to Christ (John 5:39). Remember Jesus' indictment of the counterfeit religious leaders:

> **"Woe to you, teachers of the law and Pharisees, you hypocrites! You build tombs for the prophets and decorate the graves of the righteous. (30) And you say, 'If we had lived in the days of our ancestors, we would not have taken part with them in shedding the blood of the prophets.' (31) So you testify against yourselves that you are the descendants of those who murdered the prophets. (32) <u>Go ahead, then, and complete what your ancestors started!</u>**
>
> **(33) "You snakes! You brood of vipers! How will you escape being condemned to hell** *(Gehenna)***?**
>
> **Matthew 23:29-33**

As you can see, Jesus' parable potently **symbolizes the main theme of the New Testament**. It's **a prophecy of the rejection of unrepentant Israel and the coming Church Age where reconciliation with God and eternal life are made available to the whole world**. Amazing, isn't it? It's true!

The woman who wrote me about the rich man and Lazarus asked why this story was included in God's Word; she insisted that there was *"something there."* There certainly is—**the most important theme of Holy Scripture!**

Chapter Nine

THE NEW TESTAMENT
and Sheol (Hades)

In this chapter we will examine references to Sheol (Hades) in the New Testament other than Jesus' Parable of The Rich Man and Lazarus. We'll look at direct and indirect references to Hades, as well as every passage that people cite to argue that Sheol is a state of conscious existence for human souls.

"The Gates of Hades will Not Overcome It"

Let's start with an interesting statement Jesus made in response to Peter's confession that Jesus was "the Christ, the Son of the living God":

> Jesus replied, "Blessed are you, Simon son of Jonah, for this was not revealed to you by man, but by my Father in heaven. (18) And I tell you that you are Peter, and on <u>this rock</u> I will build <u>my church</u>, and <u>the gates of Hades will not overcome it</u>.
> **Matthew 16:17-18**

What is the "rock" on which Jesus said he would build his church in verse 18? It's not Peter whose name in Greek, *petros*, means "stone." The "rock" on which Jesus would build his church is *petra*, meaning "large rock" or "bedrock." When you're driving on an interstate highway and pass through a section with sheer rock cliffs on either side it's obvious that the road workers blasted through a big hill or mountain. When I see this I can't help but marvel at the solid mass of rock underlying the topsoil. This is *petra* or bedrock. Figuratively speaking, Jesus said his church would be built on such bedrock—an incredible mass of solid rock. What is this "rock"? It's the revelation—the fact— that Jesus is the Christ or Messiah, the Son of the Living God, who died for humanity's sins and was raised to life for our justification, disarming all diabolical powers and authorities. This is the gospel or "good news." Jesus' church is built on this incredibly good news. It is through this gospel that people escape bondage to the kingdom of darkness and become part of God's kingdom (Colossians 1:13).

Why did Jesus emphasize Peter's name, *petros*? Because, although Peter was just a little "stone," he would become a part of the bedrock of the church of Jesus Christ, as are all believers. We're all little "stones" that together make up the bedrock of the church, Christ's body on earth!

Jesus adds in verse 18 that the "gates of Hades" would not overcome his church. **The "gates of Hades" was a colloquial Jewish phrase for death,** which makes sense since Hades (or Sheol in Hebrew) is the realm of the dead and consequently a person would have to physically die to go there. In other words, physical death was the "gate" to enter Hades. With the understanding that the "gates of Hades" refers to death, Jesus was saying that even death, Satan's ultimate weapon (Hebrews 2:14-15), couldn't stop the Messiah from birthing and unleashing his church. And it didn't. He was raised to life and the rest is history. Furthermore, death has no power to destroy the church, period. Every Satanic attempt to wipe out believers and stop the church's spread has failed. In fact, the blood of genuine martyrs has always served to advance God's kingdom rather than diminish it; for example, Stephan from Acts 7:59-8:4.

Peter's Reaction to the Prospect of Jesus Dying and Going to Sheol

An interesting insight on the nature of Sheol can be observed from Peter's response to Jesus' declaration that he was going to be crucified and rise again three days later:

> **From that time on Jesus began to explain to his disciples that he must go to Jerusalem and suffer many things at the hands of the elders, the chief priests and the teachers of the law, and that <u>he must be killed and on the third day be raised to life</u>.**
>
> **(22) Peter took him aside and <u>began to rebuke him</u>. "<u>Never, Lord!</u>" he said. "<u>This shall never happen to you!</u>"**
>
> **(23) Jesus turned and said to Peter, "Get behind me, Satan! You are a stumbling block to me; you do not have in mind the concerns of God, but merely human concerns."**
>
> **Matthew 16:21-23**

Notice that Jesus doesn't tell his disciples that he will be physically killed and live in a conscious state in Sheol for three days and then be raised to physical life. No, he plainly informs them that he will be killed and only raised to life *three days later*. This is in harmony with the notion that Sheol is the graveyard of souls where dead souls are housed until their resurrection. It doesn't support the idea that souls are conscious and either fellowshipping with father Abraham in paradise or suffering constant roasting torment.

This, in turn, is verified by Peter's response where he literally rebukes the Messiah: "Never, Lord!" Why would Peter have such a negative reaction to Jesus' crucifixion if it resulted in him going to paradise for three days to chum with Abraham? This is just further testimony to the fact that Jesus' Parable of the Rich Man and Lazarus is a fantastical tale given to rebuke the Pharisees and proclaim the main theme of the New Testament and not a literal accounting of the nature of Sheol.

Jesus' Transfiguration and the Appearance of Moses & Elijah

The "transfiguration" refers to the occasion where Jesus took Peter, James and John up a high mountain whereupon the Lord was gloriously *transfigured* before them. Moses and Elijah then appeared and talked to Jesus. Let's read the passage:

> **Six days later Jesus took with Him Peter and James and John his brother, and led them up on a high mountain by themselves. (2) And <u>He was transfigured before them</u>; and His face shone like the sun, and His garments became as white as light. (3) And behold, <u>Moses and Elijah appeared to them, talking with Him</u>. (4) Peter said to Jesus, "Lord, it is good for us to be here; if You wish, I will make three tabernacles here, one for You, and one for Moses, and one for Elijah." (5) While he was still speaking, a bright cloud overshadowed them, and behold, a voice out of the cloud said, "This is My beloved Son, with whom I am well-pleased; listen to Him!" (6) When the disciples heard *this*, they fell face down to the ground and were terrified. (7) And Jesus came to *them* and touched them and said, "Get up, and do not be afraid." (8) And lifting up their eyes, they saw no one except Jesus Himself alone.**
>
> **(9) As they were coming down from the mountain, Jesus commanded them, saying, "Tell the vision to no one until the Son of Man has risen from <u>the dead</u>."**
>
> **Matthew 17:1-9** (NRSV)

Did Moses and Elijah actually appear to Jesus on the mountain and talk to him? If so, how was this possible? There are two general explanations:

1. After his spectacular transfiguration, Jesus said to his disciples, "Tell the *vision* to no man" (Matthew 17:9). The Lord referred to what they saw as **a vision.** A vision is not a material reality, but a supernatural picture seen in the mind or eyes. This same Greek word for "vision" was used in reference to Peter's vision of the unclean beasts being made clean (Acts 10:3,17,19 &11:5). This leads to the possibility that Elijah and Moses were not real but a supernatural picture. If this was the case, the transfiguration was perhaps a prophetic vision of that which would take place in the distant future. Peter, James and John saw the Son of Man glorified in the Kingdom and communing with Moses & Elijah in this vision.

Although this is a plausible explanation since Jesus himself specifically called it a *vision*, it's weak in that Jesus was seen talking to Moses and Elijah. If these two figures were, in fact, a vision why would Jesus—who is real in this situation, not a vision—talk with "them"? It makes no sense.

There's a better explanation and this is the one I embrace:

2. Elijah & Moses literally came "down" from heaven and visited Jesus on the mountain. The evidence for this position is that Elijah escaped death and Sheol altogether and was spectacularly translated to heaven (2 Kings 2:11). This is apparently what happened to Enoch as well (Genesis 5:24). As for Moses, we know he wasn't translated to heaven like Elijah because the Bible shows that he died and the LORD kept his gravesite hidden, but there's evidence that he was resurrected from Sheol and went to heaven.

To explain, consider something discussed in Chapter Six' *Samuel, Saul & the Witch of Endor (and Elijah & Moses)*:

In the Old Testament period people's souls went to Sheol at the point of physical death and the animating breath of life returned to the Almighty. They subsequently 'sleep' in death until their resurrection; this included both the righteous and the unrighteous in periods preceding the ascension of Christ. Elijah and Enoch were *exceptions*. They bypassed death—Sheol—and were supernaturally translated to heaven in the same manner that believers will be during the Rapture of the church. God is the all-knowing, all-powerful Sovereign Creator of the universe who occasionally chooses to treat some differently; and he chose to spare these two from death—Sheol—for His own purposes. What was God's purpose in making these exceptions? To offer Old Testament *examples* of the resurrection of New Testament believers, specifically translation to heaven, which is what will happen when the Rapture occurs. Believers who die before the Rapture are translated as well, it's just that their souls are translated to heaven first—when they physically die—and subsequently experience a bodily resurrection at the time of the Rapture where they receive new glorified bodies.

Since Elijah was already alive in heaven it wouldn't be a problem for him to appear to Jesus on the Mountain and speak with him. The Scriptures also offer evidence that Moses was in heaven, along with Elijah and Enoch; in other words, although Moses certainly died and his body was buried, he too was resurrected to heaven after a brief time in Sheol. What proof is there of this?

Deuteronomy 34:5-6 shows that Moses physically died and his body was buried in Moab, but no one knows exactly where because the LORD—who buried him—intentionally wanted it kept hidden, likely to keep his gravesite from becoming an idolatrous shrine, which would've been a stumbling block to the Israelites. With this understanding, there's a curious passage about Moses' body in the New Testament:

> **But even the archangel Michael, when he was disputing with the devil about the body of Moses, did not himself dare to condemn him for slander but said, "The Lord rebuke you!"**
>
> **Jude 9**

This passage leaves you scratching your head. Why would Michael be arguing with Satan over Moses' body after his death? Obviously the LORD did something *extraordinary* with Moses.

As you can see in the verse, Michael is described as an "archangel," literally meaning an angel of the highest ranking. The Greek word for "archangel" is only used twice in the New Testament—here and 1 Thessalonians 4:16—the latter addressing the bodily resurrection of believers. Michael is also associated with the resurrection of the dead in Daniel 12:1-2. This offers evidence that Michael is God's chief servant in the process of the resurrection of the dead. With this in mind, Jude 9 shows Michael arguing with the devil about Moses' body, which suggests that Moses was resurrected from the dead at some point *after* his death.

The Scriptures are like a puzzle when it comes to topics like this and we have to put the pieces together based on the evidence God provides in his Word. From this evidence—even if it's scant—we can draw possible conclusions; and the evidence at hand points to Moses being bodily resurrected sometime after his death and going to heaven. Before this resurrection his soul was dead in Sheol for a time, as shown in Chapter Seven's *"Gathered to His People"*.

After Christ's transfiguration, Jesus told his three closest disciples not to mention the supernatural event to anyone else until he was resurrected from the dead (Matthew 17:9 & Mark 9:9). Why? Because they didn't yet understand the resurrection unto eternal life, which includes three general types:

1. **Believers going straight to heaven when they die and their later bodily resurrection at the time of the Rapture of the church** (1 Thessalonians 4:13-18); this type of resurrection also includes people who become believers during the Tribulation and die (Revelation 20:4-6), as well as mortal believers during the Millennium; the latter will be similar to the time of the Rapture in which dead believers will be resurrected and living believers will be transformed from mortal to immortal.

2. **The translation of physically living believers at the Rapture,** which includes the miraculous transformation of their bodies from mortal to immortal (1 Corinthians 15:51-54 & 1 Thessalonians 4:13-18). This will take place at the end of the Millennium as well.

3. **The resurrection of the righteous from periods preceding the resurrection of Christ,** which will take place at the time of Christ's

Second Coming after the Tribulation and before the millennial reign (Daniel 12:1-2 & Matthew 19:28-30); keep in mind, however, that there *may* be an earlier soulish resurrection of these Old Testament saints, which we'll consider in Chapter 11.

What Peter, James and John saw on the mountain when Jesus was transfigured were **examples of these three types of resurrections**. Think about it: Elijah was supernaturally translated to heaven while Moses and Jesus were resurrected sometime after their physical decease. As such, Elijah represents the "type 2" resurrection specifically and "type 1" generally (as does Enoch); and Moses and Jesus represent "type 3."

Another reason Moses & Elijah appeared to Jesus is that they represent the law and prophets respectively. Jesus was *The* Prophet who fulfilled the law and implemented a superior covenant (Hebrews 8:6). Again, Enoch, Moses and Elijah were types of the first resurrection, which is the resurrection of the righteous (covered in Chapter 11). Perhaps the LORD wanted types from each era of history: Enoch represented the righteous populace before the flood; Moses the deliverance of the Hebrews from Egypt and establishment of the theocracy of Israel; and Elijah the kingdom of Israel.

An Objection to Elijah & Moses Going to Heaven

Some object to the idea that Elijah & Moses (and Enoch) went to heaven based on a statement Jesus made:

No one has ever gone into heaven except the one who came from heaven—the Son of Man.

John 3:13

This statement seems to contradict the scriptural evidence above, that Elijah and Moses ascended to heaven as examples of the forthcoming resurrections of the righteous. But since God's Word is truth and cannot contradict itself we must apply the hermeneutical rules: **1.**

Scripture interprets Scripture and **2.** context is king. When we do this all will make sense and the passages will harmonize with each other.

Let's first establish what the Bible clearly says about Elijah's last moments on earth:

> **As they were walking along and talking together, suddenly a chariot of fire and horses of fire appeared and separated the two of them, and Elijah <u>went up to heaven in a whirlwind</u>.**
>
> **2 Kings 2:11**

As you can see, there's no getting around the fact that Elijah was supernaturally translated **to heaven** at the end of his earthly life because it's what God's Word explicitly says. This explains how he was available to talk to Jesus at the Transfiguration and also how he was one of the two prophets from Revelation 11:1-14, the other being Moses, which is clear in the passage (and we'll address it in the next section).

As detailed in the previous section, Elijah and Moses went to heaven as respective **types** of the resurrections of New Testament believers and Old Testament saints.

Since we know for a fact that Elijah *did* ascend to heaven as **a type** of raptured believers, how are we to interpret John 3:13? Again, Scripture interprets Scripture and context is king. Let's read the passage with the surrounding verses, which is the context:

> **I have spoken to you of earthly things and you do not believe; how then will you believe if I speak of heavenly things? (13) No one has ever gone into heaven except <u>the one who came from heaven</u>— the Son of Man. (14) Just as Moses lifted up the snake in the wilderness, so the Son of Man must be lifted up, (15) that everyone who believes may have eternal life in him."**
>
> **John 3:12-15**

The Messiah was contextually talking to Nicodemus, a leading Bible scholar of his day, and Jesus was answering the question of

Proverbs 30:4: "Who has gone up to heaven and come down?" The answer, of course, is Jesus himself—he both came down from heaven to become a man and later ascended to heaven 40 days after his resurrection. Jesus then presents the gospel message to Nicodemus in verses 14-15 and the Bible implies that he later embraced it (see John 7:50-51 & 19:38-42). As you can see, the gospel message is rooted in believing in the One the Father lifted up—Jesus Christ who ascended to heaven.

So the context of John 3:13 is that of a person who **both** came from heaven and ascended to heaven and only one person fits that description, Jesus Christ. Elijah didn't come from heaven; he was only translated to heaven as an Old Testament **example** of the raptured believer in the New Testament, as well as believers in general. Neither did Moses come from heaven; he died and went to Sheol but was later resurrected as an **example** of the resurrection of Old Testament saints.

People have to be careful not to take one passage out of its context, like John 3:13, and disregard clear scriptural evidence stated elsewhere, like the fact that Elijah was indeed translated to heaven (Enoch too); as well as the less overt evidence that Moses was resurrected and went to heaven.

"To Him (God) all are Alive"

Let's now examine a passage of Scripture sometimes cited to argue that souls in Sheol are alive and conscious:

> Some of <u>the Sadducees, who say there is no resurrection</u>, came to Jesus with a question. (28) "Teacher," they said, "Moses wrote for us that if a man's brother dies and leaves a wife but no children, the man must marry the widow and raise up offspring for his brother. (29) Now there were seven brothers. The first one married a woman and died childless. (30) The second (31) and then the third married her, and in the same way the seven died, leaving no children. (32) Finally, the woman died too.

(33) Now then, at the resurrection whose wife will she be, since the seven were married to her?"

(34) Jesus replied, "The people of this age marry and are given in marriage. (35) But those who are considered worthy of taking part <u>in the age to come</u> and in <u>the resurrection from the dead</u> will neither marry nor be given in marriage, (36) and <u>they can no longer die</u>; for they are <u>like the angels</u>. They are God's children, since they are <u>children of the resurrection</u>. (37) But in the account of the burning bush, even Moses showed that <u>the dead rise</u>, for he calls the Lord 'the God of Abraham, and the God of Isaac, and the God of Jacob.' (38) <u>He is not the God of the dead, but of the living, for to him all</u> [of these] <u>are alive</u>."

Luke 20:27-38

The topic here is the resurrection of the dead, not whether or not souls are conscious in Sheol awaiting their resurrection. Any unbiased reader who has read the previous chapters of this book realizes that God's Word makes it clear that souls in Sheol are unconscious because they're *dead* and know nothing. The remains of their souls in Sheol await **resurrection**. In this passage and the parallel passages (Matthew 22:23-33 & Mark 12:18-27) the resurrection of **the dead** is the subject, which the Sadducees *didn't* believe in. So Jesus was not arguing for the immortality of the soul apart from Christ, but rather that the righteous dead would be resurrected to eternal life and attain a full state of immortality. This is why Jesus said "and they can no longer die" in verse 36, which of course indicates that they *could* die previously.

Let's now consider verse 37. Jesus said that Moses showed at the burning bush that "the dead rise...". Again we observe that the topic is **the resurrection of the dead**, not whether or not people are conscious in Sheol. Jesus points out that Moses referred to the LORD at the burning bush as "the God of Abraham, and the God of Isaac, and the God of Jacob." To which Jesus points out: "He is not the God of the dead, but of the living, for to him all [of these] are alive." The meaning is obvious within the context of the resurrection of the dead, which the Sadducees didn't believe in: As far as God is concerned, Abraham, Isaac and Jacob were all alive because they were to be resurrected from the dead, as covered in the previous section. Just the same, the New Testament refers to unbelievers as "*dead* in their transgressions" even while they're fully alive at present (Ephesians 2:5). In other words, they're alive now, but God sees them as dead because he views reality from an eternal perspective and not a temporal one.

As you can see, Jesus' statement was a correction to the Sadducees who didn't believe in the resurrection of the dead.

"You'll be with Me in Paradise"

Some claim that righteous people of the Old Testament era experienced "paradise" in the compartment of Sheol they call "Abraham's Bosom" based on a literal reading of Jesus' Parable of the Rich Man and Lazarus (covered in Chapter Eight). They cite Jesus' statement to the repentant thief on the cross as proof of this:

> **One of the criminals who hung there hurled insults at him: "Aren't you the Messiah? Save yourself and us!"**
>
> **(40) But the other criminal rebuked him. "Don't you fear God," he said, "since you are under the same sentence? (41) We are punished justly, for we are getting what our deeds deserve. But this man has done nothing wrong."**
>
> **(42) Then he said, "Jesus, remember me when you come into your kingdom."**
>
> **(43) Jesus answered him, "Truly I tell you, today you will be with me in paradise."**
>
> **Luke 23:39-43**

Jesus obviously discerned a repentant spirit in this thief and faith for salvation (Acts 20:21). As such, he was promising the former criminal paradise when he was resurrected, possibly when Jesus later ascended (Ephesians 4:8); if not, at his Second Coming (Daniel 12:1-2 &

Matthew 19:28-30). Some argue that Jesus told the man he'd be with him in paradise **that very day**. We know, of course, that the Lord said no such thing because Christ didn't go to "paradise" the day he died; he literally died and his dead soul laid in Sheol for three days until he was resurrected. This obviously was not "paradise," but rather the penalty of sin—death—which Jesus experienced in our place as our substitutionary death.

So what "paradise" was Jesus referring to and when would he and this repentant thief experience it? The Greek word is only used three times in Scripture. Other than Jesus' statement in Luke 23:43, Paul referred to "paradise" as currently being **in heaven** in 2 Corinthians 12:4, which is substantiated by Revelation 2:7. Since the latter verse states that the tree of life is in this paradise, it's likely a reference to the Garden of Eden (see Genesis 2:9 and 3:22-24), which was evidently removed from this fallen earth after Adam's banishment, to be replaced one day when God makes the earth and universe new—new in the sense of removing the stain of evil and death, as well as other changes, like making worthless desert landscapes blossom and bloom (Revelation 21:1-4). Again, we know Jesus didn't go to paradise that day, but to Sheol. He was dead and resurrected three days later. Forty days after that Jesus ascended to heaven where this paradise is located.

As already noted, Jesus may have resurrected Old Testament saints from Sheol at this time—including this ex-thief who was crucified with him. If so, this passage seems to support this possibility:

> **"When he [Jesus] ascended on high, <u>he led captives in his train </u>and gave gifts to men."**
> **Ephesians 4:8**

When Jesus was crucified & resurrected he triumphed over the powers of darkness (Colossians 2:15). Paul said of this, "he was delivered over to death for our sins and was raised to life for **our justification**" (Romans 4:25). The apostle was referring to the justification of all those who believe according to the new covenant, of course, but also to the holy people of the Old Testament period who had already passed away. In our new covenant believers don't go to Sheol when they die because they've been born-again of the imperishable seed of Christ (1 Peter 1:3,23); as such, they bypass Sheol and go straight to heaven to await their forthcoming bodily resurrection (Philippians 1:21-24 & 2 Corinthians 5:8). Death—Sheol—has no power over believers who are born-again of the seed of Christ by the Holy Spirit (1 Corinthians 15:55-57). Old Testament saints, on the other hand, had to go to Sheol when they physically died because Jesus hadn't yet died for their sins or been raised to life for their justification. This includes the repentant thief whom Jesus informed would be with him in paradise, which—as we've seen—is located in heaven, not Sheol. As covered earlier this chapter, Enoch, Elijah and Moses were the only exceptions in the Old Testament period because they were types and shadows of the resurrection of the righteous. After Jesus was resurrected, righteous souls no longer had to go to Sheol because justification was made available.

All this renders Luke 23:43 nonsensical because Jesus said to the ex-thief, "Truly I tell you, *today* you will be with me in paradise." The idea that Jesus went straight to paradise when he died—whether in heaven or anywhere else—simply isn't supported by the rest of Scripture. This violates the hermeneutical law "Scripture interprets Scripture." The contradiction is easily solved, however, by simply placing a comma in the appropriate spot in the text. Keep in mind that there was no punctuation in the original Greek text; consequently, translators have to determine where punctuation marks go, like commas and so on. Also bear in mind that the Greek word for "today" literally means 'this day' or 'now.' With these facts in mind, the passage makes perfect sense simply by changing the placement of one comma in the English text like so: "Assuredly, I tell you this day, you will be with me in paradise."

So Jesus wasn't telling the ex-thief that he'd be with him in paradise that very day; no, he was telling him *that day* he'd be with him in paradise, meaning the ex-thief would be with Jesus in paradise in heaven when his soul was resurrected from Sheol, whether that occurred 43 days later when Jesus ascended or much later at Christ' Second Coming is regardless. Keep in mind that time is of no significance when you're dead in Sheol.

Those who disagree have to find scriptural support that Jesus went straight to some paradise upon physical death, which they can't do; so this is the appropriate way to read the verse. Of course, some cite Jesus' parable of the rich man and beggar, suggesting that "Abraham's bosom" was a paradise, but the overwhelming evidence supplied throughout this book disproves that theory.

"You will Go Down to Hades"

Jesus condemned three villages of northern Israel on the grounds that the wicked pagan cities of Tyre, Sidon and Sodom would have all repented if they experienced his miraculous ministry:

> **Then Jesus began to denounce the towns in which most of his miracles had been performed, because they did not repent. (21) "Woe to you, Chorazin! Woe to you, Bethsaida! For if the miracles that were performed in you had been performed in Tyre and Sidon, they would have repented long ago in sackcloth and ashes. (22) But I tell you, it will be more bearable for Tyre and Sidon <u>on the day of judgment</u> than for you. (23) And you, Capernaum, <u>will you be lifted to the heavens</u>? No, <u>you will go down to Hades</u>. For if the miracles that were performed in you had been performed in Sodom, it would have remained to this day. (24) But I tell you that it will be more bearable for Sodom <u>on the day of judgment</u> than for you."**
>
> **Matthew 11:20-24**

Jesus says that it will be "more bearable... **on the day of judgment**" for the wicked cities of Tyre, Sidon and Sodom than for these three Israelite towns. He was talking about the Great White Throne Judgment where people will be resurrected from Sheol (Hades), nation by nation, and judged, as shown here:

> **Then I saw a great white throne and him who was seated on it. The earth and the heavens fled from his presence, and there was no place for them. (12) And I saw the dead, great and small, standing before**

the throne, and books were opened. Another book was opened, which is the book of life. The dead were judged according to what they had done as recorded in the books. (13) The sea gave up the dead that were in it, and <u>death and Hades gave up the dead that were in them</u>, and <u>each person was judged according to what they had done</u>. (14) <u>Then death and Hades were thrown into the lake of fire</u>. The lake of fire is the <u>second death</u>. (15) Anyone whose name was not found written in the book of life was thrown into the lake of fire.

Revelation 20:11-15

Notice the sequence of events: Unredeemed souls are resurrected from Hades (Sheol) and judged according to what they had done; then death and Hades (Sheol) are cast into the lake of fire, which is defined as the "second death." Then anyone whose name is not found written in the book of life will be thrown into the lake of fire.

This massive judgment takes place right before the establishment of the "new heaven and new earth," the eternal home of righteousness where "there will be no more death" (Revelation 21:1-5 & 2 Peter 3:13). How is it that there will be no more death? Because, as you can see above, Revelation 20:14 says that death and Hades (Sheol) will be thrown into the lake of fire. As we've seen throughout this study, death and Sheol go hand in hand because when an unredeemed person dies their body goes to the grave ("death") and their soul to Sheol ("Hades"). Both are cast into the lake of fire—probably symbolically—and so "there will be no more death" in the eternal age of the new heaven and new earth.

It's important to understand this so that we understand Jesus' condemnation of Chorazin, Bethsaida and Capernaum in Matthew 11:20-24 (and Luke 10:12-15). Notice again what Jesus says to Capernaum:

And you, Capernaum, <u>will you be lifted to the heavens</u>? <u>No, you will go down to Hades</u>. For if the miracles that were performed in you had been

performed in Sodom, it would have remained to this day.

Matthew 11:23

The phrase "will you be lifted up to the heavens?" is figurative since this judgment takes place *in* God's throne room in heaven and immediately after this judgment the heavenly city of the new Jerusalem will come "down out of heaven from God" to rest on the new earth (see Revelation 21:2,10 & 3:12) and thus the eternal age of the new heavens and new earth will begin. Just the same, the phrase "you will go down to Hades" is also figurative because Hades (Sheol) will no longer exist at this time. The dead souls of Hades will have been resurrected to face this judgment and then Hades itself is cast into the lake of fire. It would have been more accurate if Jesus said, "you will go down to the lake of fire (or Gehenna)," so why didn't he? Because both Hades and the Lake of Fire (Gehenna) refer to the condition of death for human beings, the state of utter non-being. They're one and the same in this sense; the difference being that Hades is the first death and the lake of fire is the second death. Everyone will be resurrected from Hades, the first death, but no one will be resurrected from the lake of fire, the second death. In other words, those unredeemed souls who are resurrected from Hades to face judgment will be thrown into the lake of fire to suffer death forever and ever (that is, *if* their names are not written in the book of life). As the Bible says, "the wages of sin is death" (Romans 6:23). In short, for human beings Hades and the Lake of fire are one in the same in that they both involve the condition of death.

Now what about Jesus' statement that it would be "more bearable" on the day of judgment for some towns than others? The whole point Jesus is making in this section of Scripture (Matthew 11:20-24 & Luke 10:12-15) is that the unrepentant cities of Chorazin, Bethsaida and Capernaum, where he preached and performed great miracles, were guilty of even greater sins than the infamous cities of Tyre, Sidon and Sodom. Because of this, Jesus says that it's going to be "more bearable… on the day of judgment" for Sodom than those unrepentant cities. Please note that Jesus said it would be more bearable **on the day of judgment** and not more bearable for all eternity experiencing fiery conscious torment in the lake of fire. Jesus was simply pointing out that, on the day of judgment, the second death will be more bearable for the people of Sodom than for the people of Capernaum according to divine justice. Why? Because the people of Capernaum are guilty of a greater degree of sin. That's simple enough to understand. We should just allow Scripture to say what it literally says and not feel compelled to add to it or take away (Revelation 22:18-19). In this case, adherents of eternal torment read way too much into this simple statement, no doubt because they're desperate for biblical support of their position. For more details on this issue see *Hell Know* <u>Chapter Three</u>'s *Suffering Meted Out as Divine Justice Requires*.

"You will Die in Your Sins"

This is a minor point, but notice what Jesus said to the Pharisees, the fake religious leaders of 1st century Israel:

> **Once more Jesus said to them, "I am going away, and you will look for me, <u>and you will die in your sin</u>. Where I go, you cannot come."**
>
> **(22) This made the Jews ask, "Will he kill himself? Is that why he says, 'Where I go, you cannot come'?"**
>
> **(23) But he continued, "You are from below; I am from above. You are of this world; I am not of this world. (24) I told you that <u>you would die in your sins</u>; if you do not believe that I am he, <u>you will indeed die in your sins</u>."**
>
> **John 8:21-24**

The Pharisees (verse 13) were wicked religionists whom Jesus bluntly said were children of the devil (verse 44). **Three times** in this passage Jesus plainly informs them of the dismal prospects of their afterlife: "you will die in your sins."

Sometimes it's just as important to point out what the Bible *doesn't* say as it is to point out what it does say. In this case Jesus doesn't say "you will die in your sins and suffer roasting torment in Hades for a few thousand years without a drop of water for relief and then be resurrected to face judgment and condemned to fiery torture forever and ever in the lake of fire." No, he simply declares—three times—that, if they didn't believe, they would **die** in their sins. Why? Because that's what the wages of sin is—*death*.

I realize that Jesus wasn't obligated to tell them *every single detail* of their eternal fate on this public occasion, but—as "The Truth" (John 14:6)—he was certainly obliged to tell them the gist. For instance, he doesn't say anything about the resurrection of the unrighteous, the Great White Throne Judgment and being cast into the lake of fire to suffer the second death (Revelation 20:11-15), but he certainly summarizes their eternal fate if they refused to believe (three times): "You will indeed **die** in your sins."

Jesus Spoke of "Sleeping" in Death, Not Enjoying Paradise with Abraham

We addressed this point in Chapter Four, but let's look at it again from a slightly different angle: Jesus got word that his friend Lazarus was deathly ill and, later, discerned that he had died. Notice what Christ says to his disciples:

> ..."Our friend <u>Lazarus has fallen asleep</u>; but I am going there to wake him up."
> **(12) His disciples replied, "Lord, if he sleeps, he will get better." (13) <u>Jesus had been speaking of his death</u>, but his disciples thought he meant natural sleep.**
> **(14) So then he told them plainly, "<u>Lazarus is dead</u>, (15) and for your sake I am glad I was not there, so that you may believe. But let us go to him."**
> **John 11:11-15**

Lazarus died and Jesus describes it as falling "asleep," which his disciples mistook as natural sleep. So the Lord plainly informs them that Lazarus was dead.

Unlike the Parable of the Rich Man and Lazarus, which is figurative like all parables, this occasion is a *historical chronicling* and Jesus says nothing whatsoever about the real Lazarus[18] going to paradise to hang out with father Abraham, which would be the case if his parable was a literal account of the nature of Sheol. How does Jesus describe the *real* Lazarus' condition after physically dying? He describes it in explicit terms of 'sleeping' in death. This doesn't refer to literal snoozing, of course, but to the condition of non-existence in Sheol where dead souls are housed. The Lord describes it in terms of 'sleeping' simply because every soul in Sheol will be 'awoken' one day; that is, resurrected. This is in contrast to the "second death," which refers to being cast into the lake of fire (Revelation 20:13-15). Those who suffer the second death are never said to be 'sleeping' because they will never be 'awoken' from eternal death, which is why the Bible calls it an *"everlasting destruction"*—destruction that lasts forever with no hope of resurrection (2 Thessalonians 1:9).

I want to emphasize that Lazarus' death would've been the ideal occasion for Jesus to elaborate on Sheol having a paradisal compartment for righteous souls of the Old Testament period, but Jesus says nothing of the kind. Nor does the Bible mention anything at all about Lazarus being in bliss with Abraham and lamenting his return to our fallen earth after Jesus miraculously resurrects him. Why? Because it's a false doctrine based on mistaking a fantastical parable for a literal account.

Jesus also described a dead girl as being "asleep" in three accounts of the same story, as seen in Matthew 9:24, Mark 5:39: and Luke 8:52. As with the case of Lazarus, this would've been the perfect occasion for the Lord to elaborate on how the girl was in paradise in Sheol with Abraham, but—again—Jesus says no such thing. Instead, he likewise describes her condition in terms of 'sleeping' in death.

On top of this is the astounding event of "many holy people" who were raised to life when Jesus was resurrected, as shown in Matthew 27:50-53. They came out of their tombs and went into Jerusalem and were seen by many. Again, absolutely nothing is said about these righteous people being resurrected from a supposed blissful

---

[18] As opposed to the *fictitious* Lazarus in the parable.

section of Sheol where living souls commune with Abraham. Instead, the passage simply says this:

> **The tombs were opened, and many bodies of**
> **<u>the saints who had fallen asleep</u> were raised;**
> **Matthew 27:52** (NASB)

As you can see, the Bible repeatedly describes the intermediate state of unregenerated souls in Sheol in terms of 'sleeping' in death, not being comforted in paradise or suffering constant fiery torment. It's as if God is flashing the truth about Sheol in bright neon lights in His Word, but many Christians are too indoctrinated, sectarian, proud or dull to see it. WAKE UP, CHURCH!

Jesus' Disciples Did Not Believe He went to Paradise (or Torments)

This is another minor point, but there's no evidence in the New Testament that Jesus' followers believed he went to some nether-paradise to commune with father Abraham when he died. If this were so, wouldn't they celebrate his going to this supposed paradise, even while they would grieve *their* loss? Yet there's zero indication of this—none. Take, for instance, Mary Magdalene's mournful disposition in this passage:

> **Now Mary stood outside the tomb <u>crying</u>. As**
> **she <u>wept</u>, she bent over to look into the tomb**
> **John 20:11**

After Mary saw the resurrected Jesus she reported it to the other disciples who were also terribly grieving:

> **She went and told those who had been with**
> **him and who were <u>mourning and weeping</u>.**
> **Mark 16:10**

There's mysteriously no mention anywhere of the disciples celebrating Jesus going to the paradise compartment of Sheol to fellowship with Abraham and other Old Testament holy people. For those who believe that Jesus went to Sheol to suffer constant torment for three days without a drop of water for relief, there's curiously no mention of this either. Why not? Because the idea that Sheol is a place of constant torments for wicked souls and blissful comfort for righteous souls is a false doctrine; a religious myth that's utterly foreign to the Scriptures. This unbiblical doctrine is spread by people who are simply ignorant of the colossal biblical data on Sheol. Their understanding on the subject is limited to Jesus' tale of the rich man and Lazarus, which they regard as a literal accounting of the nature of Sheol. Of course this is contradicted by the entire rest of Scripture, but they don't realize this, which is why this book exists.

Understanding the Three Realms—Heaven, Earth and the Underworld

Scripture reveals that there are three basic realms or universes:

Therefore God exalted him [Jesus] **to the highest place and gave him the name that is above every name, (10) that at the name of Jesus every knee should bow, in <u>heaven</u> and on <u>earth</u> and <u>under the earth</u>, (11) and every tongue acknowledge that Jesus Christ is Lord, to the glory of God the Father.**

Philippians 2:9-11

And I saw a mighty angel proclaiming in a loud voice, "Who is worthy to break the seals and open the scroll?" (3) But no one <u>in heaven</u> or <u>on earth</u> or <u>under the earth</u> could open the scroll or even look inside it.

Revelation 5:2-3

As you can see, the three realms are:

1. **Heaven**, the spiritual realm where God's throne is located, also called the "third heaven" (2 Corinthians 12:2).
2. **The earth**, which naturally includes the physical universe that encompasses it and, as such, refers to the entire physical realm.
3. **The underworld**, which is the "dark heavenlies," as described in this passage:

> **For our struggle is not against flesh and blood, but against the rulers, against the authorities, against the powers of this dark world and against the spiritual forces of evil in the heavenly realms.**
>
> **Ephesians 6:12**

Lending further support that there are three basic realms is the fact that God's heaven is described as the "third heaven." Since God's heaven is the highest dimension where the LORD's throne is located (Psalm 115:16) and is called the *third* heaven we must naturally conclude that there are two other heavens; that is, two other universes. These other realms are the earth/universe and the underworld, as shown in the above passages.

As far as the underworld goes, there was no such realm until Satan and his band of rogue angels started a war in heaven and were subsequently booted out and fell to the earth (Luke 10:18, Isaiah 14:12 & Revelation 12:9). The devil and his minions are spiritual beings and so they obviously didn't enter into the *physical* earth & universe when they fell from heaven, but rather fell to the spiritual dimension that parallels or **underpins the earth and universe**. This is the underworld or dark heavenlies. We see evidence of this underpinning spiritual realm in the book of Job where Satan twice presents himself to the LORD in heaven to which God asks, "Where have you come from?" Both times the devil replies, "From roaming through the earth and going back and forth in it" (Job 1:6-7 & 2:1-2). Being a spiritual being, Satan wasn't roaming around the *physical* earth, but rather throughout the dark heavenlies or underworld, which underpins the earth and universe.

The dark heavenlies exist *between* the earth/universe and the third heaven. This can be observed in Daniel 10:10-14 where an angel explains to Daniel that he was the messenger who came with a response from the Almighty to Daniel's prayer, but he was hindered by a demonic entity in the dark heavenlies—"the prince of Persia"—and needed Michael the archangel's help to get through to the physical realm. There's more Scriptural evidence, but it's scant and you have to read in between the lines. "For *now* we see through a glass, **darkly**; but then face to face: *now* I know **in part**; but *then* shall I know even as also I am known" (1 Corinthians 13:12 KJV).

In the above passage, Philippians 2:10, the Greek word translated as "under the earth" is one word—*katachthonios (kat-akh-THON-ee-os)*, which means "subterranean" or "infernal." This is the underworld—the dark spiritual dimension that underpins the earth & universe, which explains why it's called the *underworld*. Notice that this passage doesn't define the underworld as Hades. Why? Because Hades— that is, Sheol—is not the underworld; it's merely a **pit** *in* the underworld where dead souls are kept.

Sheol: " The Heart of the Earth" and "the Earth Below"

The fact that Sheol is a "pit" in the underworld and is not *the* underworld can be seen in its biblical description as "the heart of the earth" and "the earth below":

> **For as Jonah was three days and three nights in the belly of a huge fish, so the Son of Man will be <u>three days and three nights in the heart of the earth</u>.**
> **Matthew 12:40**

> **"Son of man, wail for the hordes of Egypt and consign to <u>the earth below</u> both her and the daughters of mighty nations, along with those who go down to <u>the pit</u>."**
> **Ezekiel 32:18**

Since we know that Jesus' soul went to Sheol for three days and nights when he died we know that "the heart of the earth" is a description of Sheol. "The earth below" in the second passage is also a reference to

Sheol since "the pit" is a biblical synonym for Sheol, as shown in Chapter Three's *Sheol: "The Pit" or "Well of Souls"*, not to mention "the earth below" is referred to *as* Sheol in verses 21 and 27.

These descriptions of Sheol tell us where Sheol is located—in the nether regions of the earth, not in the physical realm, but the spiritual. The Hebrew word translated as "the pit" is *bowr (borr)*, which means "pit," "well" or "dungeon;" and Proverbs 7:27 suggests that there are "chambers" or orderly sections to Sheol. As such, **Sheol is a pit or dungeon in the underworld where dead souls are housed until their resurrection**. Sheol has levels and chambers where dead souls are "laid to rest" in an orderly fashion, according to nation, clan and family, much the way that bodies are buried in earthly graveyards in an orderly fashion according to citizenship, family, purchaser and sometimes religious faith (for instance, there are Catholic cemeteries and church cemeteries where only those of that specific faith can be buried). Why would we think it would be any different for dead souls in Sheol? For more info see Chapter Six' *The Longest and Most Detailed Passage on Sheol.*

So Sheol is not the underworld or dark heavenlies, it's a colossal dungeon *in* the underworld located in the nether regions of the earth. This is where Jesus' dead soul was housed for three days until his mighty resurrection.

With the understanding that Sheol is the graveyard of dead souls in the core of the earth, let's examine an Old Testament passage that also shows Sheol as being located in the heart of the earth. This text has to do with God's astonishing judgment on rebellious Korah and his followers:

> **Then Moses said, "This is how you will know that the Lord has sent me to do all these things and that it was not my idea: (29) If these men die a natural death and suffer the fate of all mankind, then the Lord has not sent me. (30) But if the Lord brings about something totally new, and <u>the earth opens its mouth and swallows them, with everything that belongs to them, and they go down alive into the realm of the dead</u>** *(sheol)*, **then you will know that these men have treated the Lord with contempt."**

(31) As soon as he finished saying all this, <u>the</u> <u>ground under them split apart (32) and the earth</u> <u>opened its mouth and swallowed them and their</u> <u>households, and all those associated with Korah,</u> <u>together with their possessions. (33) They went down</u> <u>alive into the realm of the dead</u> *(sheol)*, **with everything they owned; <u>the earth closed over them,</u> <u>and they perished</u> and were gone from the community. (34) At their cries, all the Israelites around them fled, shouting, "The earth is going to swallow us too!"**

Numbers 16:28-34

As you can see, the earth literally opened up and swallowed Korah and his followers and "they went down alive into the realm of the dead," i.e. Sheol. This doesn't mean that they stayed alive for long because the latter part of verse 33 clearly says that "the earth closed over them, and **they perished**." Physical bodies can't go to Sheol anyway since it exists in the spiritual realm—the dark heavenlies—and not the physical realm. Please notice that nothing is said about them suffering roasting conscious torment in Sheol for thousands of years until their resurrection on Judgment Day. It simply says "they **perished**."

" The Spirits in Prison"

First Peter 3:18-20 is a particularly weak "proof text" for those who say that Sheol is a place of consciousness because anyone making this argument didn't bother to really read the passage:

For Christ also suffered once for sins, the righteous for the unrighteous, to bring you to God. He was put to death in the body but made alive by the Spirit. (19) <u>After being made alive, he went and</u> <u>made proclamation to the imprisoned spirits</u>—(20) to those who were disobedient long ago when God waited patiently in the days of Noah while the ark

was being built. In it only a few people, eight in all, were saved through water,

1 Peter 3:18-20

Verse 18 says that Jesus "was put to death in the body but made alive by the Spirit." Of course, we know that Jesus wasn't "made alive by the Spirit"—that is, resurrected—*until three days after his crucifixion.* In the original New International Version, verses 19-20 read like so: "through whom also he [Jesus] went and preached to the spirits in prison who disobeyed long ago when God waited patiently in the days of Noah while the ark was being built..." As you can see above, the newer edition of the NIV cites these verses as such: "*After* being made alive, he went and made proclamation to the imprisoned spirits—to those who were disobedient long ago when God waited patiently in the days of Noah while the ark was being built." With this in mind, let me stress five things about this passage:

1. Clearly, Jesus didn't preach to these "spirits in prison" until *after* his resurrection and likely before his appearance to his disciples, but certainly before his ascension.

2. The "imprisoned spirits" spoken of in the passage refer to fallen angels or demons that were permanently bound due to their extraordinarily vile nature. Elsewhere in the Scriptures we see that unclean spirits resist such an imprisonment (Luke 8:31). Ultimately, they will be cast into the lake of fire as their eternal abode and punishment (Matthew 25:41 & Revelation 20:10).

3. What is this "prison"? Most likely what the New Testament describes as "the Abyss," the furnace-like pit where evil spirits are imprisoned, *not* human beings. See Luke 8:31, Revelation 9:1-2 and 20:1-3 for verification. As noted in the previous point, the mass of unclean spirits known as Legion begged Jesus not to sentence them to the abyss (Luke 8:31). Jude 6 also refers to this prison for fallen angels.

4. What did Jesus preach to these spirits in prison after his resurrection? Jesus' resurrection was an incredible moment of victory wherein Jesus "made a public spectacle of" the powers of darkness, which is illustrative of a Roman general parading his enemies through the

streets of Rome (Colossians 2:15 & Ephesians 1:19-22). The Lord no doubt proclaimed this crushing victory to these filthy losers and reminded them of their impending judgment and condemnation to the lake of fire. Think of a football player making an incredible touchdown in a championship game and the ensuing victory celebration, but times it to the nth degree for Jesus Christ's triumphant resurrection.

5. Verse 20 shows that these impure spirits have been captive to the Abyss since the time of Noah, which coincides with 2 Peter 2:4. They were sentenced to this prison because their wickedness overstepped the parameters of the Sovereign LORD's tolerance, which helps explain why, after 120 years of Noah's preaching while building the ark, only seven of his family members believed in the LORD. No one else in the human race could be convinced because of the vile anti-God activity of these spirits (not that this discounts human will, of course). Therefore God bound these wicked spirits in the Abyss until their final judgment.

As you can see, 1 Peter 3:18-20 in no way supports the idea that people are conscious in Sheol, including Jesus Christ who spent three days there—*dead*—until his awesome resurrection and victory over the kingdom of darkness.

1 Peter 4:6

This verse has been known to befuddle people because it causes them to wonder if it's talking about the gospel being preached to souls in Sheol, which of course implies that souls in Sheol are alive and conscious. Thankfully, **the context** of the passage clears it up:

> **Therefore, since Christ suffered in his body, arm yourselves also with the same attitude, because whoever suffers in the body is <u>done with sin</u>. (2) As a result, <u>they do not live the rest of their earthly lives for evil human desires, but rather for the will of God.</u> (3) For you have spent enough time in the past doing**

what pagans choose to do—living in debauchery, lust, drunkenness, orgies, carousing and detestable idolatry. (4) They are surprised that you do not join them in their reckless, wild living, and they heap abuse on you. (5) But they will have to give account to him who is ready to judge the living and the dead. (6) For <u>this is the reason</u> the gospel was preached even to those who are now dead, <u>so that they might</u> be judged according to human standards in regard to the body, but <u>live according to God in regard to the spirit</u>.

1 Peter 4:1-6

As you can see, the **context of the paragraph** is the believer being "done with sin" in order to live the rest of his or her earthly life "for the will of God" (verses 1-2). This is **the topic** of the passage. Verses 3-4 go on to show how unbelievers—"pagans"—are in bondage to the flesh and live in sin as a lifestyle, for which they'll be judged by God when they stand before Him to give an account of their lives on Judgment Day (verse 5).

This is **the context** of verse 6, which is obviously talking about the gospel being preached to those who were now dead and not to preaching the gospel to dead souls in Sheol. In other words, the gospel was preached to these people *before* they died, which enabled them to "not live the rest of their earthly lives for evil human desires, but rather for the will of God" (verse 2). This is, after all, the main purpose of preaching the gospel to people beyond acquiring immortality (2 Timothy 1:10)—the power of the gospel sets them free of the flesh and enables them to "participate in the divine nature" (2 Peter 1:4) via "walking in the spirit." When believers learn to be spirit-controlled rather than flesh-ruled they are free to "live according to God in regard to the spirit" (verse 6). We see this in passages like Ephesians 4:22-24. This is the thrust of the paragraph—the context—and "Context is King."

It is presumed by the wording that the people whom Peter was referring to in verse 6 "who are now dead" accepted the gospel and—as spiritually regenerated children of God—were in heaven with the Lord, a topic covered (and proven) in the next chapter.

How Can Sheol Be a State of Torment if Men Seek it During the Tribulation?

Let's look at an indirect reference to Sheol in Revelation 9. The first part of this chapter has to do with the fifth trumpet judgment during the Tribulation. "Locusts" are released from the Abyss to torment people on the earth who don't have the seal of God. As noted in a previous section, the "Abyss" is the furnace-like pit where particularly malevolent evil spirits are imprisoned (see Luke 8:31, Revelation 9:1-2 and 20:1-3). As such, we can confidently conclude that the "locusts" are wicked spirits who are given the power to torture people for five months, but not to kill:

> [The locusts] **were not allowed to kill them but only to torture them for five months. And the agony they suffered was like that of the sting of a scorpion when it strikes. (6) <u>During those days people will seek death but will not find it; they will long to die, but death will elude them</u>.**
>
> **Revelation 9:5-6**

As you can see, the agony of these stubborn, unrepentant people will be so great that they'll seek death but it will elude them.

This passage indirectly addresses the nature of Sheol in two ways: **1.** These unbelievers are seeking death and, if they die, they automatically go to Sheol; and **2.** death and Hades (Sheol) are spoken of in the same breath in Scripture; for instance:

> **I am the Living One; I was dead, and now look, I am alive for ever and ever! And I hold the keys of <u>death and Hades</u>.**
>
> **Revelation 1:18**

> **...and there before me was a pale horse! <u>Its rider was named Death, and Hades was following close behind him</u>. They were given power over a**

fourth of the earth to kill by sword, famine and plague, and by the wild beasts of the earth.

Revelation 6:8

The sea gave up the dead that were in it, <u>and death and Hades gave up the dead that were in them</u>, and each person was judged according to what they had done. (14) <u>Then death and Hades were thrown into the lake of fire.</u> The lake of fire is the second death.

Revelation 20:13-14

Why is it significant that these horribly tormented people will literally seek death? Because such a statement only makes sense if Sheol is the graveyard of souls where dead souls 'sleep' in death. In other words, Revelation 9:6 makes no sense if Sheol were a torture chamber in the heart of the earth where unredeemed souls suffer constant fiery torment until their resurrection. Let's go ahead and read this verse as if this doctrine were true:

> **During those days people will seek death** [and go to Sheol to suffer constant roasting torment where they will not receive even a drop of water for relief] **but will not find it; they will long to die** [and be tortured in flames in Sheol]**, but death will elude them.**

As you can see, the idea that Sheol is a condition of constant fiery torment for unredeemed souls doesn't fit this passage or any other passage in Scripture. It's a false doctrine that makes utter nonsense of God's Word. However, when we have a biblical understanding of the nature of Sheol—that it's the soulish graveyard in the underworld where dead souls "rest" in death—then the passage makes perfect sense. No wonder these people wanted to die.

Now someone might argue that it's not necessary for these people to know what death actually entails—i.e. suffering constant roasting torture in Sheol. In other words, they're *deceived* in thinking that death will offer them relief from the torture of the "locusts" when it will actually bring them worse agony. Supposing this is true, let's read the passage according to this line of reasoning:

> **During those days people will seek death but will not find it; they will long to die, but death will elude them** [little knowing that death will not bring them the non-existence they crave as they will suffer perpetual flaming torment in Hades only to be resurrected on the day of judgment and cast into the lake of fire where they will suffer *never-ending roasting torture forever and ever*].

Again, the eternal torture belief makes utter nonsense of the Scriptures.

One last point about this passage: If Sheol is a place of constant fiery torment for the unrighteous, why were the locusts not allowed to kill the people, as detailed in verse 5? After all, if they killed them the people would automatically go to Sheol where they'd undergo unceasing torture there until their resurrection on judgment day, right? Again, this view makes nonsense of the Scriptures.

For further commentary on this topic see *Job's View of Sheol* in Chapter Two.

Jesus Christ DIED

A central doctrine of Christianity is that Jesus **died** for our sins and was **raised to life** for our justification:

> **He was <u>delivered over to death</u> for our sins and was <u>raised to life</u> for our justification.**
> **Romans 4:25**

Moreover, the Bible explicitly says that Father God **did not spare** his Son but **delivered him over to death** for our sakes:

> **He who did not spare his own Son, but gave him up for us all—how will he not also, along with him, graciously give us all things?**
>
> **Romans 8:32**

Jesus himself plainly declared that he was going to be killed:

> **From that time on Jesus began to explain to his disciples that he must go to Jerusalem and suffer many things at the hands of the elders, the chief priests and the teachers of the law, and that he must be <u>killed</u> and on the third day be <u>raised to life</u>.**
>
> **Matthew 16:21**

> **Jesus took the Twelve aside and told them, "We are going up to Jerusalem, and everything that is written by the prophets about the Son of Man will be fulfilled. (32) He will be delivered over to the Gentiles. They will mock him, insult him and spit on him; (33) they will flog him and <u>kill him</u>. On the third day <u>he will rise again</u>."**
>
> **Luke 18:31-33**

My point is that all four passages literally say in one way or another that Jesus **died** for our sins and three of them that he was **raised to life**. How can someone be "raised to life" if he didn't actually die? Stop for a moment and consider that question again: How can someone be "raised to life" if he didn't actually die? It's a simple question with a simple and obvious answer.

Amazingly, whole segments of Christendom don't believe that Jesus really died. They only believe he died *physically* and then went to Sheol to either roast in torment for three days or hang out with Abraham in some paradise compartment; he perhaps ministered to imprisoned spirits in his spare time. Whatever the case, they don't really believe he died, nor do they believe he was raised to life since he was already very much alive in Sheol. They only believe he was raised to life *bodily*.

The Bible, however, refutes this point blank. Both the Old and New Testaments plainly show that Jesus Christ died *soulishly* as well as physically:

> Because **He** [Jesus] **poured out His soul** *(nephesh)* **unto death,**
> **And He was numbered with the transgressors,**
> **And He bore the sin of many,**
> **And made intercession for the transgressors.**
>
> **Isaiah 53:12** (NKJV)

> Then he said to them, "**My soul** *(psuche)* **is overwhelmed with sorrow to the point of death**. Stay here and keep watch with me."
>
> **Matthew 26:38**

As you can see, the Hebrew and Greek words for "soul" are used in these passages. Jesus "poured out His *soul* unto death," not just his body.

To reinforce this, the Bible over and over stresses that Jesus Christ *died* as our substitutionary death. In fact, it's often hard to get through *one chapter* of the New Testament without reading some reference to Jesus **dying** for our sins, as well as being **raised to life**. Let's look at a smattering of examples from the epistle of Romans:

> and who through the Spirit of holiness was appointed the Son of God in power by his **resurrection from the dead**: Jesus Christ our Lord
>
> **Romans 1:4**

> But God demonstrates his own love for us in this: While we were still sinners, Christ **died** for us.
>
> **Romans 5:8**

> For if, while we were God's enemies, we were reconciled to him through the **death** of his Son, how

much more, having been reconciled, shall we be saved <u>through his life</u>!

Romans 5:10

Or don't you know that all of us who were baptized into Christ Jesus were baptized into <u>his death</u>? (4) We were therefore buried with him through baptism into death in order that, just as Christ was <u>raised from the dead</u> through the glory of the Father, we too may live a new life.

(5) For if we have been united with him in <u>a death like his</u>, we will certainly also be united with him in a <u>resurrection like his</u>. (6) For we know that our old self was crucified with him so that the body ruled by sin might be done away with, that we should no longer be slaves to sin—(7) because anyone who has died has been set free from sin.

(8) Now if we <u>died</u> with Christ, we believe that we will also live with him. (9) For we know that since Christ was <u>raised from the dead</u>, he cannot <u>die</u> again; death no longer has mastery over him. (10) <u>The death he died</u>, he died to sin once for all; but the <u>life he lives</u>, he lives to God.

Romans 6:3-10

And if the Spirit of him who raised Jesus from <u>the dead</u> is living in you, he who <u>raised Christ from the dead</u> will also give life to your mortal bodies because of his Spirit who lives in you.

Romans 8:11

Who then is the one who condemns? No one. <u>Christ Jesus who died</u>—more than that, who was <u>raised to life</u>—is at the right hand of God and is also interceding for us.

Romans 8:34

> For this very reason, <u>Christ died</u> and <u>returned to life</u> so that he might be the Lord of both the dead and the living.
>
> **Romans 14:9**

> If your brother or sister is distressed because of what you eat, you are no longer acting in love. Do not by your eating destroy someone for whom <u>Christ died</u>.
>
> **Romans 14:15**

This is just *one book* of the New Testament and I'm skipping examples.

Here are more examples from other New Testament books:

> As they were coming down the mountain, Jesus instructed them, "Don't tell anyone what you have seen, until the Son of Man has been <u>raised from the dead</u>."
>
> **Matthew 17:9**

> When they came together in Galilee, he said to them, "The Son of Man is going to be delivered into the hands of men. (23) They will <u>kill him</u>, and on the third day he will be <u>raised to life</u>." And the disciples were filled with grief.
>
> **Matthew 17:22-23**

> "We are going up to Jerusalem, and the Son of Man will be delivered over to the chief priests and the teachers of the law. They will condemn him to <u>death</u> (19) and will hand him over to the Gentiles to be mocked and flogged and <u>crucified</u>. On the third day he will be <u>raised to life</u>!"
>
> **Matthew 20:18-19**

As they were coming down the mountain, Jesus gave them orders not to tell anyone what they had seen until the Son of Man had <u>risen from the dead</u>.

Mark 9:9

"We are going up to Jerusalem," he said, "and the Son of Man will be delivered over to the chief priests and the teachers of the law. They will condemn him to <u>death</u> and will hand him over to the Gentiles, (34) who will mock him and spit on him, flog him and <u>kill him</u>. Three days later <u>he will rise</u>."

Mark 10:33-34

For even the Son of Man did not come to be served, but to serve, and to <u>give his life</u> as a ransom for many."

Mark 10:45

In their fright the women bowed down with their faces to the ground, but the men [angels] said to them, "Why do you look for the living among the dead? (6) He is not here; he has risen! Remember how he [Jesus] told you, while he was still with you in Galilee: (7) 'The Son of Man must be delivered over to the hands of sinners, <u>be crucified</u> and <u>on the third day be raised again</u>.' "

Luke 24:5-7

"We are witnesses of everything he did in the country of the Jews and in Jerusalem. <u>They killed him</u> by hanging him on a cross, (40) but <u>God raised him from the dead on the third day</u> and caused him to be seen.

Acts 10:39-40

> Now may the God of peace, who through the blood of the eternal covenant brought back <u>from the dead</u> our Lord Jesus, that great Shepherd of the sheep,
>
> Hebrews 13:20

> Praise be to the God and Father of our Lord Jesus Christ! In his great mercy he has given us new birth into a living hope through the <u>resurrection of Jesus Christ from the dead</u>,
>
> 1 Peter 1:3

> Through him you believe in God, who <u>raised him from the dead</u> and glorified him, and so your faith and hope are in God.
>
> 1 Peter 1:21

> "I am the Living One; <u>I was dead</u>, and now look, <u>I am alive</u> for ever and ever! And I hold the <u>keys of death and Hades</u>."
>
> Revelation 1:18

> "To the angel of the church in Smyrna write:
> These are the words of him who is the First and the Last, <u>who died</u> and <u>came to life again</u>."
>
> Revelation 2:8

The person speaking in these last two verses is Jesus Christ Himself—"The Truth" (John 14:6). Notice that he plainly testifies that he *died*, but is now alive forever. **No where does he say that he only physically died, but was fully conscious in either bliss or torments in Sheol. No, he plainly declares that he *died* and came to life again!**

This is just a quick smattering of these types of passages. You'll find such statements in most of the books of the New Testament and, again, often every chapter. If words mean anything at all we have to conclude that Jesus Christ literally died for our sins and was raised to life for our justification. This is a **central truth of Christianity**.

Yet adherents of eternal torture don't believe this; they only believe Jesus died *physically* and then ministered to spirits in subterranean prisons for three days or hanged out with father Abraham or was tortured in flames. Whatever the case, they don't believe he really died; and they don't believe he was raised to life either, except physically, because they don't actually believe he died.

True Christianity, however, is rooted in the fact that Jesus Christ, the Son of God, gave up his deity to become a human being and became "obedient to **death**":

> **In your relationships with one another, have the same mindset as Christ Jesus:**
>
> **(6) Who, being in very nature God, did not consider equality with God something to be used to his own advantage;**
>
> **(7) rather, he made himself nothing by taking the very nature of a servant, being made in human likeness.**
>
> **(8) And being found in appearance as a man, he humbled himself by becoming obedient to death— even death on a cross!**
>
> **Philippians 2:5-8**

Jesus Christ literally died for our sins and was raised to life for our justification. When he was crucified he "gave up his spirit" (John 19:30) and the breath of life returned to the Father in heaven while Jesus' dead soul was laid to rest in Sheol—the "the assembly of the dead," as Proverbs 21:16 defines it—the graveyard of souls in the heart of the earth.

Think about that for a moment because it's a mind-blowing statement: One part of the Godhead (Father, Son & Holy Spirit) **DIED** for you and me so that we may be reconciled to the Creator and have eternal life—**God DIED**. How could God possibly die, that is, cease to exist for three days? I don't know, but that's precisely what happened: The Alpha and Omega, the Beginning and the End, became "obedient to **death**" and ceased to exist for three days; and was raised to life so that we may be justified and inherit eternal life.

What an incredible price to pay; it's *awe-inspiring!*

Pat Robertson (whom I love) objected to the idea that Jesus died completely by adamantly insisting that Jesus was God and if Christ *wholly* died—not just his body—the universe would fall apart (Robertson 72). While it's true that if the Creator died—that is, Father, Son and Holy Spirit—the universe would certainly perish with its Creator, Jesus is *one part* of the Godhead, not all three (Matthew 28:19). So, whereas Jesus is God and Jesus died completely for three days, as Isaiah 53:12 shows, the Father and Holy Spirit did not. As such, the Father and Holy Spirit naturally made up for the loss of the Son for three days. To illustrate, consider my wife, Carol, going on a trip for three days. I'd have to cover for her in the home and the ministry. If I can cover for my wife for three days why wouldn't the Father and Holy Spirit be able to do the same for the Son? This in no way diminishes the worth of my wife or the Messiah. I consider my wife invaluable, how much more so the King of kings?

One last point before moving on: We've gone over numerous passages in this section that show how Jesus died for our sins and was resurrected three days later. Isn't it interesting that there's absolutely no mention of Jesus being alive & conscious in Sheol, whether in blissful comfort with Abraham or in roasting agony? If either were true, don't you think God would mention it *somewhere* in his Word, particularly these passages that address the issue? It's not like it's an insignificant detail! And yet there's mysteriously no mention of either in any of these passages. Why not? Because Jesus' soul was literally dead in Sheol for three days. There's no getting around it, the idea that Sheol is a place of conscious existence is a false doctrine that's utterly foreign to the Scriptures.

Hades in the Book of Revelation

The Greek word for Sheol—*hades*—appears four times in the book of Revelation. Here's the first time:

> **When I saw him** [Jesus Christ], **I fell at his feet**
> **as though dead. Then he placed his right hand on me**
> **and said: "Do not be afraid. I am the First and the**

Last. (18) I am the Living One; <u>I was dead</u>, and now look, <u>I am alive</u> for ever and ever! And <u>I hold the keys of death and Hades</u>."

Revelation 1:17-18

The context of this passage is the vision John received as a prisoner on the island of Patmos when he was about 95 years old (!). In this vision John sees Jesus Christ and falls "at his feet as though dead," which *might* be a reference to the "slain in the Spirit" phenomenon. The Lord proceeds to comfort him by touching him and encouraging him not to be afraid because Jesus is the beginning and the ending of history and, in fact, the meaning of history (it is, after all, His-story).

Jesus goes on to point out that **he died**, but now he is **alive** forever and ever. This corroborates what was established in the previous section: Jesus Christ literally died for humanity; he suffered the wages of sin—**DEATH**—so that we don't have to. Religion has been lying about this for centuries, saying that he only died physically. Who are you going to believe, religion or Jesus Christ?

The Messiah then goes on to say that he holds the keys to death and Hades. What does this mean? Keys signify control or authority. If you own the keys to a facility you control who comes in or leaves. Jesus holds the keys to death and Hades. As we've seen over and over in this study, death and Hades go hand-in-hand because when un-regenerated people physically die and their bodies go to the grave or tomb their dead souls automatically go to Sheol, which is Hades. Death and Hades go hand-in-hand, which explains the next appearance of Hades in Revelation:

> **And behold, a pale horse, and he who sat on it, his name was <u>Death. Hades followed with him</u>. Authority over one fourth of the earth, to kill with the sword, with famine, with death, and by the wild animals of the earth was given to him.**

Revelation 6:8

The passage refers to the fourth seal judgment, which involves the fourth horseman of the apocalypse, which is death. Why is this fourth horseman death itself? Because, as you can see, this massive judgment entails the death of one quarter of the population on earth (!). This is why Hades follows after death because those who die go to Hades to "rest" in death until their resurrection, which takes place on judgment day, as shown here:

> **Then I saw a <u>great white throne</u> and him who was seated on it. The earth and the heavens fled from his presence, and there was no place for them. (12) And I saw the dead, great and small, standing before the throne, and books were opened. Another book was opened, which is the book of life. The dead were judged according to what they had done as recorded in the books. (13) The sea gave up the dead that were in it, and <u>death</u> and <u>Hades</u> gave up the dead that were in them, and each person was judged according to what they had done. (14) Then <u>death</u> and <u>Hades</u> were thrown into the lake of fire. The lake of fire is the second death. (15) Anyone whose name was not found written in the book of life was thrown into the lake of fire.**
>
> **Revelation 20:11-15**

As you can see, dead souls in Sheol are resurrected, as are their dead bodies from the earth and sea, and they are judged according to what they had done; *if* their names are not found written in the book of life they will be cast into the lake of fire, which is called "the second death" where Jesus said God would "destroy both soul and body" (Matthew 10:28). We address the details of this judgment in <u>Chapter Eight</u> of *Hell Know*.

With this in mind, let's go back to Jesus' statement in the first chapter of Revelation:

> **"I am the Living One; I was dead, and now look, I am alive for ever and ever! And <u>I hold the keys of death and Hades</u>."**
>
> **Revelation 1:18**

Because of Jesus' miraculous triumph over death he holds the keys to death and Hades (Sheol) and therefore is in control of the eternal destiny of the bodies (death) and souls (Hades) of every unredeemed person who has ever existed.

Now let's revisit the final two verses of chapter 20:

> Then <u>death</u> and <u>Hades</u> were thrown into the lake of fire. The lake of fire is the second death. (15) Anyone whose name was not found written in the book of life was thrown into the lake of fire.
>
> **Revelation 20:14-15**

What does it mean that death and Hades are to be thrown into the lake of fire, which is the second death? It refers to one of two things or, more likely, both: **1.** Since Jesus holds the keys to death and Hades he therefore has control over the bodies and souls of the un-regenerated. Those whose names are not found in the book of life will be cast into the lake of fire to suffer the second death; as such, death and Hades being cast into the lake of fire refers to the bodies (death) and souls (Hades) of the unredeemed who will suffer literal "everlasting destruction," as Paul described it in 2 Thessalonians 1:9. **2.** It also refers to the fact that "there will be **no more death**" in the eternal age of the new heavens and new earth as stated five verses later in Revelation 21:4. Since there will be no more death in the coming eternal age, death itself is cast into the lake of fire as is its counterpart Hades (Sheol). After all, if there's no death there's no need for Sheol either. In other words, they both cease to exist, just like the bodies and souls of the unrighteous who are cast into the lake of fire; that is, after a period of conscious suffering as divine justice dictates, which is covered in *Hell Know* <u>Chapter Three</u>.

" The Rest of the Dead Did Not Come to Life until the Thousand Years were Ended"

Let's look at one more passage from Revelation that reveals the nature of Sheol:

I saw thrones on which were seated those who had been given authority to judge. And I saw the souls of those who had been beheaded because of their testimony about Jesus and because of the word of God. They had not worshiped the beast or its image and had not received its mark on their foreheads or their hands. They came to life and reigned with Christ a thousand years. (5) (<u>The rest of the dead did not come to life until the thousand years were ended</u>.) This is the first resurrection. (6) Blessed and holy are those who share in the first resurrection. The second death has no power over them, but they will be priests of God and of Christ and will reign with him for a thousand years.

Revelation 20:4-6

In his vision, John describes what he sees **in Heaven** and says he "saw **the souls** of those who had been beheaded because of their testimony" during the Tribulation. These righteous souls are in heaven and the latter part of verse 4 says "they **came to life** and reigned with Christ a thousand years," referring to the Millennium, the thousand-year reign of Christ. This resurrection is referred to as the "first resurrection" in verses 5-6. Some argue that the phrase "they **came to life** and reigned with Christ a thousand years" suggests that these righteous souls were fully dead—that is, in Sheol—but this can't be since, again, the first part of verse 4 plainly shows these souls *in* heaven after being martyred during the Tribulation on earth, just like the martyrs in Revelation 7:9-17 and Revelation 6:9-11. Remember the hermeneutical rules: "Context is king" and "Scripture interprets Scripture." With this understanding, here's what verse 4 is saying: "they came to life [physically] and reigned with Christ a thousand years." You see? The addition of one simple word clarifies the statement and settles the matter.

So this passage is addressing the "first resurrection," which in this case is the third stage of the resurrection of the righteous (the first stage took place when Jesus was resurrected as the firstfruits and the second stage takes place at the time of the Rapture, as shown in 1

Thessalonians 4:13-18[19]), but notice the parenthetical reference to unredeemed souls in Sheol at the beginning of verse 5:

(The rest of the dead <u>did not come to life until</u> the thousand years were ended.)

Revelation 20:5

"The rest of the dead" is referring to all unredeemed souls laid to rest in Sheol throughout the course of human history. They "did not come to life" until *after* the Millennium, which is when the Great White Throne Judgment takes place, which we addressed in the previous section. If they "did not come to life" until their Judgment Day then this obviously means that they will be **dead** until then. In other words, they are in Sheol—the world of the dead—where dead souls 'sleep' in death until their resurrection.

Now, someone might argue that the reference to righteous martyrs coming to life at the end of verse 4 refers specifically to a *bodily* resurrection since the first part of the verse shows their souls alive in heaven; therefore, they argue, the reference to unredeemed people coming to life on Judgment Day would also refer only to a bodily resurrection. This argument must be rejected on the grounds that, although this passage reveals redeemed souls in heaven before their bodily resurrection, it doesn't show anything about the nature of unredeemed souls in Sheol before their resurrection on Judgment Day. In fact, all it says is that they "did not come to life" until the thousand years were ended," which shows that they were **dead** until then, dead in Sheol. Since this passage says nothing more on the nature of Sheol than what is implied by this statement we have to look to the rest of Scripture to ascertain what it's like for souls in Sheol; and the rest of this study plainly shows that souls in Sheol are dead, 'resting' in death until their resurrection.

We'll address the issue of the believer's intermediate state between death and resurrection next chapter.

---

[19] This is covered in <u>Chapter 11</u>.

What about People who Claim to have Visited Sheol Literally or in a Vision?

This question applies to books like Bill Wiese' *23 Minutes in Hell* (2006) and Mary K. Baxter's *A Divine Revelation of Hell* (1993), both claiming to have gone to Sheol (Hades) in visions. I've read another minister's testimony that he went to Sheol in a vision as well. I'm sure there are others with similar assertions.

The claim of these people is that they were given these visions in order to be used of God to evangelize the lost by utilizing the horrors of a torture chamber in the heart of the earth as a big club to convince people to repent. In other words, they believe they're end-time agents of God on an evangelizing mission.

While evangelization and genuine repentance are always good, these people's supernatural experiences beg the question: Why did the LORD wait almost 2000 years after the biblical canon was completed to reveal these insanely horrifying details about Sheol? If their visions (or experiences) are to be believed, why aren't there similar such descriptions of Sheol in the Bible, the Word of God?

I've never read Wiese's book and don't need to because a thorough study of God's Word informs us everything we need to know about the nature of Sheol, as this book testifies.

I did, however, read Baxter's book back in the 90s and was sickened by its unscriptural portrayal of the topic. Ms. Baxter cites a number of passages at the end of her book to support her hideous visions, including Matthew 10:28. There are two problems with this: **1.** Jesus was referring to Gehenna in this passage, which is the Greek word often translated as "hell" in English Bibles, and Gehenna literally refers to the Valley of Hinnom, a trash dump/incinerator located outside the southwest walls of Jerusalem (this is covered in detail in *Hell Know* Chapter Two's *The Example of Gehenna: "Hell"*). Why would Jesus use this perpetually smoking trash dump to illustrate the lake of fire or second death? Because it was something all his listeners knew about and his message was therefore clear: Those who are God's enemies will be discarded like trash and eradicated just like garbage cast into Gehenna, the Valley of Hinnom. **2.** Gehenna (the lake of fire) and Sheol (Hades) are two completely separate places. In fact, souls in Hades will be resurrected from Hades and—*if* their names aren't found in the book of life—will be cast into the lake of fire, as will Hades itself, as shown in Revelation 20:11-15.

Both of these points reveal the obvious problem with Baxter citing Matthew 10:28 to support her creative vision: The passage applies to the lake of fire and not to Sheol and, furthermore, refers to literal **destruction** of soul and body and not never-ending roasting torment. Evidently Ms. Baxter doesn't even realize that there's a difference between Sheol (Hades) and Gehenna, the lake of fire. Do you think it's wise to give credence to the visions of a person who doesn't even understand the fundamental aspects of her topic?

The bottom line is that we don't need the visions or testimonies of these types of people to understand the nature of Sheol because **everything God wants us to know about Sheol has already been revealed in his Word**. This is in line with a rule that Paul gave believers: **"Do not go beyond what is written"** (1 Corinthians 4:6), which explains why *Sheol Know* focuses exclusively on what God's Word says on the subject from Genesis to Revelation and not the dubious testimonies of people who claim to have visions that just so happen to wholly disagree with what God's Word teaches.

Enough said.

Near Death Experiences and Ghostly Phenomena

What about "near-death experiences"—NDEs—where people who claim to have died either "see the light" of heaven or suffer torments in some hellish torture chamber or some variation of either?

NDEs can be chalked up to one of four things:

1. Activity of the mind after temporarily dying, i.e. dreams, imaginations.
2. The person had a real after-death experience. This could be a child or spiritually regenerated person, like the kid in the book *Heaven is Real,* or an unbeliever whose soul and breath of life haven't separated yet.

3. We cannot discount what the Bible calls deceiving spirits.
4. Another possibility is that the person is lying.

As for apparitions/ghosts, they could be one of four things:

1. Flashes from the past, i.e. residual images of former events.
2. Demonic activity.
3. A person who has delayed entry to heaven or Sheol for whatever reason. In the event of a delayed entry to Sheol—if indeed such a thing even occurs—the soul and breath of life obviously haven't separated yet since the spirit of life gives consciousness to the mind. As such, the person would be temporarily stuck on this plane in a disembodied state. If this doesn't make sense see the Appendix.
4. As above, the person may be lying.

This covers the spectrum of possibilities, although I'm sure there are minor or mixed variants. Even if one discovers evidence that most cases can be pinpointed to one reason, that doesn't discount that *some* cases can be attributed to others. I think it's pointless and possibly even unhealthy to pursue the topic further since the Torah expressly forbids contact with the dead (e.g. Deuteronomy 18:9-14) and therefore people who are overly interested with the subject are treading the borders. As noted in the previous section, Paul gave a rule in the New Testament: **"Do not go beyond what is written"** (1 Corinthians 4:6). So, with subjects like this, my advice is to stay within the wise parameters of God's Word.

My main problems with NDEs are:

1. These people didn't actually die in the truest sense, despite what they say, since—if they were dead—they wouldn't be here, which is why these experiences are called *near*-death experiences.
2. We all know the crazy imaginations that the mind can come up with practically every night when we sleep, how much more so when we almost die or die for a brief time? Since this is so, how can we trust these stories as anything more concrete than dreams or nightmares? Even if many of them agree too many of them contradict; so we can't trust them.

3. We can't discount lying spirits. After all, the devil is the "god of this world" and his spiritual minions carry out his orders. He's the "father of lies" and is fittingly called "the deceiver" in Scripture. Consequently, his modus operandi is to **deceive**.

In light of all this, if you were the devil wouldn't you want spiritually un-regenerate people to think they have an immortal soul apart from Christ and that they'll automatically see a bright light and feeling of warm love when they die, being ushered into heavenly bliss? Of course you would. Why? Because it would steer them away from the gospel, repentance, spiritual rebirth and their Creator. For these reasons I choose to stick with what God's Word says on the subject and not go beyond it. I encourage you to do the same.

Chapter Ten

THE BELIEVER'S
Intermediate State

In this chapter we will look at the believer's intermediate state between death and resurrection. Here are the two views:

1. The commonly understood position is that the disembodied souls of believers go straight to heaven when they die, awaiting their bodily resurrection.
2. A deviating view is that, like Old Testament saints, the souls of spiritually regenerated believers go to Sheol at the point of physical decease to "sleep" in death until their resurrection.

The latter position is embraced to by many who adhere to literal destructionism, which they support by citing 1 Thessalonians 4:13-18 and John 5:28-29.

If we genuinely want to know the truth on any given biblical topic it's important to be honest with the Scriptures regardless of our current view or sectarian bias. We must staunchly follow the hermeneutical rules of "context is king" and "Scripture interprets Scripture," meaning our interpretation of a passage must harmonize with the surrounding text and with the rest of Scripture. The more detailed and overt passages naturally expand our understanding of the more sketchy or ambiguous ones.

With this understanding, the New Testament denies point blank that believers lie dead in Sheol until their resurrection and clearly supports Christians going to be with the Lord in heaven in a disembodied state. I don't expect anyone to take my word for it so let's examine evidence from the Scriptures and draw the obvious conclusion, starting with Paul's statement that...

"I Desire to Depart and be with Christ, which is Better by Far"

Paul is second only to Jesus Christ as far as New Testament characters go, and the LORD used him to write more of the New Testament than any other person, about one-third (not including Hebrews, which many believe he wrote); and *half* of the book of Acts is devoted to his missionary exploits. What did God inspire Paul to say on the issue of the believer's intermediate state between death and resurrection?

Paul made a few plain-as-day statements on the matter. Notice how clear he was about *where* born-again believers go when they die:

> **I eagerly expect and hope that I will in no way be ashamed, but will have sufficient courage so that now as always Christ will be exalted in my body, whether <u>by life</u> or <u>by death</u>. (21) For to <u>me</u>, <u>to live is Christ and to die is gain</u>. (22) If I am to go on <u>living in the body</u>, this will mean fruitful labor for me. Yet what shall I choose? I do not know! (23) I am torn between the two: <u>I desire to depart and be with Christ</u>, which is <u>better by far</u>; (24) but it is more necessary for you that I <u>remain in the body</u>.**
>
> **Philippians 1:20-24**

Paul wrote this epistle while imprisoned in Rome and the issue of living or dying comes up in verse 20, to which he declares, "to me, to live is Christ and to die is gain." For Paul and all believers, the purpose of life itself is the LORD and dying is actually *gain*, not loss. I think we can all agree that going to Sheol is not gain! In verse 23 he points out that if he "departs"—that is, he physically **dies**—he'll "**be with** Christ," which is "better **by far**" than staying. Verse 24 shows Paul disregarding his yearning to be with the Lord in order to stay and build Christ's church on earth, which he calls "fruitful labor" in verse 22.

Notice that Paul doesn't say anything at all about 'sleeping' in death in Sheol until he's bodily resurrected. No, he plainly says that dying is "gain" and that it means to "*be with* Christ, which is better by far."

Since the bodily resurrection of the righteous doesn't take place until the Rapture (1 Thessalonians 4:13-18) and the next stage right before the Millennium (Revelation 20:4-6),[20] this would mean that—if believers went to Sheol when they physically died—Paul and other believers throughout the Church Age would be dead in Sheol until the time of the Rapture. In Paul's case (and all believers from the first century) we're looking at around 2000 years of sleeping in death until their resurrection. To be frank, this makes utter nonsense of Paul's statements in Philippians 1:20-24. After all, how is being dead in Sheol for the next 2000 years "gain" over living for the Lord and producing "fruitful labor" building his church? Why would Paul "desire to depart and be with Christ, which is better by far" if, in fact, he wouldn't actually be with Christ for another 2000 years?

Those who hold the position that believer's go to Sheol when they die argue that—since believers are literally dead in Sheol—their resurrection would seem like a moment of time, even if it took 2000 years. This frankly comes across as forcing one's biased interpretation *into* a passage rather than allowing the text to say what it naturally says. The former is an example of **eisegesis** *(ahy-sah-JEE-sis)*, meaning to import *into* the Scriptures, whereas the latter is **exegesis** *(ek-sah-JEE-sis)*, to draw *out of* the Scriptures.

The plain-sense meaning of Philippians 1:20-24 is that dying is gain because Paul—and, by extension, all believers—go to be with the

---

[20] If you're not familiar with the *stages* of the resurrection of the righteous, see <u>Chapter Eleven</u>.

Lord in heaven unhindered by earthly burdens. Remember the hermeneutical rule: If the plain sense makes sense—and is in harmony with the rest of Scripture—don't look for any other sense lest you end up with nonsense.

Paul backs-up this position later in this same epistle by calling believers citizens of heaven in Philippians 3:20. Believers are born-again of the seed of Christ by the Holy Spirit and are therefore **citizens of heaven. We're not citizens of Sheol—death!** *Death has no power over the spiritually regenerated believer!*

"Away from the Body and at Home with the Lord"

Here's another clear statement by Paul about the believer's intermediate state:

> **For we know that if the earthly tent we live in is destroyed, we have a building from God, an eternal house in heaven, not built by human hands. (2) Meanwhile we groan, longing to be clothed instead with our heavenly dwelling, (3) because when we are clothed, we will not be found naked. (4) For while we are in this tent, we groan and are burdened, because we do not wish to be unclothed but to be clothed instead with our heavenly dwelling, so that what is mortal may be swallowed up by life. (5) Now the one who has fashioned us for this very purpose is God, who has given us the Spirit as a deposit, guaranteeing what is to come.**
>
> **(6) Therefore we are always confident and know that as long as <u>we are at home in the body we are away from the Lord</u>. (7) For we live by faith, not by sight. (8) We are confident, I say, and <u>would prefer to be away from the body and at home with the Lord</u>. (9) <u>So we make it our goal to please him, whether we are at home in the body or away from it</u>. (10) For we must all appear before the judgment seat**

of Christ, so that each of us may receive what is due us for the things done while in the body, whether good or bad.

2 Corinthians 5:1-10

The "earthly tent" that Paul mentions in verse 1 refers to the human body. The "eternal house in heaven" and "heavenly dwelling" mentioned in verses 1-2 do not refer to heaven itself, but rather to the glorified (heavenly) bodies that believers will receive at their bodily resurrection, which takes place when Christ snatches up his church and, later, returns to the earth (1 Thessalonians 4:13-18 & Revelation 20:4-6). The nature of these awesome immortal bodies is detailed by Paul in 1 Corinthians 15:42-44, which we'll examine in the Epilogue.

In verse 4 Paul points out that while we are in the "tent" of our earthly, mortal bodies "we groan and are burdened" because we naturally yearn to be clothed with our "heavenly dwelling," our imperishable resurrection bodies. At the time of our bodily resurrection Paul says that what is mortal will be "swallowed up by life" (verse 4). The next verse stresses that God has created us for this very purpose—to give us immortality and eternal life!

Then in verse 6 Paul says that "we are always confident and know that as long **as we are at home in the body we are away from the Lord.**" The obvious implication is that when we leave these bodies, we will be *with* the Lord, which perfectly coincides with Paul's statement in Philippians 1:23-24 from the previous section. If there's any doubt, Paul states in verses 8-9 that "we are confident... and **would prefer to be away from the body and at home with the Lord. So we make it our goal to please him, whether we are at home in the body or away from it.**"

You tell me: Doesn't verse 8 strongly suggest that being away from the body means to be at home with the Lord in heaven? And verse 6 too? To reinforce this, Paul stresses in verse 9 that we should make it our ambition to please the Lord whether in the body—that is, alive on earth—or away from it. This presents a problem for the view that believers are dead in Sheol during the intermediate state; after all, how exactly can we make it our goal to please the Lord if we're dead in Sheol and non-existent as far as conscious life goes? It doesn't make sense, but it *does* make sense if we go to be with the Lord in heaven and serve in one capacity or another, which we'll look at momentarily

There's no getting around the fact that both of Paul's statements in Philippians 1 and 2 Corinthians 5 show that being absent from the body (i.e. physically dying) means to be present with the Lord, but only for the believer who's born-again of the imperishable seed of Christ. Death—Sheol—has no hold on born-again believers. I've heard some weak attempts to explain away these two passages, but they always come off as strict sectarians (usually Adventists or JWs) grasping for straws in face of clear Scriptural proof that contradicts their position.

"Whether We are Awake or Asleep, We May Live Together with Him"

Let's observe one more statement by Paul that makes it clear that believers go to be with the Lord in heaven when they physically die and not to Sheol to 'sleep' in death until their resurrection.

> **He [Jesus] died for us so that, <u>whether we are awake or asleep, we may live together with him</u>.**
> **1 Thessalonians 5:10**

"Awake" here refers to believers alive on this earth while "asleep" refers to believers who have passed away. The latter concerns the body 'sleeping' in death and not the soul in light of Paul's clear statements above as well as further crystal-clear evidence we'll look at in a moment. With this understanding, Paul says that, whether alive on this earth or physically dead, we—believers—will "live together with him," Jesus Christ.

This of course presents a serious problem for those who say that Christians lie dead in Sheol until their resurrection, but it presents no problem for those who believe—as Paul believed—that we go to heaven to be with the Lord at the point of physical death. After all, you cannot very well "live *together* with him (Christ)" if you're dead in Sheol with no consciousness whatsoever until you are resurrected at the Rapture of the Church.

This is a crushing blow to the position that believers go to Sheol when they die.

Peter Will Soon Put Aside "the Tent of his Body"

Consider how Peter phrases his imminent physical decease in this passage:

> **I think it is right to refresh your memory as long as <u>I live in the tent of this body</u>, (14) because I know that <u>I will soon put it aside</u>, as our Lord Jesus Christ has made clear to me. (15) And I will make every effort to see that <u>after my departure</u> you will always be able to remember these things.**
> **2 Peter 1:13-15**

Notice how Peter refers to living in this world as living "in the tent of this body" in verse 13 (other translations say "tabernacle" instead of "tent," but that's what a tabernacle is—a tent). He then describes dying in terms of "putting aside" the tent of his body. Peter knew he was going to physically die soon because the Lord made it clear to him (verse 14). He then refers to dying as his "departure" in the next verse.

This agrees with Paul's statements in the previous three sections: When believer's physically die it's only the death of the body because we're born-again of the seed of Christ and have eternal life in our spirits. As such, our dying is merely a "putting aside of our earthly tent," a "departure" to go be with the Lord in heaven. Praise God!

Human Souls "Under the Altar" During the Tribulation

Let's now turn to the book of Revelation to see even more proof that believers go to heaven when they die:

> **When he opened the fifth seal, I saw under the altar <u>the souls of those who had been slain</u> because of the word of God and the testimony they**

had maintained. (10) They <u>called out</u> in a loud voice, "How long, <u>Sovereign Lord</u>, holy and true, until <u>you</u> judge the inhabitants of the earth and avenge our blood?" (11) Then <u>each of them was given a white robe, and they were told to wait a little longer</u>, until the full number of <u>their fellow servants, their brothers and sisters</u>, were killed just as they had been.

Revelation 6:9-11

The sixth chapter of Revelation involves the seal judgments that will take place during the 7-year Tribulation period that's coming at the end of this age; this passage details the fifth seal judgment. **The text plainly shows tribulation martyrs in heaven in a disembodied state, conscious and speaking to the Lord.** In fact, **each of them is given a robe and instructed to be patient.** Please notice that **they are in communion with the Lord in heaven**, which coincides with Paul's statements in previous sections that dying for the believer means to depart this earth and be "at home with the Lord" or "be with Christ," living "together with him." Revelation 6:9-11 shows this literally happening in heaven. These are obvious facts about the passage.

Now, someone may "spiritualize" the text and maintain that it's symbolic of this or that and therefore shouldn't be taken literally, but we should only spiritualize passages in this manner if there's clear indication that the language is indeed symbolic. Not to mention make sure there are no passages in the same general context that support a literal interpretation.

The obvious problem with teachers allegorizing certain passages is that there are no rules and the interpreter can spiritualize at whim according to the lens of his or her theology. This type of "methodology" can then be used to "prove" practically anything! Needless to say, if you see a minister doing this it's a big red flag.

I admit that the reference to souls being "under the altar" in Revelation 6:9-11 sounds somewhat fantastical, but two things: **1.** What do we know about the dynamics of this altar in heaven? There could be room for innumerable people under this altar. And **2.** nowhere does the passage or context indicate that the language is symbolic (as, say,

Revelation 1:20 does). Again, the text plainly shows believers in heaven—referred to as "souls"—conscious, speaking, given garments and instructed to wait. They ask the Lord a question and are instructed— by the Lord—to wait until the full number of their fellow servants are likewise martyred. It sounds like literal souls in heaven to me. Not to mention this passage is backed up by an even clearer reference to martyred believers in heaven in the very next chapter. Let's look at it...

Tribulation Martyrs "Before the Throne of God" Serving Day and Night

Notice what Christians during the Tribulation will be doing in heaven after they're martyred for Christ:

> After this I looked, and there before me was <u>a great multitude that no one could count, from every nation, tribe, people and language, standing before the throne and before the Lamb</u>. They were wearing white robes and were holding palm branches in their hands. (10) And <u>they cried out in a loud voice:</u>
> "Salvation belongs to our God, who sits on the throne, and to the Lamb."
> (11) All the angels were standing around the throne and around the elders and the four living creatures. They fell down on their faces before the throne and worshiped God, (12) saying:
> "Amen! Praise and glory and wisdom and thanks and honor and power and strength be to our God for ever and ever. Amen!"
> (13) Then one of the elders asked me, "These in white robes—who are they, and where did they come from?"
> (14) I answered, "Sir, you know."
> And he said, "<u>These are they who have come out of the great tribulation;</u> they have washed their robes and made them white in the blood of the Lamb.

(15) Therefore, "<u>they are before the throne of God and serve him day and night in his temple</u>; and he who sits on the throne will shelter them with his presence. (16) 'Never again will they hunger; never again will they thirst. The sun will not beat down on them,' nor any scorching heat. (17) For the Lamb at the center of the throne will be <u>their shepherd</u>; 'he will lead them to springs of living water.' 'And <u>God will wipe away every tear from their eyes</u>.' "

Revelation 7:9-17

This passage shows the multitude of Christian martyrs that will come out of the Tribulation now in heaven wearing the robes given them in the previous chapter. This answers the question of **when** this is taking place. The elder speaking in the passage explains **who** these people are, **where** they are and **what** they'll be doing while there (verses 14-15). There is no symbolism—these are **disembodied believers in heaven**. What are they doing? They're "before the throne of God and serve him day and night in the temple."

They're not yet on earth reigning with Christ during the Millennium because this won't take place until the second stage of the bodily resurrection of the righteous (Revelation 20:4-6). Again, the events of Revelation 7 take place during the seal judgments, which are the first in a series of three multi-faceted judgments. The second stage of the resurrection of the righteous doesn't take place until *after* the Tribulation right *before* the Millennium.

How do people who reject the idea of believers going to heaven when they die explain this passage? I've actually heard some say it applies to the Millennium or eternity. If this were the case, the passage would appear somewhere in Revelation 20-22, not Revelation 7. If it's a "flash forward," as they suggest, we'd see evidence of this in the text— even a hint—but there isn't any. The passage is an account of martyred believers **during the Tribulation serving the Lord in heaven**. It even expressly states this.

People who try to write this passage off—as well as Revelation 6:9-11—do so out of rigid sectarianism. The idea of believers going to Sheol when they die and 'sleeping' in death until their resurrection is a traditional doctrine of their sect and so they desperately try to cut & paste Revelation 7:9-17 and 6:9-11 and place them somewhere in chapters 20-22. It's sad that people resort to such unsound interpreting measures, obviously due to the pressure of religious tradition. However, *mature* believers aren't concerned with what human religion teaches; they're interested in discovering what God's Word actually says. Needless to say, cutting & pasting Revelation 7:9-17 and 6:9-11 and placing them in Revelation 20-22 is an example of un-rightly dividing the Scriptures, that is, incorrectly interpreting them. I'm not saying that we can't *consider* this as an option in our search for truth on the issue of the believer's intermediate state; I'm just pointing out why this option must be rejected.

Believers are Born-Again of the Seed of Christ by the Holy Spirit

All the above is rooted in the fact that believers are born again of the imperishable **seed** of Christ:

> **(3) Praise be to the God and Father of our Lord Jesus Christ! In his great mercy he has given us <u>new birth</u> into a living hope through the resurrection of Jesus Christ from the dead,**
> **(23) For you have been <u>born again</u>, not of perishable <u>seed</u>, but of <u>imperishable</u>, through the living and enduring word of God.**
> **1 Peter 1:3,23**

Peter's talking about *spiritual* rebirth here, which is a blatant truth of the new covenant:

> **But when the kindness and love of God our Savior appeared, (5) he saved us, not because of righteous things we had done, but because of his mercy. He saved us <u>through the washing of rebirth and renewal by the Holy Spirit</u>,**
> **Titus 3:4-5**

For further evidence, Jesus said that people *must* be born-again to enter God's kingdom and explained what he meant by saying, "Flesh gives birth to flesh but **Spirit gives birth to spirit**" (John 3:3,6). Just as your mother gave birth to you, so the Holy Spirit gives re-birth to a person's spirit when he or she turns to the Lord through the gospel. This spiritual rebirth is what Peter was referring to in 1 Peter 1:23-2:3. He even says, "Like **newborn babies**, crave pure spiritual milk, so that by it you may *grow up* in your salvation" (2:2).

Let's focus on Peter's statement that believers have "been born again, not of perishable **seed** but of imperishable, through the living and abiding word of God" (1 Peter 1:23). The "word of God" in this verse refers to the *Living* Word of God, Jesus Christ. We've been born of Jesus' imperishable "seed." Notice how this passage puts it:

> **No one who is <u>born of God</u> will continue to sin, because God's <u>seed</u> remains in them; they cannot go on sinning, because they have been <u>born of God</u>.**
>
> **1 John 3:9**

In this passage "Seed" is the Greek word *sperma* and should be translated "sperm." As such, we've been born again of the imperishable *sperm* of Christ. This is obviously a *spiritual* rebirth as our physical bodies will wither and eventually die, but we have the hope of the bodily resurrection where we'll receive a powerful, glorified, spiritual, immortal body (1 Corinthians 15:42-44), *Praise God!*

So what's my point? Due to spiritual rebirth through the sperm of Christ and power of the Holy Spirit believers *have* eternal life, which is the life-of-the-age-to-come. We don't have it outwardly yet—that is, physically—but we have it inwardly. Notice how clear this is in the Scriptures:

> **Whoever believes in the Son <u>has eternal life</u>, but whoever rejects the Son will not see life, for God's wrath remains on him.**
>
> **John 3:36**

I write these things to you who believe in the name of the Son of God so that you may know that <u>you have eternal life</u>.

1 John 5:13

Because believers intrinsically possess eternal life, death—Sheol—has no power over them. The only part of our being that can die is our body because it's not redeemed yet. Notice how Paul put it:

...we ourselves, who have the firstfruits of the Spirit, groan inwardly as we wait eagerly for our adoption to sonship, <u>the redemption of our bodies</u>.

Romans 8:23

Why does Paul specify the redemption of our bodies? Because believers are already redeemed *inwardly* via the seed (sperm) of Christ; it's our *bodies* that need redeemed. This redemption takes place at the resurrection of the righteous when we'll receive imperishable bodies (1 Corinthians 15:42-46 & Revelation 20:4-6).

Our inward self, however, possesses inherent eternal life, which is why the born-again believer doesn't go to Sheol when he or she dies. Death holds no power over us except for our aging natural bodies. As such, when our bodies die we go to be with the Lord in heaven, awaiting our forthcoming bodily resurrection.

I repeat: **Death holds no power over blood-bought, spiritually regenerated believers who intrinsically possess eternal life!**

This is not to say, however, that a believer can't lose their eternal life sometime after being born-again while still on this earth *if they choose to walk in unbelief.* After all, if it takes faith to be saved, one cannot very well be saved if he or she no longer has faith. Consider it like this: Just because a baby is born into this world doesn't mean it will make it to maturity. If the infant's not cared for properly it will perish. Just the same, someone can be genuinely born of God and not make it to spiritual maturity if they're not cared for properly, which is why the LORD holds ministers accountable (1 Corinthians 3:16-17). See my article *Once Saved Always Saved?* at the Fountain of Life website (dirkwaren.com).[21]

Believers "have Faith and PRESERVE their Souls"

The above explains something about the believer's soul:

> **But we are not of those who shrink back to destruction, but of those who have faith to <u>the preserving of the soul</u>.**
> **Hebrews 10:39** (NASB)

> **But we are not of those who shrink back and are destroyed, but of those who have faith and <u>preserve their souls</u>.**
> **Hebrews 10:39** (ESV)

> **But we are not among those who shrink back and thus perish, but are among those who have faith and <u>preserve their souls</u>.**
> **Hebrews 10:39** (NET)

> **and we are not of those drawing back to destruction, but of those believing to a <u>preserving of soul</u>.**
> **Hebrews 10:39** (YLT)

Because believers are spiritually born-again of the sperm of Christ they *have* eternal life inwardly and therefore death has no power over their inward selves—mind and spirit. Only their bodies are subject to death. Believers are "those who have faith and ***preserve* their souls**" when they physically die. As such, they escape death and Sheol

---

[21] For more info on how God holds ministers responsible for the vulnerable believers under their care see *Hell Know* <u>Chapter Eight</u>'s *The Judgment Seat of Christ—the Judgment of Believers.*

altogether and go straight to heaven when their bodies perish. Why do you think Jesus said:

> **Very truly I tell you, whoever obeys my word**
> **<u>will never see death</u>."**
> **John 8:51**

Unless they're raptured by Christ, the only death born-again believers will experience is physical death. They will never see true death—Sheol—because their souls are preserved from death. When they physically perish they don't consciously expire; they go to be with the Lord in heaven.

Objections to the Believer's Intermediate state in Heaven

I've heard the argument that there's too little elaboration on the believers' intermediate state in heaven between physical death and bodily resurrection, yet the *multiple passages* we've looked at plainly paint the picture of believers alive in heaven with the Lord serving before his throne day and night. What else needs to be said? How much more detail do we require?

I've also heard the scoffing objection: "Do we go to heaven, only to be pulled out at the time of the Rapture and then put back in heaven for seven years until the Millennium?" The clear scriptural exposition on the believer's intermediate state, bodily resurrection, the Millennium and eternal state will set people free on the matter (as Jesus said, "the truth shall set you free"). I realize that religious tradition limits the nature of eternal life to going to heaven and living on a cloud playing a harp forever and that's about it, but God's Word tells something different, something more, much more.

Believers only exist in a non-physical state in heaven until their bodily resurrection (1 Corinthians 15:42-44), which takes place at the Rapture, as shown in 1 Thessalonians 4:13-18. For Christian martyrs during the Tribulation they only exist in a non-physical state in heaven until their bodily resurrection at the end of the Tribulation, as seen in

Revelation 20:4-6. Those who are bodily resurrected at the time of the Christ's return for his church—the Rapture—do go back to heaven and later accompany Christ when he returns to the earth to establish his millennial reign, which is when the second stage of the "first resurrection" takes place, again shown in Revelation 20:4-6. This passage shows that the partakers of this resurrection—martyrs of the Tribulation and those still alive on earth at the end—don't go back to heaven but rather "reign with Christ a thousand years," which of course refers to Christ's millennial reign on earth, not heaven.

After that, believers temporarily go "back in heaven" while the LORD renovates the earth and universe, removing all vestiges of sin and death (2 Peter 3:10-13, Revelation 21:1-4 & Romans 8:21). When this is accomplished, the heavenly city, the New Jerusalem, will "come down **out of heaven from God**" to rest on the new earth (Revelation 21:2,10 & 3:12). This is the eternal home of believers, not that we'll be limited to the confines of the city any more than you're limited to the confines of your current home and neighborhood. Since God at this time makes his dwelling with humanity "and he will live with them" in this new eternal era (Revelation 21:3), you could say that heaven and the physical realm somehow intersect. And it's going to be more *awesome* than we can possibly imagine! See the Epilogue for details.

Although this is a little complicated, it's what God's Word plainly teaches and we'll examine the sequence of events in more detail next chapter, as well as provide diagrams to help you visual human eschatology. It's really not that difficult to grasp. In any case, to mock the reality of these events because they're not simplistic is irreverent and foolish. Besides, they *are* simple in a sense: There will be a resurrection of the righteous and the unrighteous, just as Jesus and Paul said (John 5:28-29 & Acts 24:15); it's the *details* of these events that get complex. Furthermore, since when do we reject the reality of something because it's complicated? Is the human nervous system simple or complex? How about the billions of galaxies in the universe? Need I go on?

1 Thessalonians 4:13-18

Let's now look at the passage people use to support the idea that Christians *don't* go to heaven when they die:

> **Brothers and sisters, we do not want you to be uninformed about those who sleep in death, so that you do not grieve like the rest of mankind, who have no hope. (14) For we believe that Jesus died and rose again, and so we believe that <u>God will bring with Jesus those who have fallen asleep in him</u>. (15) According to the Lord's word, we tell you that we who are still alive, who are left until the coming of the Lord, will certainly not precede those who have fallen asleep. (16) For the Lord himself will come down from heaven, with a loud command, with the voice of the archangel and with the trumpet call of God, and the dead in Christ will rise first. (17) After that, we who are still alive and are left will be caught up together with them in the clouds to meet the Lord in the air. And so we will be with the Lord forever. (18) Therefore encourage each other with these words.**
>
> **1 Thessalonians 4:13-18**

Although some people use this passage to support the belief that Christians 'sleep' in death in Sheol when they physically die it ironically supports the position that Christians go to heaven to await their bodily resurrection.

Let's first address the question: Who are "those who sleep in death" whom Paul mentions in verse 13? This is a reference to believers who have already died. "Sleeping in death" here only refers to the body sleeping in death in the grave (or tomb or whatever the case); it's not referring to the believer's soul sleeping in death because the New Testament repeatedly shows that believers are alive in heaven during their intermediate state between death and bodily resurrection, as we have plainly seen in this chapter. In fact, this passage itself proves that believers who have died go to heaven because verse 14 says that, at the time of the Rapture of the church, "God will **bring with** Jesus those who have fallen asleep in him." Those who have "fallen asleep in him" is a reference to believers who have already physically died—their bodies "sleeping" in the dust. Notice that these believers will come *with Jesus* from heaven at the time of the Rapture. How so? Because that's **where they already are**, not their bodies, but their souls!

Verse 16 shows that the "dead in Christ"—meaning those who have already died and whom "God brings with Jesus" from heaven—will "rise first," referring to their bodily resurrection where they'll receive their glorified immortal bodies. Then those believers who are still alive on earth at the time of the Rapture will be transformed physically, receiving their imperishable bodies:

> **I declare to you, brothers and sisters, that flesh and blood cannot inherit the kingdom of God, nor does the perishable inherit the imperishable. (51) Listen, I tell you a mystery: We will not all sleep, but we will all be changed—(52) in a flash, in the twinkling of an eye, at the last trumpet. For the trumpet will sound, the dead will be raised imperishable, and we will be changed. (53) For the perishable must clothe itself with the imperishable, and the mortal with immortality. (54) When the perishable has been clothed with the imperishable, and the mortal with immortality, then the saying that is written will come true: "Death has been swallowed up in victory."**
>
> **(55) "Where, O death, is your victory? Where, O death, is your sting?"**
>
> **(56) The sting of death is sin, and the power of sin is the law. (57) But thanks be to God! He gives us the victory through our Lord Jesus Christ.**
>
> **1 Corinthians 15:50-57**

As noted in the previous section, the resurrection of the righteous occurs in **stages**. Jesus' resurrection is the first stage, the time of the

Rapture is the second stage and the beginning (and end) of the Millennium is the third stage (Revelation 20:4-6). All three together are the resurrection of the righteous. We'll address this next chapter.

Speaking of which, the "first resurrection" that takes place right before the Millennium offers even more proof that believers go to heaven when they die awaiting their bodily resurrection. Let's look at that…

"I Saw the Souls of Those Who had Been Beheaded"

The book of Revelation shares John's revelational vision, which is actually "the revelation **of Jesus Christ**" according to Revelation 1:1. In this next passage John depicts events taking place **in heaven** after the Tribulation and before the Millennium:

> **I saw thrones on which were seated those who had been given authority to judge. <u>And I saw the souls of those who had been beheaded because of their testimony about Jesus and because of the word of God</u>. They had not worshiped the beast or its image and had not received its mark on their foreheads or their hands. They came to life and reigned with Christ a thousand years. (5) (The rest of the dead did not come to life until the thousand years were ended.) This is the first resurrection. (6) Blessed and holy are those who share in the first resurrection. The second death has no power over them, but they will be priests of God and of Christ and will reign with him for a thousand years.**
>
> **Revelation 20:4-6**

John describes what he sees **in Heaven** and says he "saw **the souls** of those who had been beheaded because of their testimony" during the Tribulation. Let me repeat: John is in heaven (via his vision) and he sees the **souls of believers** who were martyred during the Tribulation. They're in heaven! Nothing is said whatsoever about these souls being resurrected from Hades (i.e. Sheol), as is the case with unbelievers after the Millennium at the resurrection of the unrighteous, (Revelation 20:13).

Now some might argue that verse 4 says that "they **came to life** and reigned with Christ a thousand years," which of course suggests that they were fully dead, but this simply means that they came to life *physically* since **their souls are already shown alive in heaven after being martyred for the Lord,** just like the martyrs in Revelation 7:9-17 and the martyrs in Revelation 6:9-11. Remember the hermeneutical rules: "Context is king" and "Scripture interprets Scripture." With this understanding, here's what verse 4 is saying: "they came to life [physically] and reigned with Christ a thousand years." You see? The addition of one simple word clarifies the statement and settles the matter.

What more proof could anyone need? God's Word is clear on the issue: Believers go to heaven when they die—in a disembodied form— awaiting their bodily resurrection.

Jesus' Statement about the Resurrections of the Righteous and the Unrighteous

We've observed from the Scriptures that the resurrection of the righteous takes place in three stages. With this in mind, let's look at a statement Jesus made about the resurrection of both the righteous and the unrighteous:

> **"Do not be amazed at this, for <u>a time is coming when all who are in their graves will hear his voice</u> (29) and <u>come out</u>—those who have done what is good will rise to live, and those who have done what is evil will rise to be condemned."**
>
> **John 5:28-29**

Jesus mentions two resurrections here—a resurrection to life for the righteous and a resurrection to condemnation for the wicked. The Lord doesn't provide details in this simple statement and the wording makes it *seem* like there's only one resurrection of the righteous and that the resurrections of the righteous and wicked take place simultaneously.

This is why we have the hermeneutical rule "Scripture interprets Scripture" so we can interpret non-detailed passages like this one with passages that provide more exposition. The other Scriptures that we examined in this chapter prove that the resurrection of the righteous takes place in stages, starting with Jesus' resurrection, then the Rapture of the church (1 Thessalonians 4:13-18) and, lastly, the resurrection that occurs after the Tribulation (Revelation 20:4-6), which presumably includes one that occurs at the end of the Millennium. Only the last one would occur at the same general time as the resurrection of the unrighteous.

Now some will point out how Jesus says that people in **their graves** will hear his voice and come out, suggesting that believers are sleeping in Sheol, but the word for "graves" here isn't Hades but rather *mnémeion (mnay-MY-on)*, which refers to a tomb, grave or monument. Hence, for the righteous, Jesus is referring to a *bodily* resurrection. Furthermore, as we have seen in this chapter, the rest of the New Testament clearly shows that the souls of believers are in heaven awaiting their bodily resurrection.

Of course, this isn't the case with the unredeemed. They lack redemption and eternal life and therefore go to Sheol when they die to 'sleep' in death until their resurrection to face the Great White Throne Judgment where "Anyone whose name was not found written in the book of life was thrown into the lake of fire," which is the second **death** (Revelation 20:14-15).

Chapter Eleven

RESURRECTIONS:

Firstfruits, Harvest & Gleanings

To tie everything up and see the bigger picture, we'll focus on the resurrection of the dead in this chapter. Whether believers know it or not, the resurrection of the dead is one of **the six basic doctrines of Christianity**, as shown in Hebrews 6:1-2. Unfortunately, it's rarely taught and so the body of Christ is largely ignorant on the topic. This chapter will help rectify the problem.

As noted in the previous chapter, the Bible speaks of two *types* of resurrections...

The Resurrections of the Righteous and the Unrighteous

Jesus and Paul plainly declared two basic resurrections:

> **"for a time is coming when all who are in their graves will hear his voice (29) and come out— those who have done what is good will <u>rise to live</u>, and those who have done what is evil will <u>rise to be condemned</u>."**
>
> **John 5:28-29**

> having hope toward God, which they themselves also wait for, that there is about to be a **rising again of the dead**, both of **righteous** and **unrighteous**;
>
> **Acts 24:15** (YLT)

As you can see, there will be resurrections of both the righteous and unrighteous. This doesn't mean, however, that there will only be two resurrections in number, just that there are two *types* of resurrections: **1.** The resurrection of the righteous and **2.** the resurrection of the unrighteous. The former is called "first resurrection" in Scripture (Revelation 20:5-6), which makes the latter the second resurrection.

The second resurrection takes place at the time of the Great White Throne Judgment, detailed here:

> Then I saw a **great white throne** and him who was seated on it. The earth and the heavens fled from his presence, and there was no place for them. (12) And I saw the dead, great and small, standing before the throne, and books were opened. Another book was opened, which is the book of life. The dead were judged according to what they had done as recorded in the books. (13) The sea gave up the dead that were in it, and **death and Hades gave up the dead that were in them, and each person was judged according to what they had done**. (14) Then death and Hades were thrown into the lake of fire. The lake of fire is the second death. (15) **Anyone whose name was not found written in the book of life was thrown into the lake of fire.**
>
> **Revelation 20:11-15**

This massive judgment concerns every dead soul contained in Hades (Sheol) after the thousand-year reign of Christ on this earth, which means it involves every unredeemed person throughout history. It does not include Old Testament holy people because they had a covenant with the LORD and will be resurrected after the 7-year Tribulation and before the Millennium, which we'll examine later this chapter.

The second resurrection is covered thoroughly in *Hell Know*, so I encourage you to pick up a copy, if you haven't already. Not only do we examine the nature of the "second death"—i.e. being thrown into the lake of fire (verses 14-15)—we also explore the question of whether or not every person who partakes of this resurrection will automatically be cast into the lake of fire. For instance, what about those who never heard the gospel? What about those who heard the gospel but didn't understand it for one legitimate reason or another? What about those who rejected it because it was either a flawed, religionized version of the gospel or it came with serious baggage, like imperialism? Every legitimate minister of God's Word must consider these obvious questions and try to answer them based on what the Bible says and simple common sense. I would be seriously skeptical of anyone who doesn't do this, particularly those who write off such questions in preference to the official position of whatever group they adhere to, which is an example of rigid sectarianism. Staunch sectarianism actually hinders the truth and, in fact, is a form of legalism, i.e. counterfeit Christianity. Remember, Jesus said it's the truth that will set us free (John 8:31-32), so anything that *hinders* the acquisition of truth is not good.

In any event, *Hell Know* addresses these questions and others in <u>Chapter Eight</u>.

The Resurrection of the Righteous

The first resurrection is the resurrection of the righteous, meaning those in right-standing with God. Again, when Jesus and Paul spoke of two basic resurrections they were talking about *types* of resurrections and not numbers. While there's only one resurrection of the *un*righteous, the resurrection of the righteous takes place in *stages*, which correspond to the analogy of a harvest.

In biblical times the harvest took place in three basic stages: **1.** the firstfruits, **2.** the main harvest, and **3.** the gleanings. The harvest began with the **firstfruits**, which concerned the first fruits and grains to ripen in the season and were offered to the LORD as a sacrifice of thanksgiving (Exodus 23:16,19). Later came the **general harvest** (Exodus 23:16) and, lastly, the **gleanings**, which were leftovers for the poor and needy (Leviticus 19:9-10).

Let's examine the three stages:

1. **The Firstfruits.** Paul described Jesus as the firstfruits here:

    > But <u>Christ has indeed been raised from the dead, the firstfruits of those who have fallen asleep</u>. **(21) For since death came through a man, the resurrection of the dead comes also through a man. (22) For as in Adam all die, so in Christ all will be made alive. (23) But each in turn:** <u>Christ, the firstfruits</u>**; then, when he comes, those who belong to him.**
    >
    > **1 Corinthians 15:21-23**

    Just as the firstfruits of the harvest were a sacrifice to the LORD so Jesus Christ was sacrificed for our sins and raised to life for our justification (Romans 4:25); hence, he's the firstfruits of the resurrection of the righteous.

2. **The General Harvest.** Verse 23 shows that the main harvest takes place when Jesus returns for the church—his "bride"—which is the Rapture, detailed in 1 Thessalonians 4:13-18. This harvest includes physically-alive believers translated to heaven.

3. **The Gleanings** refer to the righteous who were not included in the main harvest and are, as such, "leftovers." This resurrection takes place at the time of Jesus' return at the end of the Tribulation. Jesus' return to earth to establish his millennial reign is separate from the Rapture, which is when the general harvest occurs. Remember, when Jesus comes for his church he doesn't return to earth, but rather meets believers in the sky (1 Thessalonians 4:17). We'll address this in a forthcoming section. The gleanings include the resurrection of Old Testament saints—at least a bodily resurrection, but more likely a soulish/bodily resurrection (more on this later)—as well as the bodily resurrection of believers who died during the Tribulation.

The "gleanings" will also include believers who physically die during the Millennium. Some argue that such a resurrection won't be necessary because, as Isaiah 65:19-25 shows, lifespans will return to the lengthy durations of people before the flood, like Adam and Methuselah. However, this passage doesn't actually say righteous people *won't* die during the Millennium; notice what it says:

> **Never again will there be in it** [Jerusalem] **an infant who lives but a few days, or <u>an old man who does not live out his years</u>; <u>the one who dies at a hundred will be thought a mere child</u>; <u>the one who fails to reach a hundred</u> will be considered accursed.**
> **Isaiah 65:20**

The passage simply shows that lifespans will be greatly increased, as before the flood; it doesn't say righteous people won't die. In fact, it's implied that blessed people will die by the reference to "an old man who *does not live out his years*." Moreover, verse 22 says that God's people will live as long as trees during the Millennium. Depending on the species, trees can live less than a hundred years or up to a few thousand, but they ultimately die.

Something else to consider: While it's true that many people lived to be over 900 years old before the flood, it's still not a thousand years, which is how long the Millennium will last. Also, some people died well short of 900-plus years; for instance, Lamech died at 777.

Someone might argue: How can *both* the resurrection of the righteous at the beginning of the Millennium and another resurrection at the end be considered "gleanings" since they're separated by a thousand years? Answer: Because the very word "gleanings" implies more than one gleaning; after all, the poor gleaned the harvested fields more than once in biblical times. Also, Psalm 90:4 and 2 Peter 3:8 show that a thousand years is like a day to the LORD, so the two gleanings occur only one day apart from the Divine perspective.

Why is it Called the "First Resurrection"?

The resurrection of the righteous is called the "first resurrection" in this passage:

> **I saw thrones on which were seated those who had been given authority to judge. And I saw the souls of those who had been beheaded because of their testimony about Jesus and because of the word of God. They had not worshiped the beast or its image and had not received its mark on their foreheads or their hands. They came to life and reigned with Christ a thousand years. (5) (The rest of the dead did not come to life until the thousand years were ended.) This is <u>the first resurrection</u>. (6) Blessed and holy are those who share in <u>the first resurrection</u>. The second death has no power over them, but they will be priests of God and of Christ and will reign with him for a thousand years.**
>
> **Revelation 20:4-6**

The passage refers specifically to the bodily resurrection of Christian martyrs from the Tribulation, which John calls the "first resurrection." By calling it the *first* resurrection is he saying that there were no resurrections before this? No, because Jesus Christ was resurrected at the beginning of the Church Age and believers will be resurrected bodily at the time of the Rapture while living believers will be translated; not to mention the resurrections of Enoch, Elijah and Moses as *types*, covered in <u>Chapter Nine</u>. Speaking of those three, their resurrections can be considered "taste-testing of the fruit" according to the harvest analogy.

Here's a diagram that helps visualize the first and second resurrections and the three stages of the first:

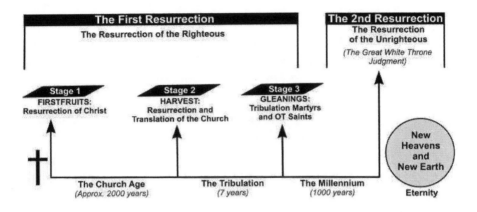

By calling the resurrection of the righteous the "first resurrection" John may mean more than just first in order. The Greek word for "first" is *prótos (PRO-toss)*, which also means principle, chief, honorable or most important. How is the resurrection of the righteous the more honorable resurrection? Because it entails the resurrection of people in right-standing with the LORD through covenant and spiritual rebirth (Titus 3:5 & Ephesians 4:22-24). Since this resurrection involves people who are in right-standing with their Creator, i.e. God's children, it's the more honorable resurrection and therefore the more important one to the LORD, just as the resurrection of your child would be more important to you than some stranger you never knew.

Someone might argue that all people are God's children, even atheists. No, all people are *creations* of God, but only those born-again of the seed (sperm) of Jesus Christ by the Holy Spirit are *children* of God (1 John 3:9). Because of the death and resurrection of the Messiah, Old Testament saints who were in covenant with God automatically become spiritually-regenerated at the time of their resurrection.

'Isn't this too Complicated?'

Some might argue that the resurrection of the righteous, as mapped out in this chapter, is too complicated. This is perhaps one of the main reasons why the so-called "father of orthodoxy," Augustine of Hippo, simplified human eschatology by inventing (or, at least, popularizing) the false doctrine of amillennialism. Believe it or not, this erroneous teaching suggests that we're currently *already* in both the

Millennium and Tribulation; and when believers or unbelievers die their immortal souls either go to heaven forever or suffer never-ending torment in hell. Incredibly, Augustine argued that biblical references to the new Jerusalem, new earth, new heavens and the believer's new glorified body are all symbolic language for heaven! Talk about adding to and taking away from the Holy Scriptures, a practice repeatedly denounced in the Bible (see Revelation 22:18-19, Proverbs 30:6 and Deuteronomy 4:2).[22]

Getting back to our question: Is the resurrection of the dead too complicated? Think about it like this: When referencing a complex subject to someone who knows little about the topic it's best to state the facts in the simplest of terms, which is how Jesus and Paul talked about the resurrection of the dead in John 5:28-29 and Acts 24:15 (both cited at the beginning of this chapter). Daniel did the same thing in Daniel 12:1-2. All three of these passages detail that there will be a resurrection of both the righteous and the unrighteous, which is true, but they don't go any further than this. As such, we have to look to the rest of Scripture for more details and that's what we're doing in this chapter. This is in line with the hermeneutical rule "Scripture interprets Scripture" wherein the more clear and detailed passages offer necessary data that helps interpret the more ambiguous and sketchy ones.

Furthermore, the argument that "this is just too complicated" implies that truth—reality—must always be simple when this simply isn't the case. Take brain surgery, for example. Is it simple or does it take years of schooling to master? How about computer technology, astronomy, world history, languages or law? How simple is the sewage system of any major city? How about the electrical grid of New York City? I could go on and on.

Yes, the resurrection of the dead is more complicated than what Augustine taught, but it's certainly not too complicated for the average person to grasp. The above diagram illustrates that it's actually not that

---

[22] See *Hell Know* for more information on Augustine and his false doctrines that corrupted the church, specifically <u>Chapter Seven</u>'s *The Augustinian Corruption of Christendom* and <u>Chapter Nine</u>'s *The Good and Bad of Orthodoxy and Traditionalism.*

complicated and it's much less complicated than any of the topics just listed.

As noted at the beginning of this chapter, the resurrection of the dead is one of the six basic doctrines:

> **Therefore let us move beyond the elementary teachings about Christ and be taken forward to maturity, not laying again the foundation of <u>repentance from acts that lead to death</u>, and of <u>faith in God</u>, (2) <u>instruction about baptisms</u>, the <u>laying on of hands</u>, the <u>resurrection of the dead</u>, and <u>eternal judgment</u>.**
>
> **Hebrews 6:1-2**

Years ago I did a six-part series on these foundational doctrines, one sermon per each doctrine. A knowledgeable minister could easily do a *series* of teachings on every one of them. Unbelievably, in most Christian camps the six basic doctrines are almost utterly ignored. And then ministers wonder why many in their congregations act like spiritual babies. It's because the pastors and teachers aren't properly feeding them! This, by the way, explains the existence and mission of my ministry, Fountain of Life—to feed the body of Christ the rightly-divided Word of God; and to do this free of the constraints (hindrances, limitations) of rigid sectarianism (Matthew 4:4).

In any case, the writer of Hebrews was lamenting that the people he was addressing needed to be taught these basic doctrines all over again when they should've been teachers by this point (Hebrews 5:11-12). Now, think about it, if the topic of the resurrection of the dead was as simple as Augustine taught—that is, people just go to heaven or hell when they die to spend eternity in either bliss or torment—why would these people need to be taught the subject again? If the subject were that simplistic it'd take just a few minutes to teach and not a whole sermon or series of sermons. Moreover, if it were that simple how could the believers *not* grasp it the first time around?

Yes, the resurrection of the dead is a complicated subject and this explains why this chapter exists, as well as the previous chapter.

The Second Coming: Jesus' Return for his Church and his Return to the Earth

I pointed out something in a previous section that should be elaborated on: Most believers don't realize that there are two phases to the Lord's Second Coming: **1.** Jesus' return for his Church, known as the Rapture, and **2.** Jesus' return to the earth to establish his millennial kingdom. The former is detailed in 1 Thessalonians 4:13-18 and the latter in Revelation 19:11-16. A comparison of these passages and other pertinent Scriptures reveal **two separate phases** of Jesus' Second Coming that can be distinguished like so:

The Lord's Second Coming	
PHASE 1 **The Rapture** **(1 Thessalonians 4:13-18)**	**PHASE 2** **Jesus' Return to the Earth** **(Revelation 19:11-16)**
Jesus appears in the air	Jesus returns to the earth
Jesus returns in secret, like a thief	Jesus returns openly
Jesus returns *for* his Church	Jesus returns *with* his Church
Jesus comes as bridegroom	Jesus comes as King
Jesus comes as deliverer	Jesus comes as warrior and judge
Jesus comes with grace	Jesus comes with wrath and grace
Jesus delivers the Church *from* wrath	Jesus delivers believers (of the Tribulation) who endured wrath
Living believers receive immortal bodies as they are taken to heaven	Living believers remain mortal on the earth during the Millennium
The world is left unjudged	The world is judged (Mt. 25:31-46)
The world continues in sin	Righteousness is established
Addresses only the saved	Addresses the saved and unsaved
Can happen at any moment	Many signs must first occur
The devil continues his evil reign	The devil is cast into the Abyss

One of the differences on the list is that the Lord's return for his Church—the Rapture—can happen at any time once the general season of the end is apparent, meaning it's *imminent*, whereas many distinct signs *precede* Christ's return to the earth. These signs include, amongst others: the global cataclysm of the Tribulation period itself (Revelation

6-19), the revealing of the antichrist (2 Thessalonians 2:1-8), the two witnesses (Revelation 11:1-12) and the institution of the mark of the beast (Revelation 13:16-17). Generally speaking, once the Tribulation begins—and it will be obvious when it does—you can be sure that Jesus will return to the earth seven years later (which is different than saying you'll be able to pinpoint the precise moment or day).

However, this isn't the case with the Lord's return for his Church because, again, it's imminent and could happen at any time with zero warning once the general season of his return is at hand, which means **now** (Matthew 24:3-14). Notice what Jesus said:

> **(36) "But <u>about that day or hour no one knows, not even the angels in heaven, nor the Son, but only the Father</u>. (37) As it was in the days of Noah, so it will be at the coming of the Son of Man.**
>
> **(42) "Therefore <u>keep watch</u>, because <u>you do not know on what day your Lord will come</u>. (43) But understand this: If the owner of the house had known at what time of night the thief was coming, he would have kept watch and would not have let his house be broken into. (44) So you also must <u>be ready</u>, because <u>the Son of Man will come at an hour when you do not expect him</u>.**
>
> **Matthew 24:36-37, 42-44**

As you can see, we are instructed to "keep watch" and "be ready" because Jesus "will come at an hour when we do not expect him." Interestingly, the Son doesn't even know the day or hour, only the Father knows (verse 36). We must be "dressed ready for service" and "keep our lamps burning" (Luke 12:35) precisely because the Lord's return for his Church is imminent. I should add that, while we don't know the day or hour, we can know the general season via Jesus' descriptions and, again, that season is *now*.

While some claim that the word "Rapture" isn't biblical, it is. It refers to a phrase used in this passage:

> After that, we who are still alive and are left will be <u>caught up</u> together with them in the clouds to meet the Lord in the air. And so we will be with the Lord forever.
>
> 1 Thessalonians 4:17

'Caught up' in the Greek is *harpazó (har-PAD-zoh)*, which means to "snatch up" or "obtain by robbery." It's translated in Latin as "rapio" in the Vulgate, which is where we get the English "Rapture." With this understanding, when the Bridegroom, Jesus, comes for his bride, the Church, he's going to obtain us by **robbing us off the earth!**

We looked at the most prominent support text for the Rapture last chapter—1 Thessalonians 4:13-18—but there's quite a bit more support:

> "Do not let your hearts be troubled. You believe in God; believe also in me. (2) My Father's house has many rooms; if that were not so, would I have told you that I am going there to prepare a place for you? (3) And <u>if I go and prepare a place for you, I will come back and take you to be with me that you also may be where I am</u>."
>
> John 14:1-3

> Listen, I tell you a mystery: We will not all sleep, but we <u>will all be changed</u>—(52) <u>in a flash, in the twinkling of an eye, at the last trumpet</u>. For the trumpet will sound, <u>the dead will be raised imperishable, and we will be changed</u>.
>
> 1 Corinthians 15:51-52

> and to wait for his Son from heaven, whom he raised from the dead—Jesus, <u>who rescues us from the coming wrath</u>.
>
> 1 Thessalonians 1:10

What is the "coming wrath" and how does Jesus "rescue" us from it? The coming wrath refers to the Tribulation and the Lord rescues the Church from it via the Rapture.

Notice what Jesus promises the faithful church of Philadelphia:

> **"Since you have kept my command to endure patiently, <u>I will also keep you from the hour of trial that is going to come on the whole world to test the inhabitants of the earth</u>."**
>
> **Revelation 3:10**

"The hour of trial that is going to come on the whole world" is referring to the Tribulation period detailed in Revelation 6-19. Jesus doesn't say he would just protect believers during the Tribulation, but that he'd "keep them from the hour of trial" altogether. Keep in mind that, while the church at Philadelphia was one of seven first century churches that Jesus addresses in Revelation 2-3; these seven churches were picked by the Lord because they typify the seven kinds of churches that exist throughout the Church Age. As such, Jesus' words were to all faithful Christians throughout the ensuing centuries of the Church Age. In fact, since the Rapture and the Tribulation didn't come at the general time of this message to the church of Philadelphia circa 90-100 AD, the passage *must* more specifically refer to a future generation of faithful believers.

Further support for the Rapture can be observed in what happens to John in the book of Revelation. Jesus gave John the threefold *contents* of Revelation at the end of chapter 1: "Write, therefore, **what you have seen, what is now** and **what will take place later**" (Revelation 1:19). This is the Contents Page of the book of Revelation: "What you have seen" refers to chapter 1 because that's what John had seen up to that point in the vision while "what is now" refers to chapters 2-3 and "what will take place later" refers to chapters 4-22.

Chapters 2-3 of Revelation cover "what is now," meaning the Church Age, as noted above. These chapters cover the seven types of churches that exist throughout the Church Age. Chapters 4-22 address "what will take place later" and chapters 4-19 specifically the period of the Tribulation, which involves the seal, trumpet and bowl judgments of God's wrath that will befall the earth and its inhabitants.

Here's my point: John was an apostle of the church and right at the beginning of Revelation 4—the beginning of his coverage of the Tribulation—Jesus says to him, "Come up here," referring to heaven (verse 1). You see? John is representative of the church and just before the Tribulation he is taken up into heaven. Why? Because the church itself will be delivered from the Tribulation via Jesus' return for his church, which is the Rapture.

Another thing to consider is that the church is referred to no less than nineteen times in the first three chapters of Revelation and not once on earth in chapters 4-19. Why? Because the existing church—all genuine believers—will be "snatched up" to heaven before the Tribulation starts. Revelation 19 details Christ's return to the earth at the end of the Tribulation. Guess who's riding with him? The church (verse 14).

This doesn't mean, however, that there won't be believers during the Tribulation because there will be multitudes; and, yes, they *are* the church because 'church' simply refers to the *ekklesia (ek-klay-SEE-ah)*, the "called-out ones" who are called out of the darkness of this world into the kingdom of light. However, the *existing church* at the time of the Rapture before the Tribulation will have been snatched away. In other words, believers *during* the Tribulation embraced the gospel *after* the Rapture. We'll address this in the next section.

The snatching up of the church before the Tribulation corresponds to the biblical pattern of the righteous being saved from destruction when God's judgment falls on unrepentant masses. Jesus noted this pattern when he taught on the Rapture:

> **For the Son of Man <u>in his day will be like the lightning, which flashes and lights up the sky from one end to the other</u>. (25) But first he must suffer many things and be rejected by this generation.**
>
> **(26) "<u>Just as it was in the days of Noah, so also will it be</u> in the days of the Son of Man. (27) People were eating, drinking, marrying and being**

given in marriage up to the day Noah entered the ark. Then the flood came and destroyed them all.

(28) "It was the same in the days of Lot. People were eating and drinking, buying and selling, planting and building. (29) But the day Lot left Sodom, fire and sulfur rained down from heaven and destroyed them all.

(30) "It will be just like this on the day the Son of Man is revealed. (31) On that day no one who is on the housetop, with possessions inside, should go down to get them. Likewise, no one in the field should go back for anything. (32) Remember Lot's wife! (33) Whoever tries to keep their life will lose it, and whoever loses their life will preserve it. (34) I tell you, on that night two people will be in one bed; one will be taken and the other left. (35) Two women will be grinding grain together; one will be taken and the other left."

Luke 17:24-35

Jesus is talking about "the day the Son of Man is revealed" (verse 30) that "will be like the lightning, which flashes and lights up the sky from one end to the other" (verse 24). In other words, it'll take place in the blink of an eye. The last two verses show beyond any shadow of doubt that Jesus was talking about his snatching up of the church: "Two people will be in bed; one will be taken and the other left. Two women will be grinding grain together; one will be taken and the other left" (verses 34-35). This, incidentally, presents a problem for those who argue that the Rapture takes place at the same time as Jesus' return to the earth at the end of the Tribulation because the impression of these verses is that of ordinary every-day life and not of people who just went through a worldwide cataclysm horrifically described in Revelation 6-19.

Observe in verses 26-29 how Jesus likens the time of the Rapture to the "days of Noah" and the "days of Lot." "Just as it was" in the days of these two "so it will be" when Christ returns for his church. What's the significance of this? In the days of Noah and Lot there were warnings of the LORD's coming judgment on masses of people if they stubbornly refused to repent. In Noah's situation the judgment concerned the entire world whereas in Lot's situation it concerned the cities of Sodom and Gomorrah. In both cases **the righteous were removed *before* God's judgment fell**. "So it will be" with the future Tribulation—those in right-standing with God will be taken out of the way *before* His wrath falls on rebellious humanity. Those who become believers during the Tribulation are those who wisely respond to the pouring out of God's wrath by repenting.

In verse 30 Jesus says "It will be just like this on the day the Son of Man is revealed." Just like what? Just like the days of Noah and Lot where people were carrying on business as usual—eating, drinking, marrying, buying, selling, planting and building (verses 27-28). This is what people will be doing when Jesus comes for his church, not enduring a global upheaval, which disproves the post-Tribulation position.

Speaking of the post-Tribulation view, how do people who hold this position explain Luke 17:24-35? They argue that Jesus only speaks of his coming *once* in this passage, not twice, and when he comes he will **1.** snatch up the righteous and then **2.** pour out his wrath on the unrighteous, citing verses 26-32. The problem with this, of course, is that *it's an explicit description of the pre-Tribulation position* (or, at least, "pre-wrath"). The only thing they're omitting is Jesus' return to the earth *after* God's wrath is poured out on rebellious humanity to set up his millennial kingdom (Matthew 25:31). As already explained, this is detailed in the book of Revelation: In Revelation 4:1 Jesus says to John—representing the church—to "come up here" to heaven. Chapters 4-19 cover the Tribulation where God's wrath is poured out and Jesus returns to the earth at the end (Revelation 19).

Here's a timeline diagram to help visualize these events:

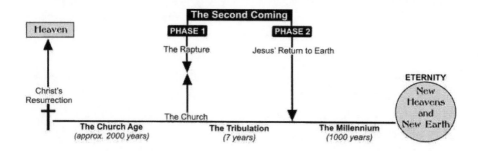

Some people suggest that the Rapture isn't part of Jesus' Second Coming and that only his return to the earth should be designated as the Second coming, but Jesus himself spoke of his snatching up of the church as "**the coming of the Son of Man**" (Matthew 24:27,37,39) and within this context are clear references to the Tribulation (verses 21-22 & 29). The Greek for "coming" in these passages is *parousia (par-oo-SEE-ah)*, traditionally translated as "advent" in Christian circles as in "the Second Advent of Christ." This is the same word used to describe the Lord's coming at the *end* of the Tribulation in 2 Thessalonians 2:8. Jesus elsewhere referred to this latter coming as "**When the Son of Man comes** in his glory" (Matthew 16:27 & 25:31). Since the Rapture of the church is clearly separate from the Lord's coming to the earth—with the Tribulation separating them—and both the Rapture and Jesus' return to the earth are described in terms of "coming" then we must conclude that **they both represent his Second Coming**, albeit two phases.

Someone might argue: "But these two phases are separated by several years, how can they both refer to the *same* Second Coming? Because it's *one* coming taking place in *two* stages. Besides, seven years isn't that long of a time to the eternal God. Let me put it in perspective: The Bible says that a thousand years is like a day to the Lord (Psalm 90:4 & 2 Peter 3:8), which means that seven years would be like 10½ minutes! So from Jesus' perspective the Second Coming—both stages— takes place in 10½ minutes. It's hard to get out of the airport without baggage in that amount of time!

"For it will Not be, Unless the Departure Comes First"

Both phases of the Lord's Second Coming are covered in this passage:

> **Now, brothers, <u>concerning the coming of our Lord Jesus Christ</u>, <u>and our gathering together to him</u>, we ask you (2) not to be quickly shaken in your mind, nor yet be troubled, either by spirit, or by word, or by letter as from us, saying that <u>the day of Christ</u> had come. (3) Let no one deceive you in any**

**way. <u>For it will not be, unless the departure comes
first, and the man of sin is revealed</u>, the son of
destruction, (4) who opposes and exalts himself
against all that is called God or that is worshiped; so
that he sits as God in the temple of God, setting
himself up as God. (5) Don't you remember that,
when I was still with you, I told you these things? (6)
<u>Now you know what is restraining him</u>, to the end
that he may be revealed in his own season. (7) For the
mystery of lawlessness already works. <u>Only there is
one who restrains now, until he is taken out of the
way</u>. (8) <u>Then the lawless one will be revealed</u>, whom
<u>the Lord will kill with the breath of his mouth, and
destroy by the manifestation of his coming</u>;**

2 Thessalonians 2:1-8 (WEB)

Verse 1 shows that this text concerns the Second Coming,
including the church being "gathered together to him," which is the
Rapture. Verse 8 details the second phase of Jesus' coming, which is
when he returns to the earth and destroys the "lawless one"—the
antichrist—with a mere word or two from his lips. (So much for Christ
being a milksop weakling as he's often maligned in modern Western
culture!) The Greek word for "coming" in both verses is the
aforementioned *parousia*. You see? The Second Coming consists of **1.**
Jesus' return for his church and **2.** His return to the earth to vanquish his
enemies and establish his millennial kingdom.

Verse 3 reveals the sequence of events, emphasizing that the
"day of Christ" will not come to pass *until* "the departure comes first,
and the man of sin is revealed." The "departure" is an obvious reference
to the snatching up of the church while the revealing of the "man of sin"
refers to the unveiling of the antichrist, a wicked, possessed man who
will obtain worldwide power during the Tribulation (Revelation 13:7).

The Greek word for "departure" is *apostasia (ap-os-tas-EE-ah)*
and is only used one other time in the Bible where it refers to departing
from the law of Moses (Acts 21:21). Interestingly, the word was
translated as "departure" or "departing" in 2 Thessalonians 2:3 in the
first seven English translations of the Bible, which changed when the

King James translators decided to translate it as "falling away." Most modern English versions have followed the lead of the KJV by translating it as "apostasy" or "rebellion," but the World English Bible (above) translates it as "departure." I believe this is the proper translation for a few reasons:

1. The verb form of the word is used 14 times in the New Testament where it predominantly means "departed." Luke 2:37 is a good example where it refers to an elderly prophetess who "never *left* the temple but worshiped night and day, fasting and praying;" Acts 12:10 is another example where it refers to an angel *leaving* Peter after helping him escape from prison.

2. It doesn't make sense in the context of 2 Thessalonians 2:3 to translate *apostasia* as "rebellion" or "apostasy"/"falling away." Concerning the former, the world has always been in rebellion against genuine Christianity (please notice I said "genuine"). Concerning the latter, there's *already* mass apostasy in Christendom with whole denominations embracing gross libertinism and rejecting the most obvious biblical axioms. In fact, this has been increasing for *decades*.

3. Translating *apostasia* as "departure" fits both the immediate context of 2 Thessalonians 2:1-8 and the greater context of the Lord's Second Coming in the Bible, the latter of which we've already covered. Concerning the former, verse 1 speaks of the Second Coming in terms of the church being gathered to Jesus, which involves believers *departing* from this earth. And verses 6-8 speak of the "restrainer" of lawlessness, which must be **removed** *before* the antichrist can rise to power. Who is this "restrainer" of lawlessness? The most obvious answer is the Holy Spirit and, by extension, the church, which is the temple of the Holy Spirit (1 Corinthians 3:16). When they depart the earth the antichrist will no longer be restrained and, in the vacuum, he will make his move. Whereas the church will remain in heaven during the Tribulation the Holy Spirit will return as masses of wise people will almost immediately turn to God after the incredible testimony of the Rapture. The Holy Spirit obviously returns because it's the Spirit who regenerates people through the gospel (Titus 3:5). As noted earlier, untold millions will be saved

during the Tribulation (Revelation 7:9,14) through the testimony of **1.** the Rapture, **2.** the 144,000 Jewish evangelists, **3.** the two witnesses, **4.** the mass divine judgments, and **5.** an angel commissioned to preach the eternal gospel to the inhabitants of the earth (Revelation 14:6-7).

As you can see, 2 Thessalonians 2:1-8 strongly supports the two phases of the Second Coming and the pre-Tribulation Rapture.

For more details on the Second Coming go to the Fountain of Life website, but let me close by stressing that I personally don't care if the Rapture takes place before the Tribulation, mid-Tribulation or "pre-wrath." I don't even care if it takes place at the same general time as Jesus' return to the earth at the end of the Tribulation. Don't get me wrong, like any sane believer I have zero desire to go through the Tribulation, but as a responsible minister of the Word of God all I care about is accurately conveying what the Bible teaches and my studies have led me to conclude what is contained in these last two sections. Bear in mind that I'm a devoted non-sectarian and therefore don't draw doctrinal conclusions based on the pressure of a certain group. I draw conclusions from the God-breathed Scriptures and, as you see, they overwhelmingly point in the direction of a pre-Tribulation Rapture.

I encourage you to unbiasedly look at the different perspectives in your studies and draw your own conclusions with the help of the Holy Spirit. I recommend David Reagan's many excellent articles, which can be found at lamblion.com, as well as the great works of Hal Lindsey and Todd Strandberg, noted in the Bibliography.

Lastly, all genuine believers who know how to read agree that the Lord will "snatch up" his church when he returns based on the clear passages we've looked at in this section, so the Rapture is a biblical fact. It's the *timing* of the Rapture that believers disagree on and this is a secondary issue; it's not something to argue about or break fellowship over. Whether pre, mid, post or pre-wrath, the Rapture *will* occur.

Distinguishing the Millennium from the New Earth

We've seen that the Bible teaches there will a thousand-year reign of Christ on this earth before the eternal age of the new heavens and new earth is established. What is the scriptural evidence for the Millennium and what differentiates it from the coming eternal age? Most importantly, what's the purpose of the Millennium?

While there are several biblical references to the Millennium, such as Zechariah 14:1-9 and Isaiah 11, Revelation 20 is the most detailed passage in the New Testament:

> **And I saw an angel coming down out of heaven, having the key to the Abyss and holding in his hand a great chain. (2) He seized the dragon, that ancient serpent, who is the devil, or Satan, and bound him for <u>a thousand years</u>. (3) He threw him into the Abyss, and locked and sealed it over him, to keep him from deceiving the nations anymore until <u>the thousand years</u> were ended. After that, he must be set free for a short time.**
>
> **(4) I saw thrones on which were seated those who had been given authority to judge. And I saw the souls of those who had been beheaded because of their testimony about Jesus and because of the word of God. They had not worshiped the beast or its image and had not received its mark on their foreheads or their hands. They came to life and reigned with Christ <u>a thousand years</u>. (5) (The rest of the dead did not come to life until <u>the thousand years</u> were ended.) This is the first resurrection. (6) Blessed and holy are those who share in the first resurrection. The second death has no power over them, but they will be priests of God and of Christ and will reign with him for <u>a thousand years</u>.**
>
> **(7) When <u>the thousand years</u> are over, Satan will be released from his prison (8) and will go out to**

deceive the nations in the four corners of the earth—Gog and Magog—and to gather them for battle. In number they are like the sand on the seashore. (9) They marched across the breadth of the earth and surrounded the camp of God's people, the city he loves. But fire came down from heaven and devoured them. (10) And the devil, who deceived them, was thrown into the lake of burning sulfur, where the beast and the false prophet had been thrown. They will be tormented day and night for ever and ever.

Revelation 20:1-10

The sequence of events is as follows: **1.** After the Tribulation the devil will be seized and locked in the Abyss for a thousand years. As such, he will *not* be able to deceive the nations, which suggests that all demonic entities will be powerless over people during the Millennium. **2.** The third stage of the first resurrection takes place wherein martyred believers will be bodily resurrected and reign with Christ for a thousand years. Other passages show that mortal believers will not receive their glorified bodies, but will enter the Millennium as mortals (Isaiah 65:20-25). We'll consider why momentarily. **3.** Glorified believers will be priests of God and will reign with Christ during the Millennium. Such believers will not be able to propagate because, as Jesus taught, "they will neither marry nor be given in marriage... for they are like the angels" (Luke 20:34-36). **4.** At the end of the Millennium Satan is released and immediately deceives the nation, inciting a mass attack on the righteous government of Christ in Jerusalem. **5.** The rebellion is easily defeated and the devil is cast into the lake of fire forever.

Those who deny a literal thousand-year reign of Christ on this earth argue that Revelation is full of symbols and therefore the millennial reign is symbolic of one thing or another. While it's true that Revelation contains a lot of symbolism, the symbols are usually interpreted. For instance, the first chapter of Revelation speaks of seven stars and seven golden lampstands, which Jesus later explains are seven designated angels and seven churches of Asia Minor (verse 20).

Another example of symbolism from Revelation 1 can be observed in verse 16 where a sharp, double-edged sword is said to be coming out of Jesus' mouth. Since this is obviously a symbolic statement, what does the symbolism refer to? Ephesians 6:17 shows that it's a reference to the Word of God. Scripture interprets Scripture.

Secondly, not everything in Revelation is symbolic. After all, Is Jesus Christ symbolic? Is God symbolic? Heaven? The earth? John?

So how do we know the "thousand-years" *isn't* symbolic? Several reasons: **1.** There's nothing about the phrase "the thousand years" that would indicate it's figurative as is the case with the sharp sword coming out of Jesus' mouth. In other words, you don't interpret something allegorically when there's no indication in the passage or elsewhere that it's non-literal. **2.** Nowhere does the book of Revelation say that the "thousand years" refer to something altogether different, like it does with the seven stars and seven churches in 1:20. **3.** Since there's no interpretation of what the "thousand years" refer to then it must refer to—you guessed it—a thousand years! **4.** Lastly, notice that I underlined "thousand years" six times in verses 2-7 above. Keep in mind that, while this is John's vision, it's actually the "revelation of Jesus Christ" *to* John via the vision he's given (Revelation 1:1). The point? **The Lord stresses six times in six verses that there will be a thousand year reign of Christ on this earth.** What more do we need to know that Jesus is referring to a literal thousand years? It goes without saying that anyone who uses theological mumbo jumbo to say that there *won't* be a literal Millennium is getting precariously close to "taking words away" from this divine prophecy (Revelation 22:18-19).

With the understanding that a literal Millennium is scriptural, what distinguishes it from the eternal age of the new heavens and new earth? Several things, including:

1. While believers with glorified bodies will reign with Christ during the Millennium, there will be nations of mortal people who will breed throughout the thousand years. These people are the "sheep" and their ensuing offspring that Jesus allows to enter the Millennium after the Judgment of Living Nations detailed in Matthew 25:31-46.[23] The "sheep" are promised eternal life and are allowed to enter the

---

[23] Also called the Sheep and Goat Judgment or the Pre-Millennial Judgment of Christ.

Millennium—as mortals—because they assisted believers during the Tribulation, which would include the 144,000 Jewish evangelists and their innumerable converts. These mortals will breed throughout the thousand years all over the world and, despite the completely righteous government of Christ, many of these will be susceptible to the devil's deception when he's released from the Abyss at the end of the Millennium to "deceive the nations in the four corners of the earth" (Revelation 20:7-8). Thankfully, this won't be the case in the eternal age-to-come because there won't be any mortals with ungodly natures.

2. While life during the Millennium will be a veritable utopia compared to our current age because of **1.** the righteous government of Christ and **2.** the absence of the devil and his filthy spirits to deceive people, there will still be sin because mortals will still have sinful natures, which explains why many of them will be open prey to Satan's deceptions when he's released from the Abyss. There will also be aging, pain and death. Not to mention the earth and universe will yet be burdened by the bondage to decay, which is entropy.

3. Lastly, the function of glorified believers during the Millennium will be focused on assisting the King of kings as priests of God, reigning in love over the nations of the earth (Revelation 20:6). While this is wonderful, it's a limited purpose compared to the literally universal scope of eternal life detailed in the Epilogue.

There are other differences, of course, but these are the most obvious.

God's Purpose for the Millennium

Finally, what's the purpose of the Millennium? Some answer this by saying that the Millennium is the fulfillment of Scripture prophecy in that promises to Israel, the church and Jesus Christ will be fulfilled. While this is true it doesn't satisfactorily answer the root question: What is God's actual purpose for the Millennium? I've heard it said that the Millennium is a transitional phase between this present evil age (Galatians 1:4) and the eternal righteous age-to-come (Luke 18:29-30).

While this is also true (not to mention obvious) it still doesn't answer the root question.

Hal Lindsey offers a fascinating explanation: The Millennium is the LORD's irrefutable proof to humanity that the religion of secular humanism is a lie. As you may or may not know, secular humanism is atheistic in nature and therefore anti-God. To those who embrace this godless religion there's no sin problem because there's no God with whom to sin against. To them, the problem of evil isn't humanity's sin nature and alienation from our Creator, but rather a negative environment. As such, they believe evil, crime, poverty, war and other ailments will largely be eradicated when the right government is in place and every person is provided an education, a decent job, a nice living environment, protection from crime, and so on. While these things are good they don't actually remedy the sin problem or reconcile people to their Creator. After all, a white collar man living in a rich suburb is still perfectly able to commit fraud due to a greedy heart, not to mention be a drunkard, drug addict, wife-beater, slanderer, hypocrite, adulterer, murderer, blowhard, oppressor, porn addict or practicing homosexual.

In the Millennium the LORD is going to provide nations of mortals the perfect government and environment—a veritable worldwide utopia. Since Jesus will be the King over all the earth and his assistants will be glorified believers who don't have a sin nature there will be zero corruption in the government (imagine that!). Yet as the population increases over the course of the Millennium many of the offspring of the original "sheep" will just go through the motions of being faithful to Christ while their hearts aren't in it. This is legalism—putting on the airs of godliness without the heart of godliness. Because legalism is an "outward job" it's decidedly inauthentic. As such, when the devil is unleashed at the end of the thousand years these covert rebels will naturally embrace the lies of the kingdom of darkness and unite for war in an insane attempt to take over the completely righteous government of Christ!

Of course the rebellion is quickly quelled (Revelation 20:9) and, after the Great White Throne Judgment, the eternal age of the new heavens and new earth will manifest (Revelation 21-22).

So the Millennium is the Most High's eternal showcase in disproving the religion of secular humanism. Chew on that!

The Resurrection of Old Testament Saints from Sheol

NOTE: This section involves a technical issue and is therefore recommended only for detail-oriented readers. All others are encouraged to jump to the next chapter.

In regards to the resurrection of holy people from periods preceding the resurrection of Christ, what evidence is there that righteous people of the Old Testament era were—or will be—resurrected from Sheol and when will their bodily resurrection take place? Or does their soulish resurrection from Sheol take place at the same time as their bodily resurrection?

Amazingly, *many* Old Testaments saints were resurrected from Sheol when Jesus was resurrected:

> **And when Jesus had cried out again in a loud voice, he gave up his spirit.**
>
> **(51) At that moment the curtain of the temple was torn in two from top to bottom. The earth shook, the rocks split (52) and the tombs broke open. <u>The bodies of many holy people who had died were raised to life</u>. (53) <u>They came out of the tombs after Jesus' resurrection and went into the holy city and appeared to many people</u>.**
>
> **Matthew 27:50-53**

These holy people were "raised to life" and came out of their tombs, just like Lazarus when Jesus raised him from the dead (John 11:11-44). These saints were raised from Sheol—death—which is why it says they were "raised to life" and not "they were raised from life with father Abraham in the paradise compartment of Sheol." Again we see that this bizarre belief of righteous people consciously dwelling with Abraham in a blissful section of Sheol makes utter nonsense of the Scriptures, which shows that Jesus' tale of the Rich man and Lazarus is a *parable*—a figurative story—and not a literal depiction of the nature of Sheol (see Chapter Eight).

I bring up Matthew 27:52-53 to plainly show that "many" Old Testament saints were resurrected from Sheol when Jesus was resurrected. This was a temporary resurrection, of course, in that they'd have to sooner or later physically die again, but **they would never again have to go to Sheol since Jesus was resurrected for our justification and ascended to heaven forty days later.**

Since these holy people who were resurrected from Sheol went to heaven when they later physically died, like all new covenant believers, what about the rest of the Old Testament saints held captive to death in Sheol? Asked another way, if Jesus delivered "many" righteous people from Sheol when he was resurrected what about when he ascended? Would he deliver the rest of them then—taking their souls directly to heaven with him (like believers' souls go straight to heaven when they die, as proven in Chapter Ten)?

This is why I leave room for the *possibility* that Jesus resurrected the Old Testament Saints from Sheol when he ascended to heaven forty days after his resurrection. Here's potential support for this:

> **But to each one of us grace has been given as Christ apportioned it. (8) This is why it says:**
> **"When he ascended on high, he took many captives and gave gifts to his people."**
> **(9) (What does "he ascended" mean except that he also descended to the lower, earthly regions? (10) He who descended is the very one who ascended higher than all the heavens, in order to fill the whole universe.)**
>
> **Ephesians 4:7-10**

Although this passage might refer to Jesus resurrecting righteous "captives" of Sheol when he ascended, there are a couple of other possibilities.

For instance, the "captives" in verse 8 *could* be referring to vanquished evil spirits whom Jesus brought to heaven in a victory parade. To explain, generals back then would bring their defeated enemies to Rome and parade them around the streets as the people cheered and mocked. This is the visual we get from Colossians 2:15 with

Jesus' victory over the powers of darkness through his crucifixion and resurrection. With this in mind, observe the Amplified Bible's rendering of verse 8: "When He ascended on high, He led captivity captive [He led a train of vanquished foes]". Please keep in mind, however, that when words appear in brackets in the Amplified version it's the author's *opinion* and not the Word of God, scholarly though it may be. As such, the Amplified Bible is a paraphrase. Regardless, this is a possibility we need to keep in mind.

Another possibility is that the captives in this passage simply refer to all believers who die after Jesus ascends to heaven and who essentially "follow him up," which corresponds to the biblical evidence contained in Chapter Ten.

If the souls of Old Testament saints were not resurrected to heaven when Jesus ascended and aren't resurrected at some other point, we can be sure that they'll be resurrected at the time of their bodily resurrection when the Lord returns to the earth to establish his millennial reign, which takes place at the end of the Tribulation, as shown in the following two passages:

> **"At that time Michael, the great prince who protects your people, will arise. There will be a time of distress such as has not happened from the beginning of nations until then. But at that time your people—everyone whose name is found written in the book—will be delivered. (2) Multitudes who sleep in the dust of the earth will awake: some to everlasting life, others to shame and everlasting contempt."**
>
> **Daniel 12:1-2**

Daniel prophesies that the resurrection of the Israelites will not take place until after a "time of distress" so great that such a thing never occurred before in the history of humanity. This refers to the Tribulation detailed in the book of Revelation (chapters 6-19). Daniel speaks in general terms of the righteous who will be delivered or resurrected at this time. He refers to them as "your people"—i.e. God's people—and **"everyone whose name is found written in the book,"** which would of course include more than just old Testament holy people; it would include Christian martyrs during the Tribulation, as well as living believers.

Jesus gets more specific about the resurrection of Old Testament saints at the end of the Tribulation in this passage:

> **Jesus said to them, "Truly I tell you, at the renewal of all things, when the Son of Man sits on his glorious throne, you who have followed me will also sit on twelve thrones, <u>judging the twelve tribes of Israel</u>. (29) And everyone who has left houses or brothers or sisters or father or mother or wife or children or fields for my sake will receive a hundred times as much and will inherit eternal life. (30) But many who are first will be last, and many who are last will be first."**
>
> **Matthew 19:28-30**

Some might inquire why Old Testament saints are not resurrected at the time of Jesus' return for his church—that is, the Rapture—which is when believers are bodily resurrected or translated (1 Thessalonians 4:13-18), but this idea is negated by the obvious fact that the Rapture concerns the Lord's return for his church—his bride—and not his return for holy people of the Old Testament period.

If Ephesians 4:8 *is* referring to Jesus delivering holy souls from Sheol when he ascended, some people inevitably argue that they're not shown ascending with Jesus, as seen in this passage:

> **After he said this, he was taken up before their very eyes, and a cloud hid him from their sight.**
>
> **(10) They were looking intently up into the sky as he was going, <u>when suddenly two men dressed in white stood beside them</u>. (11) "Men of Galilee," they said, "why do you stand here looking into the sky? This same Jesus, who has been taken from you into heaven, will come back in the same way you have seen him go into heaven."**
>
> **Acts 1:9-11**

If holy people were rescued from Sheol—death—when Jesus ascended, the reason they wouldn't be seen by witnesses in this passage is because it wasn't a bodily resurrection, but rather a soulish one. As such, they naturally *couldn't* be seen by people on earth. Their souls would've been resurrected from Sheol and gone straight to heaven just like the many holy people who were resurrected when Jesus died would also go to heaven when they eventually physically perished.

Now, notice something interesting about the above passage: Verse 10 shows "two men" suddenly appearing to the disciples and speaking to them. Who were these two men? I suppose this could be a reference to two non-descript angels but, if so, they wouldn't likely be designated as "men" in the text. Who were they? Perhaps Moses & Elijah who appeared to Jesus and the three disciples on the mountain.

Incidentally, Moses & Elijah are almost certainly the two prophets who will appear during the second half of the 7-year Tribulation period, detailed in Revelation 11:1-13. What evidence is there that these witnesses were Moses & Elijah? Verse 6 plainly says that these prophets "have power to shut up the heavens so that it will not rain during the time they are prophesying; and they have power to turn the waters into blood and to strike the earth with every kind of plague as often as they want." This is evidence that these prophets were Elijah & Moses since it was Elijah who miraculously stopped the rain (James 5:17) and Moses who turned the Nile River into blood (Exodus 7:20). For further evidence, Elijah stopped the rain for three and a half years and this was the same amount of time the two prophets will be functioning during the Tribulation.

Another objection to the possibility that the souls of Old Testament saints were resurrected when Jesus ascended is this passage where Peter addresses a crowd in Jerusalem shortly after Christ's ascension:

> **"Fellow Israelites, I can tell you confidently that the patriarch David died and was buried, and his tomb is here to this day... (34) For David did not ascend to heaven... "**
>
> **Acts 2:29, 34**

All this passage says is that David died and was buried in a tomb and that he did not ascend to heaven, but Peter was technically referring to the general time of David's death and not to the time of Christ's ascension. As for David's tomb, it would remain unchanged even if his soul ascended to heaven at the time of Jesus' ascension.

Regardless, the theory that the souls of Old Testament saints were resurrected from Sheol at the time of the ascension of Christ is just that—a theory—a *possibility* based on scant evidence. Please keep this in mind. If the theory isn't true then both their souls and bodies will be resurrected when Jesus returns to the earth at the end of the Tribulation.

Chapter Twelve

CONCLUSION ON SHEOL,
the Intermediate State

The most amazing thing about Sheol (Hades) is how blatantly obvious God's Word is on the topic. The truth about Sheol isn't hidden whatsoever, but people have been hindered from seeing it due to the power of religious tradition and sectarian allegiance.

To illustrate how "blatantly obvious" the Bible is on Sheol, let's recap the highlights from each chapter and then conclude. For details on any point simply go to the chapter in question. If you're not interested in reading the highlights just jump to the final section.

What is Sheol? (The Two Basic Views)

In <u>Chapter One</u> we discovered that there are two basic views of Sheol:

1. Unrighteous souls in Sheol are in a state of constant torment desperately yearning for less than a drop of water for relief, which won't be granted, while righteous souls hang out with father Abraham in a "paradise" compartment. These two compartments are separated by a great chasm.

2. Souls in Sheol lack God's breath of life and therefore lie dead until their resurrection. For the unrighteous this resurrection will take place after Christ's thousand-year reign on earth at the White Throne Judgment where "Anyone whose name was not found written in the book of life [will be] thrown into the lake of fire;" "the lake of fire is the second death" where the unrepentant will suffer "everlasting destruction," as Paul described it (Revelation 20:11-15 & 2 Thessalonians 1:9).

The sole biblical verification for the first position is a literal interpretation of Jesus' tale about the rich man and beggar. The second position, by contrast, is supported by literally hundreds of plain passages, as this study has shown, including the LORD's own descriptions.

We also saw that both wicked and righteous souls alike went to Sheol in periods preceding the resurrection of Christ. When Jesus was resurrected from the dead justification was made available for the repentant.

We further discovered that a lot of misunderstanding about Sheol can be traced to the translators of the influential King James Bible who subscribed to the curious practice of translating the Hebrew word Sheol as "hell" when it applied to wicked people and as "grave" when it applied to righteous people. In other words, their rendering of 'Sheol' in the KJV was determined purely by whether the passage referred to the wicked or the righteous. Scholars agree that there is simply no justification for this lack of uniformity in translating Sheol.

Jacob, Job & Solomon's View of Sheol

In Chapter Two we observed how these three great men from the Old Testament viewed Sheol, summarized as follows:

1. Sheol is a condition that every spiritually un-regenerated person will experience immediately following physical decease, which included godly men and women in Old Testament periods preceding the ascension of Christ. It includes the rich and the poor, the small and the great, the pure and the profane. In other words, **Sheol is the**

common destiny of anyone who is spiritually dead to God and therefore un-redeemed.

2. Sheol is a condition of **unconsciousness, likened unto sleep**, where there is no work, thought or knowledge of any kind. **It is not a place or state of conscious suffering and misery** and it is likened to sleep because everyone will one day be resurrected—i.e. "awoken"—from there, which explains the third point...

3. Sheol is a **temporary condition** and all consigned to Sheol will ultimately be **resurrected**.

Sheol in the Book of Psalms, Part I

In Chapter Three we observed a number of enlightening things about Sheol from the Psalms:

- David and others, like Hezekiah, equated Sheol with **death** and described it as **a place (or condition) where a person couldn't remember or praise God**.

- Other passages from the Psalms reveal Sheol to be a "**land of silence**" where souls "**lie silent**" rather than cry out in torment for a tiny bit of water or enjoy blissful communion with father Abraham.

- Other verses in the Psalms describe Sheol as a "Pit" in the underworld, derived from the Hebrew *bowr*, which can also be translated as "well," "cistern" or "dungeon." As such, Sheol is **the well of dead souls** or **dungeon** in the underworld where lifeless souls 'await' resurrection. It's the immaterial graveyard of souls.

- Elsewhere we discovered that **Sheol is a condition of the human soul—the mind**—and not of the spirit or body.

- Amazingly, we even discovered that the unrighteous are "**appointed for Sheol**" "**like sheep**" and explored the theological ramifications of such a statement.

- Lastly we observed David declaring that the LORD would "ransom" his soul from Sheol and take him to Him. 'Ransom' means to "redeem the captive." This shows that righteous souls would ultimately be resurrected from Sheol at some point after Jesus' resurrection wherein justification for the repentant was acquired.

Sheol in the Book of Psalms, Part II

In Chapter Four we continued looking at Sheol in the book of Psalms and explored many questions, like: Why would David pray for his ex-buddy to go to Sheol if, in fact, it was a fiery subterranean torture chamber?

We also explored the biblical metaphor of "sleep" to describe the condition of dead souls in Sheol, which was a figure of speech even Jesus used to describe people who passed away. We discovered why this metaphor is used and that it differentiates Sheol, the first death, from the lake of fire or Gehenna, which is the second death (Revelation 20:6,14, 21:8 & 2:11): **Everyone will be resurrected from the first death (Sheol), but no one will be resurrected from the second death (Gehenna)**. This is why the second death is described as an **"eternal** punishment" (Matthew 25:46) or **"everlasting** destruction" (2 Thessalonians 1:9) because there is no hope of recovery or resurrection from it—it's a fatal destruction of such complete and final magnitude that it lasts forever and ever. Sheol, the first death—by contrast—is a **temporary condition** from which every soul will be "awoken;" that is, resurrected.

Sheol in the Book of Proverbs

In Chapter Five we explored the nature of Sheol as detailed in the book of Proverbs and discovered a number of things:

- Sheol and death are synonymous concepts in that unredeemed people who die go to Sheol and experience the condition of death, the state of non-being. **The God-breathed Scriptures repeatedly equate Sheol with death and destruction, not fiery conscious torture**.

- Sheol is a condition **to be avoided as long as possible**, which utterly contradicts the position that righteous souls go to Sheol and become bosom buddies with Abraham in some nether-paradise.
- Sheol is never satisfied with its increasing population of dead souls, yet it will one day stop receiving souls, and every lifeless resident there will be resurrected to face judgment; in fact, Sheol itself—that is, "Hades"—will ultimately be thrown into the lake of fire, as shown in Revelation 20:11-15.

The Prophets and Sheol

In Chapter Six we looked at what the prophets had to say about the nature of Sheol, including the longest and most detailed passage on the subject where the LORD himself describes the nature of Sheol in explicit terms of death, not perpetual conscious roasting or blissful comfort with Abraham. As such, this passage coincides with the multitude of other biblical texts that describe Sheol in clear terms of death—the graveyard of dead souls in the nether realm.

We took note that the LORD Himself—YHWH—was speaking in this long passage, as well as a few other texts, and God described Sheol in explicit words of death, which disproves the unsound theory of "progressive revelation." This theory was concocted by advocates of eternal torture in order to unsoundly write off the multitudes of passages that support Sheol being what it is: The soulish graveyard in the heart of the earth.

The erroneous theory of "progressive revelation" is based on the idea that there was an evolution of understanding concerning Sheol and that Jesus' story of the rich man and beggar is the culminating revelation. We observed that this desperate theory can be discarded for a number of reasons: **1.** There is no "evolution of understanding" concerning Sheol in the Bible; all the myriad passages point to Sheol being the **realm of the dead** in the nether-realm where dead souls "rest" in death "awaiting" their resurrection. Only a literal reading of Jesus' Parable of the Rich Man and Lazarus contradicts these other passages. **2.** God Himself is speaking in the longest, most detailed passage on Sheol in the Bible, not to mention three other passages, and what he says corresponds to the position that Sheol is the graveyard of dead souls in the underworld where unredeemed souls lie dead. Does the LORD need "progressive revelation" on the nature of Sheol or did he always know precisely what it is and the state of souls there? **3.** All the evidence points to Jesus' tale being a parable—a symbolic story—not a literal account of life in Sheol, which is further proven in Chapter Eight.

Various Biblical Descriptions of Sheol/Hades

In Chapter Seven we looked at some enlightening Old Testament descriptions of Sheol, such as it being contrasted with the "land of the living." If life on earth is the land of the living then it naturally follows that Sheol is the land of the dead, which is precisely how the Bible defines it—"the realm of the dead."

We also saw how Sheol is often paralleled with the physical grave or tomb; and also dust, which is what corpses revert to. It goes without saying that graves, tombs and dust signify death, not fiery conscious torture.

One of the most informative descriptions of souls in Sheol is that of being "no more," meaning they don't exist in any conscious sense whatsoever.

Another enlightening description is that of souls being "gathered to his people" or "resting with his fathers," the latter being used in reference to the wickedest kings of Israel and Judah. If Sheol is a state of roasting torment for the unrighteous then surely these thoroughly wicked kings would suffer accordingly, but that's not what the Bible teaches. Their dead souls went to Sheol and simply "rested with their fathers" until their resurrection and judgment in the distant future.

Jesus' Parable of the Rich Man and Lazarus

In Chapter Eight we examined Jesus' imaginative tale of the rich man and beggar and discovered that it's clearly a symbolic story—a fantastical parable—and not a literal account of two men in Sheol after they die. For one thing, it comes in a long line of parables and opens with *the same exact words as the previous parable.* Secondly, it clearly uses fantastical and symbolic language. Thirdly, if taken literal it contradicts what the entire rest of the Bible details about the nature of Sheol, including Yahweh's very own unmistakable descriptions (!). Fourthly, the tale is a classic reversal of fortunes story that mimics the Pharisee's Hellenistic belief in the immortality of the soul apart from redemption in Christ. Fifthly, it rebukes the corruption of the legalistic Judaic leaders, including the Pharisees' greed. And, sixthly, it amazingly symbolizes the main theme of the New Testament—the end of the old covenant and the beginning of the new wherein the Gentiles have access to spiritual riches through the gospel while unrepentant Hebrews languish in unbelief.

The New Testament and Sheol/Hades

In <u>Chapter Nine</u> we explored numerous direct and indirect references to Sheol in the New Testament and found nothing that contradicts the Old Testament position. In fact, we saw how over and over again the New Testament explicitly says that **Jesus died** for our sins and was **raised to life** for our justification, often in every chapter.

Interestingly, with all these references to Christ's death there's mysteriously zero mention of Jesus being conscious in Sheol (Hades), whether hanging out with Abraham in bliss or suffering constant roasting torture without a bit of water for relief. No, the Messiah *died* and his dead soul was in the "heart of the earth" for three days before being miraculously resurrected for our justification. The "heart of the earth" is a reference to Sheol, which is the "pit" in the underworld where dead souls are housed until their resurrection.

Furthermore, when Mary and Martha's brother, Lazarus, died Jesus plainly said he was "sleeping" in death, not hanging out in paradise with Abraham, not to mention when Lazarus was raised to life absolutely nothing is said about his being raised from this curious "paradise compartment" of Sheol. Why? Because it's a false doctrine. It's the same thing with the death and resurrection of Jairus' daughter, detailed in the three synoptic gospels.

The Believer's Intermediate State

In <u>Chapter Ten</u> we looked at the believer's intermediate state between physical death and bodily resurrection and saw that the souls of believers do not die—that is, go to Sheol—because they're born-again of the imperishable seed (sperm) of Christ by the power of the Holy Spirit. As such, death—Sheol—has no power over believers and they consequently go straight to be with the Lord in heaven to serve and await their bodily resurrection, which takes place at the Lord's return for his church, i.e. the Rapture.

The fact that believers are alive in heaven in a disembodied state awaiting their bodily resurrection is so blatantly detailed in the New Testament that it's baffling some people argue otherwise. This just goes to show the power of tradition and denominational bias—they override plain Scripture when there's a contradiction, no matter how obvious the truth.

Resurrection from Sheol

In <u>Chapter Eleven</u> we saw that unredeemed souls will be resurrected from Sheol to face the Great White Throne Judgment. If anyone's name is not found in the book of life he or she will be cast into the lake of fire to suffer the "second death."

As for the souls of Old Testament righteous people, we amazingly discovered that many of these were resurrected back to temporal life on earth when Jesus was resurrected. When they eventually physically died their souls, as believers, would go to heaven with the promise of a future bodily resurrection, as is the case with all believers. As for other Old Testament saints, they will be resurrected and judged when Jesus returns to the earth to establish his millennial kingdom, although I leave room for the *possibility* that their souls were resurrected from Sheol and ascended to heaven when Christ ascended.

We also discovered that the resurrection of the righteous, called the "first resurrection," takes place in *stages* corresponding to the allegory of a biblical harvest—firstfruits, general harvest and gleanings. Jesus was the "firstfruits," while the Rapture refers to the main harvest and gleanings refer to the resurrection of Old Testament saints and Tribulation martyrs, not to mention any righteous people who die during the Millennium.

Conclusion on Sheol (Hades)

This study proves beyond any shadow of doubt that Sheol is not a place of conscious existence in the nether-realm where people are either tormented in flames crying out for a tiny bit of water or, if they're righteous, in a nether paradise chummin' around with father Abraham. This ludicrous error can be traced to a literal interpretation of Jesus' parable of the rich man and beggar, which contradicts the entire rest of the Bible. The very fact that a literal interpretation of this tale is at variance with the rest of the Bible shows that it was never meant to be taken literally, but rather figuratively.

God's Word overwhelmingly supports the view that Sheol is the world of the dead in the nether realm where dead souls lie in death 'awaiting' their resurrection. In other words, it's the graveyard of dead souls. This is so blatantly obvious in Scripture it's a wonder that so few Christians see it, but this explains the power of religious tradition and sectarian allegiance. When unrighteous souls are eventually resurrected from Sheol they will be judged and "Anyone whose name is not found written in the book of life [will be] thrown into the lake of fire" "The lake of fire is **the second death**" (Revelation 20:11-15).

It goes without saying that making sure your name is written in the Lamb's book of life is of the **utmost importance**. Any other earthly pursuit, no matter how important, is like playing trivial pursuit by comparison.

Amen and Praise God!

Epilogue

ETERNAL LIFE:
What Will It Be Like?

I think it's only fitting that this two-part study on human damnation—*Hell Know* and *Sheol Know*—should close on a positive note by looking at what the Bible says about eternal life in the new heavens and new earth, traditionally referred to as "heaven." Allow me to breach the topic in an unconventional way by referencing something most of us are familiar with, even if it's just a little bit.

One invigorating aspect of science fiction shows, films and books is the exciting notion that humankind will one day be able to explore the vast expanses of the universe. I don't know about you, but when I look up into the night sky and see the vast starry panorama I am filled with awe and reverence! Is it possible that we will one day be able to explore and inhabit the incalculable planets and solar systems in our galaxy and beyond as these sci-fi works hypothesize?

The Incredible Size of the Universe

Most people don't realize how incredibly vast the universe really is; it's beyond our finite comprehension. To get an idea consider these mind-blowing comparisons: If the thickness of one sheet of paper represented the distance from the Earth to the sun—93 million miles— the distance to the nearest star would be represented by a stack of paper *71 feet high;* and the diameter of our Milky Way galaxy would be represented by a stack of paper *310 miles high!* To reach the edge of the known universe would take a stack *31 million miles high!*

Or consider these awe-inspiring facts: The sun is so huge that if it were hollow, it could hold *1 million earths!* The star Antares could contain *64 million suns!* There's a star in the constellation Hercules that could contain *100 million 'Antares!'* And the largest known star, Epilson, could easily contain *several million stars the size of the star in the constellation Hercules!* (Kirkwood 374-375).

Sci-fi visionaries like Gene Roddenberry postulate that humanity will one day unite together in mutual acceptance and respect to peaceably explore and inhabit these unfathomable reaches of space. This is all well & good and certainly explains part of the appeal of space-exploring fictional works, but their grand vision is glaringly tainted...

The Shortcomings of Sci-Fi Visionaries

As hopeful and exciting as the future of humanity is depicted by sci-fi luminaries, it's a far cry from paradise. The shortcomings are plainly observed in these shows, movies and novels all over their fictional galaxies: hostility, violence, war, disease, evil, aging and death; not to mention more trifling ailments like arrogance, envy, jealousy, prejudice and lust. These maladies are shown to be universal—literally— to the human condition in these fictional works. No matter how many light years we travel, we cannot escape that which is intrinsic to human nature, which brings to mind the saying "wherever you go, there you are."

Yet, could you imagine a future for humanity without such maladies? Could you imagine exploring and inhabiting the vast expanses of the universe without ever experiencing hostility, war, disease, evil, aging or death? Could you imagine living *forever* and *never* running out of exciting things to do on earth or in the furthest reaches of space?

Believe it or not, this is part of the magnificent hope that is envisioned for humanity as disclosed in the biblical Scriptures. Yes, a much grander vision of humanity's future was written thousands of years *before* modern science fiction works. The reason I relate the Christian notion of eternal life to sci-fi visionaries is because I think these people sense on some instinctual level humankind's calling and blessing. What am I talking about? I'm talking about the nature of eternal life in the everlasting age-to-come, as revealed in the Scriptures.

A New Earth and Universe

The Bible teaches that God will one day create "a new heaven and new earth" where there will be "no more death or mourning or crying or pain, for the old order of things has passed away" (Revelation 21:1-4). "Heaven" in this context refers to the physical universe and not to what is commonly understood as 'heaven;' that is, the spiritual dimension where God dwells. You see, the sky and universe are often referred to as "heaven" or "the heavens" in the Bible; for example, Psalm 19:1 states: "The **heavens** declare the glory of God; **the skies** proclaim the work of his hands." This is an example of Hebrew poetry known as synonymous parallelism where the second part of the verse simply repeats the first part in different words. In this case, "the heavens" in the first part is confirmed as "the skies" in the second. The context of the passage will determine the proper definition, which is the hermeneutical rule "context is king."[24]

God's heaven—which is referred to as "the *third* heaven" in Scripture (2 Corinthians 12:2)—is perfect and has no reason to be made new. It's the earth and the physical universe that will be made new— "new" in the sense that the maladies of evil, death, pain, disease and decay will be forever eradicated. As declared in Romans 8:21: "the creation itself [the earth and universe and all living things] will be *liberated* from its bondage to decay and brought into the glorious *freedom* of the children of God." You see, God's goal is to ultimately *liberate* humanity, and the earth & universe as well, from our miserable confinement to decay, pain, aging and death, not to mention evil itself.

---

[24] See Chapter Nine of *Hell Know* for further info on the four rules of hermeneutics, the science of Bible interpretation.

Will We "Spend Eternity in Heaven"?

We've all heard it said that those blessed of God will "spend eternity in heaven." Whether this is true or not depends on your definition of heaven. If 'heaven' refers *exclusively* to the spiritual dimension where God's throne is located—that is, the spiritual realm that gave birth to our physical dimension—then the answer is no, we will not spend eternity in heaven. If, on the other hand, 'heaven' refers to what the Bible calls "the new heavens and new earth, the home of righteousness" (2 Peter 3:13) then, yes, we will spend eternity in heaven.

However, since **the phrase "spend eternity in heaven" is *not* found anywhere in Scripture**, I think it's important to stick to actual biblical expressions when discussing eternal life so there's no misunderstanding. After all, it's *the truth* that will set us free, not clichéd religious sayings.

This is especially important when you consider the fact that when 99.9% of people hear the term 'heaven' they automatically think of the blissful ethereal realm where angels dwell; and understandably so since that's its primary definition. As such, when they hear the phrase "spend eternity in heaven" they naturally think of living on a cloud playing a harp forever. There are two problems with this: **1.** It's not true and the problem with false beliefs is that they can't set people free; only the truth can set us free. **2.** Since error is incapable of setting us free it's incapable of giving us life. In other words, the truth will always excite and inspire the spiritual soul, whereas falsities do the precise opposite— they won't inspire us or excite us; in fact, they'll bore us, limit us or ruin us in one way or another. Why? Because truth equals life and freedom while error equals death and bondage. Consider, for example, the conventional imagery of eternal life—hanging out on a cloud playing a harp forever. Although this would surely be fun for a few days or weeks, we're talking about *eternity* here—forever and ever. Is this all we have to look forward to? If so, no wonder so few Christians are excited about the notion of eternal life. They find it *boring!*

Thankfully, the plain truth of God's Word is exhilarating and fascinating.

The New Jerusalem will come "Down out of Heaven from God"

Consider this example: We've all heard about the gates of heaven referred to as "the pearly gates;" yet in the Bible this is actually a description of the twelve gates of the new Jerusalem, a very large city that is presently in the spiritual realm of God, i.e. heaven (Revelation 21:21). Guess what ultimately happens to this city? After God recreates a new earth and universe, the new Jerusalem will come "down *out of heaven* from God." This is clearly stated *three times* in Scripture: Revelation 3:12 and 21:2 & 10. My point is that this awesome city will not stay in heaven; it will come down "out of heaven" to rest on the new earth. Who knows? It may even be able to hover over the planet and more, like traverse the galaxies (after all, it's going to travel from heaven to earth *intact*).

This city, the new earth and the entire new universe will be the eternal home of all those who partake of God's gift of eternal life. Note for yourself:

> **"Blessed are the meek for they will inherit the Earth."**
>
> **Matthew 5:5**

> **The righteous will inherit the land** [the earth] **and dwell in it forever.**
>
> **Psalm 37:29**

We clearly see here that the "meek" and the "righteous" will inherit the *earth* and dwell in it *forever*. This would naturally include the physical universe where the earth resides as well (more on this momentarily). My point is that humanity will inherit the new earth and universe as its **eternal home**. Notice what the Bible plainly states in this regard:

> **The highest heavens belong to the LORD, but the earth he has given to man.**
>
> **Psalm 115:16**

We see here that "the highest heavens" belong to God. This refers to the highest spiritual realm where God's throne is located, which, as previously noted, is called "the third heaven" in Scripture. Although, believers are indeed "seated... in the heavenly realms" in Christ in a *positional* sense (Ephesians 2:6), humankind will *not* inherit this highest heavens. This spiritual dimension belongs to God (which isn't to say that we can't visit there, etc.). What believers *will* inherit is the earth and the physical universe in which it resides. This is why Peter said redeemed men and women are to be "looking forward to a new heaven and new earth, the *home* of righteousness" (2 Peter 3:13). Once again, the "new heaven" in this text is referring to a new *physical universe* not the spiritual dimension where God's throne is located; although it *could* also be referring to a fusion of these two realms, a possibility we'll consider shortly.

Between Physical Death and Bodily Resurrection

Someone might understandably point out that Paul said "to be absent from the body is to be present with the Lord" (2 Corinthians 5:8), which is why he desired "to depart and be with Christ, which is far better" (Philippians 1:23). They cite these passages to argue that Christians go to heaven when they die. This is absolutely true. These passages and a few others (e.g. Revelation 6:9-11 & 7:9-17) refer to what theologians call the "intermediate state" of the Christian soul, which pertains to the state of the believer *after* physical death and *before* bodily resurrection. Clearly, the believer will be with the Lord in heaven in a conscious disembodied state, "before the throne of God" and serving him "day and night in his temple" (Revelation 7:15). This is covered in detail in Chapter Ten.

As you can see, there's *some* truth to this notion of "going to heaven" and being in the LORD's presence, but over the centuries it's been blown way out of proportion to the extent that the average Christian thinks eternal life is all about spending eternity in an incorporeal state in an ethereal dimension, reclining on a cloud playing a harp. The more one studies the God-breathed Scriptures, however, the more you realize this simply isn't true. The truth is so much more than that.

There are three important facts about the believer's intermediate state that should be emphasized:

1. **It's a *temporary* state**—only extending to the aforementioned bodily resurrection or "first resurrection," which takes place in stages, one at the time of Christ's return for his church (1 Thessalonians 4:13-18) and the other at the Lord's return to the earth (Revelation 20:4-6) and likely another at the end of the Millennium. This is covered in detail in Chapter Eleven.

2. **It's an *incomplete* state.** God purposely created the human soul/spirit to dwell in a body (Genesis 2:7, 1 Thessalonians 5:23, etc.). If the disembodied human soul/spirit is fine as is, that would naturally make the bodily resurrection unnecessary, to say the least.

3. Lastly, **the intermediate state of the Christian soul/spirit in heaven is *de-emphasized* in Scripture**. Other than the passages noted above, you won't read many references to the intermediate state in the Bible. The bodily resurrection and eternal life are more emphasized. For instance, in Acts 17:18 you'll notice that Paul preached "the good news of Jesus *and* the resurrection." You see, the resurrection is a fundamental part of the gospel of Christ. For Paul's "*hope in* the resurrection of the dead" he was put on trial (Acts 23:6). What was Paul's hope in? Not the temporary intermediate state, as wonderful as that will be, but the resurrection of the righteous where believers receive imperishable, glorified, powerful, spiritual bodies! Read it yourself in 1 Corinthians 15:42-44. More on this in a moment.

So, as wonderful as the believer's intermediate state between physical death and bodily resurrection will be, it's a *temporary* and *incomplete* state that's *de-emphasized* in Scripture, although not ignored. Other than serving in the Lord's presence in heaven in an incorporeal condition, we don't know much about it. It will be a glorious period, for sure, but the impression in Scripture is that this will be a time of anticipation—anticipating our bodily resurrection, anticipating reigning with Christ on this earth for a thousand years, and, of course, anticipating our everlasting inheritance of the "new heaven and new earth, the home of the righteous" and everything that involves (2 Peter 3:13).

Quality of Life in the New Earth and Universe

What does the Bible say about this *eternal* age? The quality of life in the new earth and universe will be wholly magnificent, to say the least.

Firstly, the new Jerusalem will be unimaginably huge and glorious: The city will be 1400 miles long and wide (Revelation 21:16). That's approximately the distance from New York to Wichita, Kansas. Can you imagine a city that big? It would take a trip of about 6000 miles just to travel around it! What's more, the magnificent golden buildings will extend up into space 1400 miles—these will be skyscrapers indeed! How would you like to live on the top floor?

Revelation 21 describes the city in some detail: The city walls will be made of jasper and will be *200 feet thick*. Each of the huge twelve gates will be made of *a single pearl*. (Where did such huge pearls come from? I don't know. All I can say is there must be a planet out there with some really *big* oysters). The main streets of the city will be of pure gold; in fact, the whole city itself will apparently be made of pure gold—so pure it's transparent!

Secondly, notice what the Bible says about our quality of life in the age-to-come:

> **Now the dwelling of God is with men, and he will live with them. They will be his people, and God Himself will be with them and be their God. (4) He will wipe every tear from their eyes. There will be no more death or mourning or crying or pain, for the old order of things has passed away.**
>
> **Revelation 21:3-4**

We see here that we will be able to see, talk to and walk with God Almighty face to face! This is in perfect harmony with what Jesus Christ said concerning the main characteristic of eternal life:

> **"For you** [Father God] **granted him** [Jesus] **authority over all people that he might give eternal**

life to all those you have given him. (3) Now this is eternal life: that they may know you, the only true God, and Jesus Christ whom you have sent."

John 17:2-3

Some suggest that Jesus was defining eternal life here, but this isn't true because 'eternal life' *means* "eternal life." That's its definition. In the Greek it's *aionios zoe (aay-OH-nee-us ZOH-aay)*, which literally means "age-lasting life" (*aion* is where we get the English 'eon', meaning "age"). Since the age-to-come is an eternal age scholars usually render *aionios* as "eternal;" hence, "eternal life." *Aionios zoe* could also be translated as "the life of the age to come." This is the "abundant" or "full" life Jesus said he came to give people in John 10:10.

Receiving this "life of the age to come" is a two-phase process:

1. Believers receive eternal life in their spirits at the point of spiritual regeneration, which is why John the Baptist said: "Whoever believes in the Son *has* eternal life [present tense], but whoever rejects the Son will not see life, for God's wrath remains on him" (John 3:36; see also 1 John 5:11-12). The fact that believers presently have the abundant life-of-the-age-to-come in their regenerated spirits reveals why it's so important that we learn to put off the "old self"—the flesh—and put on the "new self"—the spirit (Ephesians 4:22-24), meaning living (or walking) in the spirit, not in the flesh. When we do this, **we tap into that full life of God and are able to manifest it in this dark, dying, lost world**.

2. Attaining eternal life is completed at the resurrection of the righteous, which—again—occurs in stages, as shown in <u>Chapter Eleven</u>. This is when we'll receive new imperishable, glorified, powerful and spiritual bodies. The fact that the believer's eternal life is *completed* at the resurrection is confirmed by Jesus when he plainly said that believers will receive eternal life "**in** the age to come" (Mark 10:29-30). This is verified by other passages like Titus 1:2, 3:7 and Jude 21.

So, when Jesus said "Now this is eternal life: that they may know you," he wasn't defining the life-of-the-age-to-come, **he was**

emphasizing its most important quality, which is *knowing God*. Every believer can grow in this quality simply by tapping into the eternal life that's in our spirits, but we have to put off the flesh to do this; it's also necessary to "throw off" every weight or distraction that hinders (Hebrews 12:1). The Bible says, "Come near to God and he will come near to you" (James 4:8). Think about it: We can have as much of God as we want!

Getting back to Revelation 21:3-4, verse 4 plainly says that in the era of the new earth and universe there will be no more pain, crying, aging or death—all such maladies will have been eliminated! This makes perfect sense. After all, what good is paradise if one has to suffer pain, aging and death? The passage even says that God Himself will personally console us regarding the many pains, heartaches and injustices we've experienced in our lives in "this present evil age" (Galatians 1:4).

Thirdly, as noted above, the Bible promises new glorified and immortal bodies to those who accept God's gift of eternal life (1 Corinthians 15:42-54) and, although we cannot fully comprehend now how wondrous life will be in these new resurrection bodies, we can get an idea simply by observing what the Bible says about Jesus *after* his resurrection. After all, we're going to receive the same type of glorified body he did, that is, *if* you're a believer. In light of this, we'll evidently be able to walk through solid objects (John 20:26), instantly appear out of nowhere and disappear (Luke 24:31,36-37); in other words, we'll be able to *teleport* at will. With this understanding, we'll no doubt be able to take "quantum leaps" to anywhere on the new earth, moon, Mars or universe—*distances and space will no longer limit us.*

For those who argue that Christ is deity and therefore our glorified bodies may not have the same capacity as his, the Bible blatantly says that we are "*co-heirs* with Christ," which means 'joint heirs' or 'joint participants' (Romans 8:17). Besides, why would the LORD reveal to us the incredible abilities of the glorified body through Jesus' actions after his resurrection if He didn't intend for us to have the same incredible capacity when we're bodily resurrected?

Lastly, the text says that "the dwelling of God is with men, and he will live with them. They will be his people, and God Himself will be with them and be their God" (Revelation 21:3). Since "the dwelling of God" *is* heaven, this seems to suggest some kind of fusion between the spiritual realm (heaven) and the natural realm (earth and universe). As co-heirs with Christ, I'm sure we'll have access to both realms. So perhaps "spending eternity in heaven" is true in this sense.

There will be Nations and Kings on the New Earth

This passage provides additional insights about life in the eternal age-to-come:

> **I did not see a temple in the city, because the Lord God Almighty and the Lamb are its temple. (23) The city does not need the sun or the moon to shine on it, for the glory of God gives it light, and the Lamb is its lamp. (24) The nations will walk by its light, and the kings of the earth will bring their splendor into it. (25) On no day will its gates ever be shut, for there will be no night there (26) The glory and honor of the nations will be brought into it.**
>
> **Revelation 21:22-26**

The passage shows that there will be nations of peoples with kings over them on the new earth. The Greek word for "nations" is *ethnos (ETH-nos)*, meaning "a race, a people or a nation that shares a common and distinctive culture." In short, peoples on the new earth won't be look-alike drones under the supervision of the Most High. Variety is the spice of life, *Praise God!*

Plus there will be kings over these nations; that is, national authorities. And if there are national authorities there will be subordinate authorities, like governors of territories and mayors of cities and so on. Of course, there will also be authority structures in the vast new Jerusalem.

Who will be placed in these authority positions? This parable shows:

"Again, it will be like a man going on a journey, who called his servants and entrusted his wealth to them. (15) To one he gave five bags of gold, to another two bags, and to another one bag, each according to his ability. Then he went on his journey. (16) The man who had received five bags of gold went at once and put his money to work and gained five bags more. (17) So also, the one with two bags of gold gained two more. (18) But the man who had received one bag went off, dug a hole in the ground and hid his master's money.

(19) "After a long time the master of those servants returned and settled accounts with them. (20) The man who had received five bags of gold brought the other five. 'Master,' he said, 'you entrusted me with five bags of gold. See, I have gained five more.'

(21) "His master replied, 'Well done, good and faithful servant! <u>You have been faithful with a few things; I will put you in charge of many things</u>. Come and share your master's happiness!'

(22) "The man with two bags of gold also came. 'Master,' he said, 'you entrusted me with two bags of gold; see, I have gained two more.'

(23) "His master replied, 'Well done, good and faithful servant! <u>You have been faithful with a few things; I will put you in charge of many things</u>. Come and share your master's happiness!'

(24) "Then the man who had received one bag of gold came. 'Master,' he said, 'I knew that you are a hard man, harvesting where you have not sown and gathering where you have not scattered seed. (25) So I was afraid and went out and hid your gold in the ground. See, here is what belongs to you.'

(26) "His master replied, 'You wicked, lazy servant! So you knew that I harvest where I have not sown and gather where I have not scattered seed?

(27) Well then, you should have put my money on deposit with the bankers, so that when I returned I would have received it back with interest.

(28) "'So take the bag of gold from him and give it to the one who has ten bags. (29) <u>For whoever has will be given more</u>, and they will have an abundance. Whoever does not have, even what they have will be taken from them. (30) And throw that worthless servant outside, into the darkness, where there will be weeping and gnashing of teeth.'

Matthew 25:14-30

The Lord invests in every believer and expects a return on his investment when he returns. The two men in the story who doubled what was invested in them are praised by the master and told, "You have been faithful with a few things; I will put you in charge of many things." This is figurative of the judgment seat of Christ, which is the judgment believers undergo (2 Corinthians 5:10-11).[25]

Notice how a similar parable puts it:

"He was made king, however, and returned home. Then he sent for the servants to whom he had given the money, in order to find out what they had gained with it.

(16) "The first one came and said, 'Sir, your mina has earned ten more.'

(17) " 'Well done, my good servant!' his master replied. '<u>Because you have been trustworthy in a very small matter, take charge of ten cities</u>.'

(18) "The second came and said, 'Sir, your mina has earned five more.'

(19) "<u>His master answered, 'You take charge of five cities</u>.' "

Luke 19:15-19

---

[25] For more details on the judgment seat of Christ, also called the *bema* judgment, see the last section of *Hell Know* <u>Chapter Eight</u>.

The mina was a unit of currency worth three months' wages. The first man was given ten minas and earned ten more while the second man was given five minas and earned five more.

Notice what these men are rewarded with: The first one is put in charge of ten cities and the second five cities.

Both stories are figurative of the literal truth that believers will be rewarded according to what they do or don't do with the talents the Lord has invested in them. Those who are "faithful with a few things" will be "put you in charge of many things." The phrase "put in charge" indicates a position of authority; and the second parable specifies being put in charge of cities.

When and where will faithful believers be put in charge of "many things," including "cities"? On the new earth for sure, but other planets in the new universe as well (we'll look at scriptural support for this in the next section).

With this understanding, your faithfulness *now* with the few small things the Lord has put you in charge of has eternal ramifications! What has God put you in charge of? Several things: Your body, your mind (thoughts), your family, your job, your Christian service, your money, your talents and the people linked to you.

The Entire Universe will be Under Humanity's Control

It goes without saying that living on the paradise of the new earth will be utterly magnificent, but—and this is an important "but"—the new Jerusalem and new earth will only be our **home base**; in other words, *we'll be able to explore and inhabit the unfathomable reaches of the universe!*

We know this because, again, the Bible doesn't just encourage us to look forward to the new earth as our eternal home of righteousness, but **to the new heavens as well**, which refers to the new universe:

> **But in keeping with his promise <u>we are looking forward to a new heaven and a new earth</u>, the home of righteousness.**
>
> **2 Peter 3:13**

We are encouraged to look forward to the new universe because it's part of our eternal inheritance, just as much as the new earth is. In fact, the verse lists the new universe *first*, which gives the impression that we're to look forward to it even more than the new earth. Why? Because *the new earth is merely one planet in an incomprehensibly vast universe!*

Don't think for a second that God, our Almighty Creator, formed the incomprehensibly vast universe—the billions of galaxies and incalculable stars & planets for nothing. Be assured that the *whole universe* will be under humanity's subjection to explore, inhabit, rule, enjoy and who knows what else? As it is written:

> **For You (God) have put everything in subjection under his (humanity's) feet. Now in putting everything in subjection to man, He left nothing outside [of man's] control. But at present we do not yet see all things subjected to him [man].**
>
> **Hebrews 2:8** (The Amplified Bible)

"Everything" in the physical universe will be put in subjection to redeemed humanity; "everything" will be put in our control. It's interesting to note that 'everything' can also be translated as "the universe," which is how the Weymouth New Testament translates it. In other words, *nothing in the entire universe will be outside of our control.* As stated above, we will be able to explore, inhabit and rule the unfathomable reaches of the physical universe!

Remember, God originally blessed humankind to "be fruitful and multiply," to "subdue" and "have dominion" over all the earth:

> **And God BLESSED them, and said unto them, "Be fruitful, and multiply, and replenish the earth, and subdue it: and have dominion over the fish of the sea, and over the fowl of the air, and over every living thing that moveth upon the earth."**
>
> **Genesis 1:28** (KJV)

This blessing/directive is inherent in the psycho-spiritual DNA of humankind. There's no escaping it; it's our Divine mission; it's part of who we *are*. Unfortunately, the sin nature inevitably twists this blessing and it becomes a curse, resulting in abuse, slavery, wars, environmental raping, etc. Yet, this doesn't take away from the fact that the intrinsic blessing is wholly *good* and was intended to *empower* humanity to fulfill its Divine mandate—to be fruitful, multiply, replenish, subdue and take dominion. In other words, the LORD didn't create humankind to be servants of the earth, but to be lords over it, which is befitting since Father God is "Lord of heaven and earth," as Jesus Christ Himself acknowledged (Matthew 11:25). Keep in mind that humanity is created in God's image and believers are called to be "imitators of God" (Ephesians 5:1).

Before I go any further, I want to stress that the LORD doesn't want us to "subdue" and take "dominion" in a negative sense. I have to emphasize this since many people equate "dominion" with carnal control because the devil naturally tries to pervert whatever God creates, commands or blesses. God's mandate was to subdue and hold dominion in LOVE, because "God is love" (1 John 4:7-8,16). This helps make sense of this proverb:

Love and faithfulness keep a king safe;
through love his throne is made secure.
Proverbs 20:28

A "king" refers to an authority figure. In our day and age it would apply to anyone who has authority in any given environment: a father or mother, a teacher or professor, an employer or supervisor, a president or governor, a pastor or apostle, a police officer or security guard, etc. This proverb reveals the godly way of keeping one's position of authority—one's "throne"—safe and secure: Through love and faithfulness. So, when the Bible talks about "subduing" and taking "dominion" it's talking about doing so in love and faithfulness, not being an abusive tyrant. Are you with me?

Now, here's something interesting: The Garden of Eden was only about the size of California according to the specifications shown in Genesis. It was already a paradise, which is the way God created it, but the rest of the earth wasn't. The rest of the planet had potential, but it was untamed and uncultivated, which is why the LORD empowered humankind to subdue it and take dominion. In other words, God blessed humanity to make the rest of the planet the same paradise as that of the Garden of Eden, which is why Genesis 1:28 above twice stresses replenishing and subduing "the earth" and not the Garden of Eden since the latter was already replenished and subdued.

The paradise of the Garden of Eden was God's blueprint for humankind to expand on until the entire planet was a paradise. Once 'Project Earth' was complete they could go on to subdue and replenish every planet in the solar system, the galaxy, and ultimately the furthest reaches of the universe! Why do you think all those innumerable barren planets are there for? They're there for us to reach and subdue, in love and faithfulness. This is supported by Hebrews 2:8 above: God has placed *"everything"* in the natural universe in subjection to humanity— *"nothing"* is outside of redeemed humanity's control! Chew on that.

Doesn't this remind you of various science-fiction shows, films and books—humanity uniting together and going out to the furthest reaches of space to peaceably explore and inhabit? The visionaries of these sci-fi works are people created in God's image who instinctively grasp the Creator's blessing/directive because it's part of our spiritual DNA. The significant difference in the biblical model is that there will be no pain, hostility, war, disease, aging or death, not to mention the presence of the Almighty. All humanity will truly be united together in love, mutual respect and acceptance under the perfectly just govern-ship of the Creator of All.

Aging and death are the ailments that taint the optimistic visions of these sci-fi works the most. After all, what good is envisioning such a grand future for humanity and all living beings if we're dead and not able to see it? And even if we were to live in the distant era depicted in these works, no matter how utopian it would be, we'd all still ultimately succumb to the universal curse of aging and death.

But, Praise God, the glorious gospel settles this problem; believers escape death through the death and resurrection of Jesus Christ, reconciling with the Almighty and attaining everlasting life!

Where the Error Started

As you can see, the Bible is very explicit concerning *where* redeemed people will spend eternal life. Most theologians will agree with this biblical data but you'll rarely hear these fascinating scriptural facts taught in Christian circles. More likely you'll hear about "spending eternity in heaven," which, again, gives the impression of sprouting wings and living in an ethereal dimension forever, playing a harp, etc. This is the *religious* version of the wonderful truths of God's Word, the *counterfeit* version. Needless to say, the religious version isn't invigorating; it isn't interesting. It's too fantastical and one-dimensional. In a word, it's *boring*.

This misleading religious error can be traced to Augustine of Hippo (354-430 AD), one of the most influential theologians in Christian history. Unfortunately, Augustine was strongly influenced by Greek philosophy, a belief system that viewed the physical universe, including the body, as evil. Consequently, the biblical teaching that redeemed people will spend eternity in glorified *bodies* in a *literal* new Jerusalem on a *literal* new earth in a *tangible* new universe was a blasphemous concept. Augustine solved this problem by spiritualizing what the Bible plainly taught, suggesting that biblical references like "the new Jerusalem" and "new earth" are merely symbolic language for heaven. This is how the false doctrine of amillennialism developed (detailed in *Hell Know* Chapter Nine's *The Good and Bad of Orthodoxy and Traditionalism*). His views were officially accepted by the Council of Ephesus in 431 AD and are held by many professing Christians today (Reagan 324-325). This doesn't mean that they're not legitimate believers, of course, just that they're ignorant of what the Bible plainly teaches on the nature of eternal life. What a testimony to the formidable, blinding force of religious tradition and indoctrination!

This explains, incidentally, my purpose in including this epilogue on eternal life—to set the captives FREE.

The Coming Universal Utopia

So, according to the biblical scriptures, what these sci-fi luminaries write about in their fictional works *will* essentially come to pass: humanity *will* indeed unite together to peaceably explore and inhabit the far reaches of the universe, but we'll be free of the maladies that forever mar their stories—evil, pain, disease, aging and death.

Unfortunately, it's going to get worse before it gets better, as detailed in Chapter Eleven. The Bible promises a great Tribulation for humanity and the earth before the establishment of the new earth and universe. The Scriptures also speak of a great judgment where all humanity will be divinely judged; those who reject reconciliation with their Creator will suffer the "second death" which is described as "everlasting destruction" (2 Thessalonians 1:9 & Revelation 20:11-15). Why? Because of the axiom: "The wages of sin is death"; thankfully, the passage goes on to say "but the gift of God is eternal life in Christ Jesus our Lord" (Romans 6:23). This is the 'good news.'

Allow me to stress that Christianity is not a legalistic drudgery, as those steeped in life-stifling religiosity give the impression. At its core Christianity is an exciting *relationship* with the Creator of the universe, which is why the gospel is referred to as "the message of *reconciliation*" in the Bible (2 Corinthians 5:18-19). The primary purpose of the 'good news' is to reconcile people to their Maker. Immortality in the new earth and universe is merely a byproduct of this reconciliation or, we could say, "icing on the cake."

The most popular verse in the Bible says "For God so loved the world that he gave his one and only Son, that whoever believes in him shall not perish but have eternal life" (John 3:16). God is clearly extending his love to all humanity and definitely wants *everyone* to accept His gracious offer of eternal life. As we have seen, this "eternal life" does not consist of sitting on a cloud playing a harp forever as religion has erroneously told us; no, it's far more invigorating, far more purposeful and far more adventurous. In fact, the Scriptures state that, "No eye has seen, no ear has heard, no mind has conceived what God has prepared for those who love him" (1 Corinthians 2:9). The nature of our existence in the new universe will be so awe-inspiringly wonderful that it's presently beyond our finite comprehension! The biblical descriptions we've witnessed in this study are but a "poor reflection as in a mirror" (1 Corinthians 13:12). In other words, we're seeing solid pieces of the truth, but they're only the tip of the iceberg. Praise God!

Will there be Animals in the New Heavens and New Earth?

I'd like to close this epilogue by looking at what the Scriptures say about the eternal fate of animals. Will animals be resurrected in the eternal age-to-come? This is a legitimate question because some people naturally wonder about their beloved pets and other animals. Actually, I have an ulterior motive in pursuing this question as it provides us the opportunity to address aspects of eschatology that we haven't yet looked at, such as "the final restoration of all things" (Acts 3:21).

Let's start with the question: Will there be animals in the new heavens and new earth? Answer: Why wouldn't there be? After all, there are animals galore in our current age and there will be animals during the Millennium, as this passage shows:

> **The wolf will live with the lamb, the leopard will lie down with the goat, the calf and the lion and the yearling together and a little child will lead them.**
>
> **(7) The cow will feed with the bear, their young will lie down together, and the lion will eat straw like the ox.**
>
> **(8) The infant will play near the cobra's den, and the young child will put its hand into the viper's nest.**
>
> **(9) They will neither harm nor destroy on all my holy mountain, for the earth will be filled with the knowledge of the Lord as the waters cover the sea.**
>
> **Isaiah 11:6-9**

As you can see, carnivorous animals will become herbivorous during the Millennium just as they were before the fall of creation.

Furthermore, there are animals in heaven right now, as verified by passages like this one:

> **I saw <u>heaven</u> standing open and there before me was <u>a white horse</u>, whose rider is called Faithful and True. With justice he judges and wages war. (12) His eyes are like blazing fire, and on his head are many crowns. He has a name written on him that no one knows but he himself. (13) He is dressed in a robe dipped in blood, and his name is the Word of God. (14) The <u>armies of heaven</u> were following him, <u>riding on white horses</u> and dressed in fine linen, white and clean. (15) Coming out of his mouth is a sharp sword with which to strike down the nations. "He will rule them with an iron scepter." He treads the winepress of the fury of the wrath of God Almighty. (16) On his robe and on his thigh he has this name written:**
> **King of kings and Lord of lords.**
>
> **Revelation 19:11-16**

This passage details the Second Coming of Christ. The Lord is riding a white horse, as are the armies of heaven following him (Jude 14 & Matthew 25:31).

Someone might argue that these horses are symbolic due to the symbolism contained in Revelation in general and particularly because verse 15 shows a "sharp sword" coming out of the Lord's mouth to strike down the nations, which we know isn't literal. Bear in mind, however, that symbolism in the Bible is obvious within the immediate context, as well as the context of the entire Bible. This is how we know the "sharp sword" coming out of Jesus' mouth isn't a literal sword, but rather is figurative of the word of God (Ephesians 6:17). Also, the usage of *some* symbolic language in a passage doesn't necessarily mean that every aspect of the passage is figurative when it's clear some elements are literal. For instance Jesus Christ and the armies of heaven that follow him are obviously literal in the above passage. As for the horses they ride, I see no indication that they're symbolic. Other biblical passages suggest that they're literal, like this one:

When the servant of the man of God got up and went out early the next morning, an army with horses and chariots had surrounded the city. "Oh no, my lord! What shall we do?" the servant asked.

(16) "Don't be afraid," the prophet answered. "Those who are with us are more than those who are with them."

(17) And Elisha prayed, "Open his eyes, Lord, so that he may see." Then the Lord opened the servant's eyes, and <u>he looked and saw the hills full of horses and chariots of fire all around Elisha.</u>

2 Kings 6:15-17

Although these horses dwell in heaven—the highest spiritual realm—and are therefore different than the horses we're familiar with, they *are* horses.

Since there are currently animals on earth and in heaven, and there will be animals during the Millennium, why wouldn't there be animals in the eternal age of the new heavens and new earth? After all, God originally created all types of animals to fill the earth before the fall of creation, why would this change when creation is fully restored? It wouldn't.

God's Cares about Animals too!

Whether people are aware of it or not, there are several passages in the Bible that show God's concern for animals, like this one:

"And should I not have concern for the great city of Nineveh, in which there are more than a hundred and twenty thousand people who cannot tell their right hand from their left—<u>and also many animals</u>?"

Jonah 4:11

The LORD proposed this question to Jonah, who objected to God's mercy for the people of Nineveh. Nineveh was the capital of Assyria, Israel's worst enemy, and the prophet wanted the LORD to destroy the city and its people, not mercifully forgive them when they repented (Jonah 4:1-2).

As you can see, the passage shows that God wasn't just concerned about the fate of the 120,000 Ninevites, who were spiritually ignorant and couldn't "tell their right hand from their left," he was also concerned about the numerous animals in the city.

Here are several other passages that reveal the Creator's concern for animals:

- **Job 12:10:** Job points out that the "life" of every creature is in God's hands. The word 'life' is *nephesh (neh-FESH)* in the Hebrew, which is often translated as "soul" in English Bibles. The King James Version translates the passage like so: "In whose hand [is] the **soul** of every living thing, and the breath of all mankind." Enough said.
- **Psalm 24:1** says that every living thing on the earth is the LORD's, which includes the animals.
- **Psalm 50:10-11** reveals that every animal in creation is God's and He *knows* every bird in the mountains.
- **Psalm 104:21-30** goes into detail about how the LORD created all animals with wisdom and how the whole earth is filled with God's creatures; it also shows how the Almighty provides them with food at the proper time and takes away their breath when they die.
- **Proverbs 12:10** stresses that righteous people care about the needs of their animals.
- **Matthew 6:26** shows how our heavenly Father feeds the birds of the air.
- **Matthew 10:29 & Luke 12:6** reveal that when even sparrows die not one of them is forgotten by God!
- **Revelation 4:11** shows the Mighty One being worshipped for creating all things for his good purpose and pleasure.

Someone might argue: If God cares about the animals so much why did he sanction the killing of them for food? This wasn't part of the LORD's original plan, notice:

> **Then God said, "I give you every seed-bearing plant on the face of the whole earth and every tree that has fruit with seed in it. They will be yours for food. (30) And to all the beasts of the earth and all the birds in the sky and all the creatures that move along the ground—everything that has the breath of life in it—I give every green plant for food." And it was so.**
>
> **(31) God saw all that he had made, and it was very good.**
>
> **Genesis 1:29-31**

All living beings on the earth were herbivores before the fall of creation, including people, meaning their diet was strictly vegetarian.

Verse 31 shows the Creator viewing all he had made and "it was very good." There were no carnivores at this time because, as Michelle Shannon points out, a carnivorous diet necessitates suffering and death of other living creatures and this wouldn't be good. Unfortunately, Adam & Eve's sin brought a curse on the physical universe and the sins of their descendants perpetuate it:

> **The earth is defiled by its people; they have disobeyed the laws, violated the statutes and broken the everlasting covenant.**
>
> **(6) Therefore a curse consumes the earth;**
>
> **Isaiah 24:5-6**

As such, no part of creation functions entirely as originally designed. The ground is cursed, as shown in Genesis 3:17-19, which is a reference to the plant kingdom; and the animals are also negatively affected:

> **Because of [sin] the land dries up, and all who live in it waste away; the beasts of the field, the birds in the sky and the fish in the sea are swept away.**
>
> **Hosea 4:3**

> **For <u>the creation was subjected to frustration</u>, not by its own choice, but by the will of the one who subjected it, in hope (21) that the creation itself will be liberated from its <u>bondage to decay</u> and brought into the freedom and glory of the children of God.**
>
> **Romans 8:20-21**

The "bondage to decay" is entropy and includes death. As such, every living thing in creation must die, including plant life. It wasn't until after the fall and the ensuing curse that animals began to fear people (Genesis 9:2).

"The Final Restoration of All Things"

The awesome news is that creation will be redeemed and, in fact, *yearns* for it:

> **For the creation waits <u>in eager expectation</u> for the children of God to be revealed.**
>
> **Romans 8:19**

What does creation wait in eager expectation for? The children of God to be revealed, which is part of the "restoration of all things":

> **For he [Jesus] must remain in heaven until the time for <u>the final restoration of all things</u>, as God promised long ago through his holy prophets.**
>
> **Acts 3:21**

This restoration of all things takes place in stages. One key stage is when Jesus returns for his church where believers' bodies are finally redeemed:

> **We know that <u>the whole creation has been groaning as in the pains of childbirth right up to the present time</u>. (23) Not only so, but we ourselves, who have the firstfruits of the Spirit, groan inwardly as we wait eagerly for our adoption to sonship, <u>the redemption of our bodies</u>.**
>
> **Romans 8:22-23**

Christ's return for the church is the Rapture and is detailed in 1 Thessalonians 4:13-18 (covered in <u>Chapter Eleven</u>).

The restoration continues after the 7-year Tribulation when Jesus returns to earth and establishes his millennial kingdom. Tribulation martyrs and Old Testament saints will be resurrected at this time and the lifespans of mortal humans will return to the lengthy lifespans of people before the flood.

In a previous section we looked at Isaiah 11:6-9, which shows what life will be like during the Millennium: Carnivorous animals will become herbivorous and therefore wolves will live with lambs and leopards will lie together with goats; calves and lions will hang out and be led by little children. Cows and bears will feed together and formerly carnivorous beasts like the lion will eat straw like an ox. Furthermore, children will play by the cobra's den and the viper's nest without fear because poisonous creatures will no longer be poisonous.

As wonderful as the thousand-year reign of Christ will be, it's just another stage in the "restoration of all things." The final stage takes place when God wholly renovates the earth & universe and the heavenly city, the new Jerusalem, comes "down out of heaven from my God" to rest on the new earth, as detailed earlier.

The Greek word for 'restoration' in the phrase "the final restoration of all things" is *apokatastasis (ap-ok-at-AS-tas-is)*, which appears only once in the Bible, Acts 3:21. The root word is *apokathistémi (ap-ok-ath-IS-tay-mee)*, which means "to set up again" and "restore to its original position or condition." That's what the "restoration of all things" is about—restoring the earth and universe to its original condition before the fall, which is the way God originally intended it to be.

The Messiah spoke of this restoration in this passage:

> **Jesus said to them, "Truly I tell you, at <u>the renewal of all things</u>, when the Son of Man sits on his glorious throne, you who have followed me will also sit on twelve thrones, judging the twelve tribes of Israel.**
>
> **Matthew 19:28**

The Greek word for 'renewal' here is *paliggenesia (pal-ing-ghen-es-EE-ah)*, which means "new birth, regeneration or renewal." It's only used twice in Scripture. The second time is in Titus 3:5 where it refers to the ***regeneration** of the human spirit* when a believer accepts the gospel (John 3:3,6). This shows that the "renewal of all things" is actually being jump-started in this current age through the spiritual rebirth of believers. This culminates with Christ's return for his church, detailed above. The next stage of the "renewal" takes place when Christ returns to the earth to establish his millennial reign, which is what Jesus was specifically referring to in the above passage, Matthew 19:28. This renewal climaxes with the re-creation of the new heavens and new earth, the eternal age to come.

I want to stress that the animal kingdom and even the plant kingdom are partakers in this redemption of the physical universe. Why else would all creation "wait in eager expectation" for this great restoration if they were not included in it (Romans 8:19)? No, animals and trees aren't literally yearning for this renewal, but they yearn for it in a figurative sense because *they're included in it.*

David Reagan shared an interesting insight on his TV program, Christ in Prophecy: When the high priest sprinkled animal blood on the cover of the Ark of the Covenant once a year to atone for the sins of the Israelites, this blood covered God's law, which was represented in the Ark via the tablets of the ten commandments. This ritual resulted in God's mercy year to year, covering the Israelites' sins. But the blood of animals could only temporarily cover sin, not cleanse it away forever

(Hebrews 10:1-4). The good news is that Jesus Christ, who is the believer's High Priest, offered his own blood when he went to the Most Holy Place in heaven, not merely the blood of animals (Hebrews 9:23-28). David Reagan pointed out that Leviticus 16:15 shows the high priest sprinkling blood on the ground in front of the Ark after sprinkling it on the cover. At the time the Ark was housed in the tent tabernacle and so the blood was literally poured on the ground. Why's this significant? Because the entire ceremony pointed to Christ's blood atonement in heaven and the priest didn't just sprinkle blood on the lid of the Ark for the redemption of humanity, but also on the ground for the redemption of all physical creation (*Will Our Pets Be in Heaven?*).

Were there animals before the fall? Yes. Therefore there will be animals after the fall. The question is, will the LORD create new animals or will he simply resurrect animals that have already lived and died? Or both?

Will God Resurrect Animals from Sheol?

In Chapter Three we saw that animals go to Sheol, as shown in this passage:

> **Such is the fate of the foolhardy, the end of those who are pleased with their lot.**
> **(14) Like sheep they are appointed for Sheol; death shall be their shepherd; straight to the grave they descend, and their form shall waste away; Sheol shall be their home.**
> **(15) But God will ransom my soul from the power of Sheol, for he will receive me.**
> **Psalm 49:13-15** (NRSV)

I encourage you to brush up on the two sections in Chapter Three that cover this passage in detail: *Sheol: A Place where Sheep Go?* and *Do Animals Have Souls? Do They Go to Sheol When They Die?* These sections show that **1.** animals have souls, and **2.** they go to Sheol when they die. I'm not going to repeat the material here except to say that verse 14 states point blank that sheep go to Sheol. This makes perfect sense when you have a biblical understanding of the nature of Sheol rather than a religious understanding. Sheol is the graveyard of dead souls where the immaterial DNA of lifeless souls is stored. As such, God can resurrect these life-forms when and if he deems fit. This includes the souls of animals.

Animal souls are, of course, stored in a separate compartment of Sheol than humans, just as pet cemeteries on earth are separate from human graveyards.

In the previous section we saw that the Bible speaks of "the final restoration of all things" (Acts 3:21), which refers to the LORD *restoring everything in creation to its original condition*. The Greek word for 'all things' is *pas (pass)*, which means "all, the whole, every kind of." So God is going to restore *all* creation to its original condition, as he originally intended it to be. Revelation 21:5 adds an interesting insight in that God will be "making everything new" and not making new things. Chew on that.

Of course, the LORD *won't* restore those condemned to the lake of fire, which includes damned human beings, the devil and his filthy angels and anything else cast into the lake of fire, such as death and Hades:

> **The sea gave up the dead that were in it, and death and Hades gave up the dead that were in them, and each person was judged according to what they had done. (14) Then death and Hades were thrown into the lake of fire. The lake of fire is the second death. (15) Anyone whose name was not found written in the book of life was thrown into the lake of fire.**
>
> **Revelation 20:13-15**

I bring this up because those who adhere to the doctrine of universal restoration—i.e. universalists—believe that everything thrown into the lake of fire will be purged of evil and restored. If this is so, why did Jesus use the example of weeds thrown into fire in reference to damned people who will suffer the second death (Matthew 13:40)? Are weeds restored when they're cast into fire or do they burn up? What about Jesus' example of a king's enemies brought before him and *executed* in front of him from Luke 19:27? Does this example leave any room for his executed enemies being restored?

Revelation 20:14 shows that death and Hades will be cast into the lake of fire. Does this mean that they'll be eliminated forever in the coming eternal age or that they'll be restored? If the latter is true, will death—the grim reaper—be restored and become a friendly reaper? Will Hades morph from a dungeon-like pit where dead souls are housed into a beautiful park where people frolic in paradise?

The answers are obvious: Death and Hades are cast into the lake of fire to be exterminated from existence forever, just as crying and pain will be eliminated (Revelation 21:4).

One of the reasons we're exploring this topic is because people naturally wonder about their beloved pets and animals. Will they ever see them again? Will they be reunited with them in the new heavens and new earth? While the Scriptures don't directly address the question, the answer is obvious based on the passages we've looked at and others. For instance, how could it be the "restoration of all things" if one's beloved pets are omitted? If Jesus said we are to ask and receive so our joy might be complete on *this* imperfect earth (John 16:24), how much more so on the new earth, which will be perfect? Doesn't the Bible say that those who delight themselves in the LORD will receive the desires of their hearts (Psalm 37:4)? If this is so in this wicked age, how much more so in the righteous age to come? Really, it's just common sense.

Will the LORD resurrect all animal souls in Sheol or just some? Again, the question isn't addressed in the Bible, but we can use common sense in deducing a plausible answer: Why would God create new animals when he can just resurrect ones already created over the course of earth's history? Of course, the resurrected animals will be perfected when they're resurrected—restored to their original design—like straw-eating lions and snakes that are no longer poisonous. This would, again, be part of the "restoration of all things." How would it truly be a universal restoration of creation if innocent animals are omitted? And how is it that "creation waits in eager expectation" if large quantities of creation—living creatures—aren't included?

Someone might understandably argue that there wouldn't be enough space on earth to resurrect every animal that has died since the fall of creation. However, since astronomers estimate there are at least one hundred billion galaxies in the universe (!) and therefore incalculable planets with earth-like environments this won't be a problem whatsoever. Another thing to consider is that there will likely be much more land area on the new earth in light of Revelation 21:1 (currently 71% of the earth's surface is water).

If God doesn't resurrect all the animals then obviously the dead souls of the ones that aren't resurrected will still be in Sheol (Hades) when it's cast into the lake of fire. In short, the soulish remains of these animals will be wiped out of existence at this time.

You'll notice that I didn't say anything about "pets going to heaven" in these last few sections. That's because such a statement isn't biblically accurate. For one thing, the Bible doesn't describe the eternal age to come as "heaven" but rather as the "new heavens and new earth," which is "the home of righteousness" (2 Peter 3:13). 'Heaven' technically refers to the spiritual realm where God's throne is located. As pointed out earlier in this epilogue, many Christians refer to the eternal age to come as "heaven," but this is erroneous terminology that can be traced back to Augustine's false doctrine of amillennialism.

But do the souls of animals go to heaven when they die like the souls of spiritually-regenerated believers in the New Testament era? We don't see any evidence of this in the Bible, but we do see evidence of animal souls going to Sheol, as cited above. As such, your dead pets aren't likely hanging out in heaven awaiting your coming, but they will be resurrected in the coming age of the new heavens and new earth, *if* that's your desire. And why wouldn't it be?

Appendix

HUMAN NATURE:
Spirit, Mind & Body

Since human nature is inextricably linked to the topics of Sheol, damnation, etc. this appendix is for readers who desire to dig deeper in their biblical studies on spirit, mind & body and how they relate.

There has been much debate in the church on the subject of human nature. Some teach that people are essentially a dichotomy (two-part) consisting of the inner person—soul/spirit—and the outer person—body. Others maintain that we are a trichotomy (three-part) consisting of two separate inner facets—spirit and soul (mind)—and an outer facet—body. Others insist that human beings are essentially one psychosomatic unit by nature and therefore terms that the Bible uses, such as "soul," "spirit," "mind," "body" and "heart," are ways of looking at the individual from different angles and so on.

One popular description of human nature that I hear often is "man is a spirit that possesses a soul and lives in a body." Although this description isn't entirely biblically accurate, it is a workable description as long as we understand that "soul" in this context refers to the mind.

Most of the confusion over the subject of human nature can be traced to two problems: **1.** Lack of depth in biblical studies, and **2.** a narrow view of the Hebrew and Greek words for "soul," "spirit," etc. The purpose of this appendix is to see what the Bible has always clearly taught on the subject and avoid these two interpretational ruts. In doing this, the scriptural truth should be plain to see.

Human Beings are "Living Souls"

Naturally the best place to start a study on human nature is "the creation text." This is the passage in the first book of the Bible that describes precisely how God created human beings:

> **And the LORD God formed man of the dust of the ground, and breathed into his nostrils the breath of life; and man became a living <u>soul</u> (nephesh).**
>
> **Genesis 2:7** (KJV)

> **The LORD God formed the man from the dust of the ground and breathed into his nostrils the breath of life and the man became a living <u>being</u> (nephesh).**
>
> **Genesis 2:7** (NIV)

We see here that God created the human body out of "the dust of the earth"[26] breathed into it "the breath of life" and so man became "a living soul" (KJV) or "living being" (NIV).

The Hebrew word for "soul" or "being" is *nephesh (neh-FESH)*. We know that *nephesh* is equivalent to the Greek *psuche (soo-KHAY)* because when this creation text is partially quoted in 2 Corinthians 15:45 *nephesh* is translated by the Greek word *psuche*. The Greek *psuche* is incidentally where we get the English words psychology, psychiatry and psyche.

As you can see, this foundational passage plainly states that human beings are ***living*** **souls**. Biblically, "Soul" *(nephesh/psuche)* in its

---

[26] It's a scientific fact that the human body is made up of the same essential chemical elements that are in the soil. Interestingly, humanity did not discover this until recent times, but the Creator revealed it here *thousands of years ago*.

broadest sense refers to the entire human person. We *are* living souls. We see this clearly in such passages as these:

> **All the <u>souls</u>** *(nephesh)* **that came with Jacob into Egypt, which came out of his loins, besides Jacob's sons' wives, all the <u>souls</u>** *(nephesh)* **were threescore and six.**
>
> **Genesis 46:26a** (KJV)

"Souls" in this verse simply refers to the *people* who accompanied Jacob to Egypt. The New International Version translates *nephesh* in this passage as "those" and "persons" respectively.

> **And that day Joshua took Makkedah, and smote it with the edge of the sword, and the king thereof he utterly destroyed, them, and all the <u>souls</u>** *(nephesh)* **that were therein; he let none remain:**
>
> **Joshua 10:28** (KJV)

"Souls" here likewise refers to the *people* that Joshua and his troops slew. The NIV translates *nephesh* in this passage as "everyone."

In both these examples, and numerous other passages, it is clear that "soul" does not refer to the immaterial facet of human beings, which is how "soul" is popularly understood, but rather to the *whole person*. It's understandable why the average Bible reader would fail to see this because in most translations *nephesh* is **not** translated as "souls" in such passages, but rather as "those," "persons," "everyone," "people," etc.

Here are a couple examples from the New International Version where *nephesh* is translated as "people:"

> **... and the <u>people</u>** *(nephesh)* **they had acquired in Haran,**
>
> **Genesis 12:5b**

> **There were 4,600 <u>people</u>** *(nephesh)* **in all.**
>
> **Jeremiah 52:30b**

And here's an example from the New Testament where *psuche,* the Greek equivalent to *nephesh,* is translated as "people:"

> **In it only a few <u>people</u> *(psuche)*, eight in all, were saved…**
>
> **1 Peter 3:20b**

Once again we see that "soul" *(nephesh/psuche)* **in its broadest sense** clearly refers to *the whole person, the whole human being—spirit, mind and body.* When *nephesh/psuche* is used in this **broad sense** "being" is perhaps the best translation. This is why the NIV translators decided to translate *nephesh* as "being" in the creation text, Genesis 2:7—the first man was a "living being."

The Human Soul: Mind, Body, Spirit

According to Scripture, human beings (souls) have three facets—spirit, mind and body. This will become clearer as our study progresses. All three of these facets are interconnected though not necessarily inseparable. God designed these facets to function as one unit. The Hebrew and Greek words for "soul"—*nephesh* and *psuche*—can refer to *any one* of these three facets depending upon the context of the passage.

For evidence of this, let's start with passages where *nephesh*—"soul"—refers specifically to the *body*:

> **" 'He** [the high priest] **must not enter a place where there is a <u>dead body</u>** *(nephesh).' "*
>
> **Leviticus 21:11a**

> **"Whoever touches the <u>dead body</u>** *(nephesh)* **of anyone will be unclean for seven days."**
>
> **Numbers 19:11**

The Hebrew word *nephesh* in these passages refers to the body, but not to mind or spirit. This is obvious because a dead body possesses neither mind nor spirit. There are many other such examples in the Bible.

Nephesh/psuche—"soul"—can also refer specifically to the human *mind.* The mind itself possesses three powerful qualities: **volition** (will), **emotion** (feeling) and **reason** (thinking). The mind is the decision-making center of our being. Here are a couple examples of *nephesh/psuche* used in reference to the mind:

> **"And you, my son Solomon, acknowledge the God of your father, and serve Him with wholehearted devotion and with a willing <u>mind</u> *(nephesh)*, for the LORD searches every heart and understands every motive behind the thoughts.**
>
> **1 Chronicles 28:9a,b**

> **But the Jews who refused to believe stirred up the Gentiles and poisoned their <u>minds</u> *(psuche)* against the brothers.**
>
> **Acts 14:2**

The first text speaks of Solomon's "willing mind." We know that *nephesh* here refers to the mind because the mind is the center of volition and will. It is the mind that makes willful decisions.

The second passage speaks of the Jews who poisoned the minds of the gentiles. We know that *psuche* in this verse refers to the mind because the Jews obviously corrupted the reasoning faculties of the Gentiles so they would make a willful decision to reject the gospel.

Nephesh/psuche—"soul"—can also refer specifically to the *human spirit*:

> **And Mary said: "My <u>soul</u> *(psuche)* glorifies the Lord (47) and my <u>spirit</u> *(pneuma)* rejoices in God my savior."**
>
> **Luke 1:46-47**

This is an example of synthetic parallelism, a type of Hebraic poetry where the second part of the passage explains or adds something to the first. In this case, Mary says that her **"soul"**—*psuche*—glorifies the Lord (verse 46). Exactly what part of her being glorifies the Lord? Verse 47 specifies that it is her *spirit* that rejoices in Him. Thus "soul"—*psuche*—a broad term for the whole human being, refers here *specifically* to the spirit. Likewise *nephesh* is translated as "spirit" five times in the Old Testament in the New International Version.

"Soul" Used in Reference to the Entire Immaterial Being—Mind & Spirit

The Hebrew and Greek words *nephesh* and *psuche* at times refer to both mind and spirit—the entire immaterial being as *separate* from the body:

> **And he [Elijah] stretched himself upon the [dead] child three times, and cried unto the LORD, and said, O LORD my God, I pray thee, let this child's <u>soul</u> *(nephesh)* come into him again.**
> **1 Kings 17:21 (KJV)**

Elijah is praying to God here that the boy's immaterial being ("soul")—his mind and spirit—return to his dead body. Our whole immaterial being—mind and spirit—is our **life force, our very life**. It is the mind and spirit that gives life to a fleshly body that would otherwise be dead. This is why the New International Version translates Elijah's prayer as "O my God, let this boy's **life** *(nephesh)* return to him."

Here are a few other examples of *nephesh/psuche* used in reference to the **entire immaterial being** as separate from the physical body:

> **Be merciful to me, O LORD, for I am in distress; my eyes grow weak with sorrow, my <u>soul</u> *(nephesh)* and body with grief.**
> **Psalm 31:9**

> The glory of his forest and his fruitful land
> the LORD will destroy, both <u>soul</u> *(nephesh)* and body,
> and it will be as when an invalid wastes away.
>
> **Isaiah 10:18** (NRSV)

> "Rather, be afraid of the One who can
> destroy both <u>soul</u> *(psuche)* and body in hell."
>
> **Matthew 10:28**

All three of these passages describe human nature as decidedly two separate parts—"soul and body"—non-physical and physical—immaterial and material. "Soul" in such cases clearly refers to **the whole immaterial being, both mind and spirit**.

Perhaps the best proof that *nephesh/psuche* can refer to the entire immaterial being is found in the book of Revelation where disembodied saints are described as **"souls"** *(psuche)* in John's vision:

> When he opened the fifth seal, I saw under
> the altar the <u>souls</u> *(psuche)* of those who had been
> slain because of the word of God and the testimony
> they had maintained. (10) They called out in a loud
> voice, "How long, Sovereign Lord, holy and true,
> until you judge the inhabitants of the earth and
> avenge our blood?"
>
> **Revelation 6:9-10**

> I saw thrones on which were seated those who
> had been given authority to judge. And I saw the
> <u>souls</u> *(psuche)* of those who had been beheaded
> because of their testimony for Jesus and because of
> the word of God.
>
> **Revelation 20:4a,b**

Whether these passages are literal or symbolic isn't important to our study (I believe they're literal for reasons detailed in <u>Chapter Ten</u>). What is important is that *psuche* ("souls") is the biblical word used to describe disembodied people. It therefore refers to their **entire immaterial being, both mind and spirit**.

The fact that "soul"—*nephesh/psuche*—can refer to the mind in certain passages (and to the spirit on rare occasions), and to **both** mind & spirit in others, explains the *seeming* interchangeability of these terms in Scripture.

The Narrow View of "Soul" Must Be Rejected

In light of this data, to properly understand what the Bible teaches about human nature, the narrow view of the term "soul" *(nephesh/psuche)* must be rejected. I say this because many ministers and theologians give the impression that "soul" only refers to the mind or that it only refers to the immaterial part of human beings. We've just seen clear biblical proof that both of these views are narrow and erroneous. To recap our study, "soul" *(nephesh/psuche)* in its broadest sense refers to the *entire* human being. Depending on its context it can also refer specifically to each one of the three facets of human nature—body, mind or spirit. It can also refer to the entire immaterial being—mind and spirit. Thus the views that *nephesh/psuche* **only** refer to the mind or **only** refer to mind & spirit are only true in certain contexts.

Consider, for instance, Paul's statement here:

> **May God Himself, the God of peace, sanctify you through and through. May your whole spirit, soul** *(psuche)* **and body be kept blameless at the coming of our Lord Jesus Christ.**
> **1 Thessalonians 5:23**

Even though *psuche*—"soul"—in its broadest sense refers to the entire human person, in this context it obviously refers to the mind. We know this because spirit, mind and body are the three interconnecting facets of human nature. Thus *psuche* must refer to the mind in this verse. This is in line with the hermeneutical rule: "Context is king."

Or consider this passage:

> For the word of God is living and active,
> sharper than any double-edged sword, it penetrates
> even to dividing <u>soul</u> *(psuche)* and spirit, joints and
> marrow; it judges the thoughts and attitudes of the
> heart.
>
> **Hebrews 5:12**

It's obvious here that "soul" refers to the mind because spirit and mind can be "divided" but spirit and the whole person cannot be divided since the whole person naturally includes the spirit. A person that lacks a spirit is no longer a whole person, are you following?

The Struggle of the Mind between Flesh and Spirit

In 1 Thessalonians 5:23 (cited above) Paul, by the inspiration of the Holy Spirit, describes human nature as having three basic facets— spirit, mind and body. Let's observe further support for this in Paul's inspired letter to the Romans:

> For I know that nothing good dwells within
> me, that is, in my <u>flesh</u>. I can will what is right, but I
> cannot do it. (19) For I do not do the good I want, but
> the evil I do not want is what I do. (20) Now If I do
> what I do not want, it is no longer I that do it, but sin
> that dwells within me.
>   (21) So I find it to be a law that when I want
> to do what is good, evil lies close at hand. (22) For I
> delight in the law of God in my <u>inmost self</u> [i.e. spirit],
> (23) but I see in my members another law at war with
> the law of my <u>mind</u>, making me captive to the law of
> sin that dwells in my members.
>
> **Romans 7:18-23** (NRSV)

Paul speaks of three facets of human nature in this passage. In verse 18 he mentions his **"flesh"** (or "sinful nature" in the NIV) and states that "nothing good dwells within" it.

In verse 22 he mentions his "inmost self" and says that this part of his being delights in God's law. Paul is speaking of his **spirit** here; this will be more obvious in a moment.

In verse 23 he mentions his **"mind"** and the "war" that it is fighting. The precise nature of this "war" is made clearer just a few verses later:[27]

> **For those who live according to the <u>flesh</u> set their <u>minds</u> on the things of the <u>flesh</u>, but those who live according to the <u>spirit</u>[28] set their <u>minds</u> on the things of the <u>spirit</u>. (6) To set the <u>mind</u> on the <u>flesh</u> is death, but to set the <u>mind</u> on the <u>spirit</u> is life and peace.**
>
> **Romans 8:5-6** (NRSV)

These divinely inspired words reveal two truths: **1.** That there are three basic facets to human nature—flesh, mind and spirit; and **2.** that the mind is caught in a struggle between the other two opposing facets—flesh and spirit. This is the "war" Paul is talking about in verse 23 above.

What exactly is the **mind?** The mind is our **center of being.** The Greek for "mind" is *nous (noos)* meaning "The intellect, i.e. the mind (divine or human; in thought, feeling or will)" (Strong 50). This definition reveals the aforementioned three qualities of the human mind: **volition** (will), **intellect** (reason) and **emotion** (feeling):

---

[27] Keep in mind that Paul's original letter to the Romans had no chapter and verse divisions. These divisions were added centuries later for convenience in scriptural study and citation.

[28] Since there is no capitalization in the biblical Greek, translators must determine if "spirit" should be capitalized, in reference to the Holy Spirit, or not capitalized, in reference to the human spirit. Many translations capitalize "spirit" in these passages and some do not (for example The New English Bible). I believe these passages (and other such passages) are plainly referring to the human spirit and therefore "spirit" should not be capitalized. This will be made clearer as our study progresses. In a way it makes no significant difference since our born-again human spirit is **indwelt and led by the Holy Spirit** (Ephesians 3:16).

The Human Mind

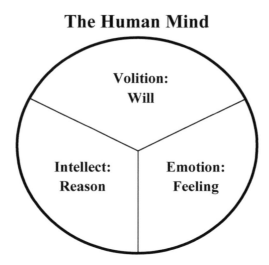

Since the mind is the center of volition and will, it is the mind that *decides* whether to live according to the flesh or according to the spirit, as the above passage shows.

What exactly are flesh and spirit? The flesh and spirit, once again, are **the opposing facets of our being**. In Romans 7:18 above Paul describes the flesh as the part of his being where "nothing good dwells." In verse 22 he describes his spirit as the side of him that delights in God's laws. We could therefore define flesh and spirit as follows: The "flesh" is that part of us that veers toward what is negative, destructive and carnal. The "spirit" is that part of us that inclines toward what is positive, productive and godly.

These contrasting facets of our being are repeatedly mentioned in Scripture:

> **"Watch and pray, lest you enter into temptation. <u>The spirit</u> indeed is willing, but <u>the flesh</u> is weak.**
>
> **Matthew 26:41** (NKJV)

> **I say then: Walk in the spirit, and you shall not fulfill the lust of the flesh. (17) For <u>the flesh</u> lusts against <u>the spirit</u>, and <u>spirit</u> against <u>the flesh</u>; and**

these are <u>contrary to one another</u>, so that you do not do the things that you wish.

Galatians 5:16-17 (NKJV)

It's interesting to note that the formulator of psychoanalysis, Sigmund Freud, was able to discover these three basic facets of human nature through his studies. The mind is comparable to Freud's "ego;" likewise the flesh coincides with his "id;" and the spirit corresponds to the "superego." Although I'm obviously not an advocate of Freud, pointing this out may help readers who are familiar with psychological theories to better understand the biblical model of human nature—spirit, mind and body. I just find it fascinating that, with little or no biblical knowledge, Freud was able to discover these three basic facets of human nature through sheer scientific analysis, which shows that human nature is obvious to anyone who cares to honestly examine it from either an unbiased scientific or biblical approach. I am reminded of M. Scott Peck, the psychiatrist and bestselling author, who converted to Christianity not long after publishing his first book, *The Road Less Traveled*, at the age of 43. One of the main factors contributing to this decision, Peck said, was the Bible's brutally honest and accurate depiction of human nature, as illustrated here:

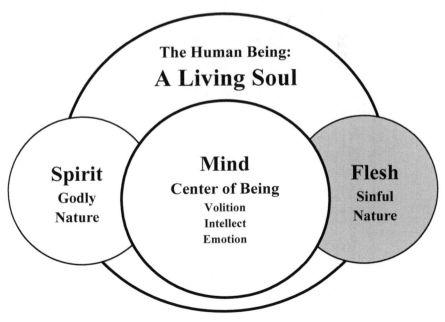

With the understanding that the human being is a living soul consisting of spirit, mind and body, let's take a closer look at the two opposing facets of human nature—flesh and spirit.

Body *(Soma)* and Flesh *(Sarx)*

The biblical Greek for "body" is *soma* (e.g. 1 Corinthians 6:19). This word can also refer metaphorically to the sinful nature:

> **For we know that the old self was crucified with him so that the <u>body</u> *(soma)* of sin might be done away with, that we should no longer be slaves to sin.**
>
> **Romans 6:6**

The Greek word for "flesh" is *sarx*. Although *sarx* is most frequently used in the Bible in reference to the literal flesh of a person (e.g. John 6:6), it is often figuratively used in reference to **the sinful nature**. In such cases the New International Version understandably translates *sarx* as "sinful nature":

> **I know that nothing good lives in me, that is, in my <u>sinful nature</u> *(sarx)*. For I have the desire to do good, but I cannot carry it out.**
>
> **Romans 7:18**

> **The acts of the <u>sinful nature</u> *(sarx)* are obvious: sexual immorality, impurity and debauchery; (20) idolatry and witchcraft; hatred, discord, jealousy, fits of rage, selfish ambition, dissensions, factions (21) and envy; drunkenness, orgies, and the like. I warn you, as I did before, that those who live like this will not inherit the kingdom of God.**
>
> **Galatians 5:19-21**

Both of these examples show *sarx*—"flesh"—being used as a metaphor for our carnal, sinful nature. In the first text Paul says that "nothing good lives in" his *sarx*. He's obviously not talking about his body here. Likewise the second passage reveals the various sinful manifestations of the *sarx*.

Because *sarx*—"flesh"—plainly refers to the **sinful nature** in such cases, I use "flesh" and "sinful nature" interchangeably throughout this study.

Soma (body) and *sarx* (flesh) seem to be very closely related in Scripture:

> **And in him [Christ] you were also circumcised with a circumcision made without hands, in the removal of the <u>body</u> *(soma)* of the <u>flesh</u> *(sarx)* by the circumcision of Christ.**
> **Colossians 2:11 (NASB)**

Soma (body) and *sarx* (flesh) are so closely related in this passage that the NIV translators decided to translate them both simply as "sinful nature":

> **In him you were also circumcised in the putting off of the <u>sinful nature</u> *(soma/sarx)*,[29] not with a circumcision done by the hands of men but with the circumcision done by Christ.**
> **Colossians 2:11 (NIV)**

The conclusion we draw from this biblical information is this: Although body and flesh are not technically one and the same, it's obvious that the flesh—the sinful nature—is most closely related to the body rather than mind and spirit. In fact, the Bible tends to use body and flesh interchangeably. Because of this, I will do the same in this study.

---

[29] The NIV translators would technically say that their decision in this specific text was to not translate *soma* and simply render *sarx* as "sinful nature."

The Human Spirit

Even though the flesh is most closely related to the body in Scripture, we know that it is somehow interwoven with the mind as well. We know this for certain because, if the sin nature were merely a condition of the body, then physical death would be the ultimate and absolute solution to humanity's sin problem. Needless to say, this would render Christ's death for humanity's sins pointless.

So the flesh is somehow interwoven with the mind, but it also renders the spirit dead to God. Jesus thus taught that the first step in solving our sin problem is to have a spiritual rebirth. The human spirit must be regenerated. Once the spirit is born-again and becomes a "new creation" the mind needs to be "renewed" and trained so that it submits its will, intellect and emotions to the spirit and not to the flesh. This is the second step. The third and final step to solving the sin problem is to receive a new imperishable glorified body.

Before we get into all that, let's define specifically what the human spirit is and what it desires to do.

The Koine Greek word for "spirit" is *pneuma (NYOO-mah)*, which corresponds to the Hebrew *ruwach (ROO-ahk)*. We've already seen in Scripture that the human spirit is that part of our being that "delights in God's law." It is that part of our nature that inclines toward what is positive, productive and godly. We could also add that the human spirit is that facet of our being that is aware of a spiritual dimension to reality and thus naturally attempts to "connect" with that dimension. Only this spiritual side of our being can know of God and desire to connect with Him because, as Jesus pointed out, "God is spirit" (John 4:24). Since the flesh is our "sinful nature," we could properly define our spirit as our "godly nature."

Both the non-believer and the spiritually born-again believer have a human spirit. The difference is that the non-believer is spiritually dead to God whereas the born-again believer is spiritually alive to God. Because born-again Christians are spiritually alive to the LORD they can have a relationship with Him, but because non-believers are spiritually dead to the Creator it is *impossible* for them to have a relationship with Him.

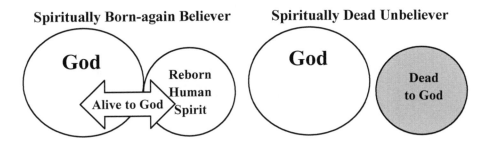

Non-Christians indeed have a spirit and therefore can be *aware* of God (or a spiritual dimension) and desire to "connect" with God (or the spiritual dimension) but they cannot connect with Him and have a relationship unless they are spiritually born-again. This universal attempt by humanity to connect with God (or a spiritual dimension) explains the existence of the world's numerous religions. Because we have a spiritual side to our being, human beings are—as a race—incurably religious.

The difference between religion and biblical Christianity is that **religion is humanity's attempt to connect with God**, whereas **Christianity is God connecting with humanity**. Religion is humanity's way, but biblical Christianity is God's way. Although it is certainly commendable that religious people are aware of a spiritual dimension to reality, and are attempting to connect with it—as they understand it— their attempt to connect with the Creator ultimately fails because they are spiritually dead to Him. It is therefore, once again, impossible for them to have a relationship with Him. This is why when Jesus' disciples asked him who could be saved, he said: **"With man this is impossible**, but not with God; all things are possible with God." (Mark 10:27). You see, salvation through the flesh—through religion—is impossible. But with God it's not only possible, it's available to all. That's Christianity—*real* Christianity, not the counterfeit legalism.

The Human Spirit Must be "Born Again" in Order to Connect with God

Biblical Christianity teaches that, in order to successfully connect with God and have a relationship with Him we need to be spiritually regenerated. As Jesus plainly taught:

> "I tell you the truth, no one can see the kingdom of God <u>unless he is born again</u>."
>
> (5) "I tell you the truth, no one can enter the kingdom of God unless he is born of water and the Spirit. (6) Flesh gives birth to flesh, but <u>Spirit gives birth to spirit</u>."
>
> John 3:3,5-6

Jesus makes it clear in verse 3 that, in order to have a relationship with God, we must be "born again." In verse 6 he clarifies specifically what kind of rebirth we need—*spiritual* rebirth. When a person is spiritually born again the Holy Spirit gives birth to a new human spirit—the spiritual facet of his or her being is born anew! This is the "new creation" that Paul writes about:

> Therefore, if anyone is in Christ, he is a <u>new creation</u>; the old has gone, the new has come.
>
> 2 Corinthians 5:17

"New Creation" in the Greek literally means "a new species of being which never existed before." The born again spirit is "God's workmanship" (Ephesians 2:10) "created to be **like God** in true righteousness and holiness" (Ephesians 4:24). The intrinsic character of the new born-again spirit is righteous and holy, just as God is righteous and holy. When the apostle Paul spoke of the "treasure in jars of clay" that he and other born-again believers have, he was referring to the new born-again spirit, which is housed in the body or "jar of clay" (2 Corinthians 4:7).

I'm always amazed when I come across believers who either play down spiritual rebirth or deny it altogether when it's actually a **fundamental Christian doctrine** (see Titus 3:3 and 1 Peter 1:23).

The Mind Needs Renewed—Trained to Live by the Spirit

Once a person's spirit is born anew something has to be done with the mind and body, the two remaining facets of the human soul:

> **Therefore, I urge you, brothers, in view of God's mercy, to offer your <u>bodies</u> as living sacrifices, holy and pleasing to God—this is your spiritual act of worship. (2) Do not conform any longer to the pattern of this world, but be <u>transformed by the renewing of your mind</u>. Then you will be able to test and approve what God's will is—his good, pleasing and perfect will.**
>
> **Romans 12:1-2**

> **You were taught with regard to your former way of life, to put off your <u>old self</u> [flesh], which is being corrupted by its deceitful desires; (23) to <u>be made new in the attitude of your minds</u>; (24) and to put on <u>the new self</u> [born-again spirit], created to be like God in true righteousness and holiness.**
>
> **Ephesians 4:22-24**

After a person is spiritually born again, his or her body needs to be offered to God as a "living sacrifice." This means that we make a conscious decision to no longer offer the parts of our body to sin as instruments of unrighteousness but to God's service as instruments of righteousness (Romans 6:13,19). This simply means we turn away from—repent of—behaviors that God informs us are unproductive or negative and start putting into practice positive and productive behaviors approved of Him. Repentance should never be viewed as a negative thing as it essentially means "to change for the better."

As far as the mind is concerned, it needs to be "renewed." As we are faithful and diligent to "be made new in the attitude of our minds" we will start to be "transformed." "Transformed" is the Greek word *metamorphoo (met-ah-mor-FOH)* which means "to change into another form." This is obviously where we get the English word metamorphosis. Just as an ugly worm-like caterpillar is transformed in its cocoon and emerges as a beautiful butterfly, so a wondrous metamorphosis will take place in our lives as we renew our minds.

The second passage above shows how to successfully do this: We put off the "old self"—the flesh—by stop setting our minds on this carnal side of our being. Instead we put on the "new self"—the born-again spirit "created to be like God in true righteousness and holiness"—by training our minds to live according to our born-again spirit:

> **Those who live according to the <u>sinful nature</u> have their <u>minds</u> set on what that nature desires; but those who live in accordance with the <u>spirit</u> have their <u>minds</u> set on what the <u>spirit</u> desires. (6) ...the mind controlled by the <u>spirit</u> is life and peace.**
> **Romans 8:5-6**

There's so much life, energy and peace when we train our minds to live according to our new born-again spirits as led of the Holy Spirit! Speaking of which, Ephesians 3:16 shows that the Holy Spirit indwells the believer's regenerated spirit. The only reason the *Holy* Spirit can do this is because our reborn spirit was "created to be *like God* in true righteousness and *holiness*," as shown in Ephesians 4:24. Chew on that.

When we successfully learn to be spirit-controlled the born-again spirit acts as a sort of "sixth sense," tuning us in to God and enabling us to perceive reality from the "divine viewpoint." People who are spiritually dead are limited to their five senses and consequently only perceive reality from the "human viewpoint" (sadly, this is also true of many legitimately born-again Christians who fail to train their minds to live according to their new born-again spirits). Intimate knowledge of God can only be attained through this sixth sense. With this understanding, it becomes increasingly clear why Jesus stressed that we must be spiritually born again to *"see* the kingdom of God."

It should be every Christian's goal and desire to be spirit-controlled; unfortunately, many never adequately learn to do this. They instead settle for being body-ruled Christians, thus cutting themselves off from the divine viewpoint and limiting themselves to the human perspective. A more common name for this is "carnal Christian." Of course there are degrees to this limiting condition and not every carnal Christian is frothing at the mouth with extreme iniquity, but they *are* body-ruled and therefore impeded from the divine viewpoint. Carnal Christians can become so hardened in heart by their sin that they naturally become hostile toward God and Christianity. As it is written:

> **The sinful mind is hostile to God. It does not submit to God's law, nor can it do so. (8) Those controlled by the sinful nature cannot please God.**
>
> **Romans 8:7-8**

Some body-ruled Christians become so hardened in heart by their sin that they end up denying Christ (!!). This is the ultimate result of unrepentant and deceptive sin—it **destroys** your relationship with God. This is spiritual death—being dead to God—and explains why the Bible says: "The mind governed by the flesh is death" (Romans 8:6).

It should be pointed out that it takes time and effort to properly train the mind to habitually live according to the new born-again spirit with the help of the Holy Spirit. Most Christians will naturally need support from more mature brothers and sisters to learn to do this. In fact, the very reason God appoints and anoints spiritually mature believers to ministerial positions—like pastor, teacher or prophet—is so that believers might be encouraged and equipped to successfully discern and fulfill God's will for their lives (see Ephesians 4:11-15).

The Positive Nature of the Flesh when Submitted to the Spirit

Allow me to add one important detail on this matter: When the mind is properly controlled by the spirit (which is, in turn, led by the indwelling Holy Spirit) the appetites and inclinations of the body actually become a positive force in a person's life. This is naturally because the body is properly submitted to the spirit-led mind.

To illustrate, consider the sexual appetites of the body. If, in our mind, we choose to be flesh-ruled, the sexual appetite can be very destructive. For instance, unbridled sexual lust can lead us into fornication, adultery and perversion resulting in broken relationships, broken families, illegitimate children, horrible diseases, prison and even death. Yet when we choose to allow our mind to be spirit-led, our natural sexuality becomes a very positive and productive force in our lives. There's nothing inherently wrong, for example, with the God-given male sex drive. The sex drive submitted to the spirit will compel a man to find a suitable wife, physically love her and produce children.

Another good example would be anger. Anger stems from our carnal nature. We all realize that uncontrolled anger can be quite destructive, even provoking people to murder. Yet, when we choose to allow our minds to be spirit-led rather than body-ruled, anger can be utilized for righteous and productive purposes, rather than childish temper tantrums. A mother's anger over drunk driving is a fitting example; her anger, properly submitted to the spirit, will compel her to seek social justice. Or consider the biblical example of Jesus when he, in righteous anger, got out a whip (!) and drove everyone out of the temple—overturning tables, scattering coins and yelling (see John 2:13-17 and Mark 11:15-18). Needless to say, the common assumption that a good Christian must be a spineless doormat for other people is a lie. There's something called *tough* love and it's thoroughly biblical.

The Heart: The Core of the Mind

Many scriptural passages speak of the human "heart" (e.g. Mark 7:6,21). What exactly is the heart? And how does it fit into the biblical model of spirit, mind and body?

The Greek word for "heart" is *kardia (kar-DEE-ah),* which is where we get the English 'cardiac.' Like the English word "heart," *kardia* literally refers to the blood-pumping organ but figuratively to the **core thoughts or feelings of a person's being or mind** (Strong 39). E.W. Bullinger describes the heart as "**the seat and center** of man's personal life in which the distinctive character of the human manifests itself" (362). The heart could therefore be best described as the core of the mind, the center of our being. It is part of the mind, but specifically refers to the deepest, most central part, i.e. **the core.**

What's in your heart is determined by whether **your mind has** *decided* to live by the flesh or by the spirit. Jesus said, "The good man brings good things out of the good stored up in his heart, and the evil man brings evil things out of the evil stored up in his heart. For out of the overflow of the heart the mouth speaks" (Luke 6:45). If we, in our mind, *decide* to dwell on carnal thoughts, then carnal, negative, destructive things will naturally store up in our heart. If, on the other hand, we *choose* to dwell on spiritual thoughts, then good, positive, productive things will store up in our heart. The paraphrase of Proverbs 4:23 puts it like this: **"Be careful what you think for your thoughts run your life"** (NCV). Take heed—truer words have never been spoken!

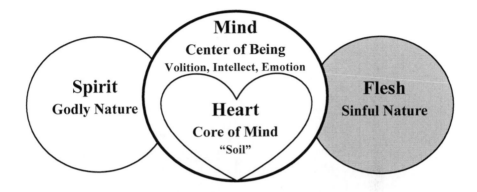

The bottom line is that **we** *decide* what's stored up in our hearts depending on whether we're governed by the flesh or spirit.

I think it's important to point out that carnal and crazy thoughts will at times flash through your mind; yet this doesn't mean these thoughts are stemming from your heart. Having carnal and crazy thoughts flash through the mind is natural to the human experience; in other words, if you're human, it will happen. Sometimes you may even be bombarded with such thoughts. These thoughts may originate from the flesh, unclean spirits, ungodly people, the environment you're exposed to, or otherwise, but just because such thoughts flash through your mind it does not mean they're in your heart. These thoughts *are not you*, and *are not originating from your heart;* but they can become *you* if you allow them to get lodged in your heart by dwelling on them and giving them life. Such thoughts should just be ignored or, if that doesn't work, taken "captive" and made "obedient to Christ," the Word of God (see 2 Corinthians 10:3-5). Otherwise they will become a weed with the potential of growing into a big, ugly tree of destructive bad fruit (e.g. bitterness, immorality, frustration, sloth, depression, arrogance, abuse, gossip/slander, rage, etc.).

The Resurrection Body: Imperishable, Glorified, Powerful & Spiritual

Even the most mature spirit-led Christian will fail to reach perfection as long as he or she dwells within a perishable flesh and blood body. Absolute escape from the sin nature will not be complete until the resurrection where God's people will receive a new imperishable, glorified, powerful and spiritual body:

> **(35) But someone will ask, "How are the dead raised? With what kind of <u>body</u> will they come?"**
> **(42) The body that is sown is perishable, it is raised <u>imperishable</u>; (43) it is sown in dishonor, it is raised in <u>glory</u>; it is sown in weakness, it is raised in <u>power</u>; (44) it is sown a natural body, it is raised a <u>spiritual</u> body.**
>
> **1 Corinthian 15:35,42b-44**

This passage describes the new bodies that born-again Christians will receive at the resurrection of the righteous, which takes place in stages, as detailed in <u>Chapter Eleven</u>. It should be emphasized that this passage contextually only refers to spiritually born-again believers, not spiritually dead pagans. The latter will of course be resurrected later in order to be judged and "If anyone's name is not found written in the book of life, he [will be] thrown into the lake of fire" (Revelation 20:11-15).

One of the best benefits of this new body will be that it will not have a flesh; that is, a sin nature. That's why it's called a *spiritual* body. Granting us such new bodies is God's final measure in our obtaining freedom from sin. The power of sin and death will be "swallowed up in victory" (1 Corinthians 15:54-57)!

The above passage describes these new bodies as **imperishable, glorified, powerful** and **spiritual** in nature. We obviously know what "imperishable" means—our new bodies **will never die** (i.e. we will possess unconditional immortality); but what exactly do the other descriptive words mean? We of course don't have all the answers since we presently "see through a glass darkly," but to take a peek at how wondrous it will be in our new bodies, all we have to do is observe what the Bible says about Jesus after his resurrection. After all, we're going to receive the same type of resurrection body he did. In light of this, we'll evidently be able to walk through locked doors (John 20:26), instantly appear out of nowhere (Luke 24:36-37) and disappear (24:31). With this understanding we'll no doubt be able to take instant "quantum leaps" to anywhere on the new earth or new universe—including planets and galaxies millions of light-years away. I personally find this extremely invigorating and excitedly look forward to it (unlike the traditional boring concept of living on a cloud playing a harp forever).

Spiritual Death Leads to Absolute Death

The strongest proof that the born-again believer is spiritually *alive* to the LORD—and, by extension, the non-believer is spiritually *dead* to God—can be found in 1 Corinthians 6:17 and this passage:

> **You, however, are controlled not by the sinful nature but by the spirit, if the Spirit of God lives in you. And if anyone does not have the Spirit of Christ, he does not belong to Christ. (10) But <u>if Christ is in you</u>, your body is dead because of sin, yet <u>your spirit is alive</u> because of righteousness.**
>
> **Romans 8:9-10**

The key statement for our subject is verse 10: "If Christ is in you... your spirit is **alive**". The obvious implication is that, if the human spirit of a spiritually born-again believer is *alive*, the human spirit of a non-believer must be *dead*.

As noted in <u>Chapter Six</u> of *Hell Know*, spiritual death is a present state in the non-Christian's life. They *are* spiritually dead to God and this explains why Paul described the Ephesian & Colossian believers as being "dead in their sins" *before* they accepted the Lord (see Ephesians 2:1 and Colossians 2:13). These believers were spiritually dead before their born-again experience. This is in contrast to all the many scriptural texts examined in *Hell Know* which clearly state that the second death—the literal destruction of soul and body in hell—is an experience that will take place in the future. In other words, the second death is not a present state but a future experience that will eventually occur, but only if the individual fails to reconcile with God and receive His gracious gift of eternal life.

We see this contrast between spiritual death and the second death in Romans 8:10 and 8:13. Romans 8:10 (above) clearly implies, once again, that the spirit of a non-believer is presently dead. Notice what Paul says about the second death a mere three verses later:

> **For if you live according to the sinful nature you _will_ die; but if by the Spirit you put to death the misdeeds of the body, you will live.**
>
> **Romans 8:13**

Do you see the clear contrast between spiritual death and the second death here? Paul says that people who choose to live according to the flesh will eventually have to reap the wages of their actions and die. This is the second death—absolute destruction of soul and body in hell. This, again, is a future event, not a present state.

The bottom line is that **spiritual death ultimately results in absolute death**. That's why God sent His Son so that "whoever believes in him shall **not perish** but have eternal life" (John 3:16).

Can Non-Christians Live by Their Un-Regenerated Spirit?

The material we've been covering so far brings up an interesting question: Can a person who is spiritually dead to God train his or her mind to live according to his/her (unregenerated) human spirit? Absolutely, and this explains the many non-Christian people we run into regularly who display noble characteristics even though their spirit is dead to God.

We have to remember that Adam didn't eat of the tree of the knowledge of evil; he ate of the tree of the knowledge of *good* and evil (see Genesis 2:17 and 3:11-12). The entire human race, as Adam's descendants, therefore possesses the capacity for both good and evil. However, even though we have the capacity for good, Adam passed on to us a sin nature (flesh)—the carnal proclivity to rebel against good, i.e. God's righteous laws (Romans 7:12). As already determined, this sinful nature is largely a condition of the body, but negatively affects the rest of our being as well. As such, the unbeliever's spirit is rendered dead to God—incapable of connecting with the Creator, unless it is born-again of the Holy Spirit via the seed (sperm) of Christ (1 John 3:9).

Because Adam ate of the tree of the knowledge of both good and evil, most people who are not spiritually regenerated are a mishmash of spiritual and carnal qualities; that is, they possess both good and bad traits.[30] Only a relatively small number of unbelievers could be designated as *wholly* wicked; and even they no doubt have *some* good qualities. (Although I sometimes wonder how "good" people would be if there were no human laws to keep them in check;[31] in other words, if they could "get away" with raping, murdering or stealing, would they do it? Only God knows their hearts).

In any event, we regularly come across non-Christian individuals who are quite developed in character. Even though they're spiritually dead to God, they appear to be humble, intelligent, loving, positive, moral, compassionate, etc. Such people have somehow trained their minds to live according to their spirit which, even though it's dead to God and thus in dire need of regeneration, is still the facet of their being that inclines toward what is positive, productive and godly, as opposed to the flesh which veers toward negativity, destruction and perversion.

There's always some training or discipline that enables people to do this. It could simply be the result of how they were raised, in which case they were trained by their parents or guardians to be loving and moral. It could also be the result of their exposure and submission to various "disciplines;" for example, religion, meditation, martial arts and generally positive philosophies, such as Sciencefictionology. Such

---

[30] Spiritually born-again believers are also a mishmash of both good and bad traits; I'm not suggesting otherwise, but our topic here is individuals who are *not* spiritually reborn.

[31] If people don't fear God's law, the only law they have left to fear is human law; but if there's no human law to constrain their lower impulses they would naturally have nothing to fear. This would be the ultimate test of character.

disciplines could be considered good in that they inspire people to be the best that they can be, yet they ultimately fail to solve the sin problem and reconcile people to their Creator. For this reason they have the potential for harm as these disciplines can delude people into thinking they can attain righteousness by their own efforts or works without spiritual regeneration. This notion is rooted in human pride and arrogance, sins the LORD "hates" (Proverbs 8:13).

The message of the Bible is that humankind is cursed with a sin nature and a spirit that is dead to God. Thus no amount of human effort to attain righteousness can adequately remove our sinfulness and reconcile us to the Almighty. Although it is certainly commendable that a person makes a conscious decision to live by his/her spirit, in a sense it's all flesh to God because the sin nature has tainted the human spirit and rendered it dead. It is utterly incapable of doing what it was originally designed to do—commune with God. Theologians refer to this as "total depravity;" not that human beings are as bad as we could possibly be, but that we are unable to contribute to our salvation in any way because we are spiritually dead in our fallen condition. The obvious exception is humble repentance & faith in response to the gospel (Acts 20:21).

It should be added that there is a danger in attempting to live out of the un-regenerated spirit. Anyone who does so will naturally become increasingly in tune with the spiritual realm. The problem with this is that there are both good and evil spirits. If a person's spirit is dead to God it naturally stands to reason that the spiritual realm they're more prone to get in tune with would *not* be of God. Unless intercessory prayer is made on their behalf—releasing the Holy Spirit to draw them to God—they are vulnerable to the deception and misleading of impure spirits. This is how false religions and philosophies develop. Their message is always the same: There's *another way* to God besides the gospel of reconciliation through Christ. Perhaps the ultimate satanic deception is that humankind can somehow attain righteousness apart from God's gift of righteousness in Christ. As already pointed out, this notion—that we can be good without God, that we don't need our Creator—is rooted in human arrogance. Thus the human attempt to be righteous apart from God is a fleshly stench to the all-knowing LORD who knows the secrets and motivations of the heart.

The popular message of the day is that there are many paths to God, none superior to any other, so what I'm teaching here will be rejected by those who embrace the spirit of this age. The bottom line is that God loves the whole world and has provided a way to spiritual regeneration, reconciliation and eternal life. Let's be wise and go with **God's way** (biblical, Spirit-led Christianity), and reject **man's way** (religion). Amen?

So, to answer the question, can spiritually un-regenerated persons learn to live out of their human spirit and consequently produce good works and develop in character? Certainly. This is commendable, but whatever discipline they follow ultimately fails to heal their sinful condition and reconcile them to the LORD. This is "total depravity."

"Spirit" and "the Breath of Life"

In our study we've determined that the human spirit is the facet of human nature that is opposed to the flesh; it is the part of our being that compels us toward what is positive & godly and inspires our desire to connect with our Creator. It should be pointed out that in certain contexts 'spirit' refers to "the breath of life." The breath of life could also be referred to as the spirit of life because "breath" is translated from the same Hebrew and Greek words for "spirit"—*ruwach* and *pneuma* respectively.

The "breath of life" describes the human spirit on the most basic level as separate from mind and body: The human spirit is essentially a breath of life from God. As such, **the breath of life is not our being; it is the life force from God that gives consciousness to our being**. In other words, **the very reason we have consciousness is because of the breath of life, but the breath of life is not our consciousness**.

We could draw a parallel to the human body. The body is the facet of human nature that enables our being to dwell in the physical realm. It is indeed a part of our being, but it is not our consciousness, rather it enables our consciousness to dwell in the physical realm. Separate from spirit and mind, the body is just a carcass, a slab of nonliving flesh. This is what the body is on the most basic level separate from spirit and mind. Likewise, **separate from mind and body, the human spirit is simply a breath of life from God**.

We've discovered from the Scriptures that the mind is the center of our being. Our mind has the power of will and therefore makes decisions. The mind is also the emotional and intellectual seat of our being; we therefore feel and reason with our mind.

The breath of life gives consciousness to the mind, the center of our being. The breath of life, or spirit of life, could thus be described as **the animating spiritual life force from God**. You see, our being consists of material and immaterial facets, physical and non-physical. Our immaterial being is our mind (disembodied soul). We could describe the mind as spiritual in nature and substance. **Our spiritual being (mind) requires a spiritual breath of life to live just as our physical being requires a physical breath of life to live**. In fact, "breath of life" often refers simultaneously to both spiritual and physical breath in the Scriptures. This will be made clear as we continue.

The Scriptures reveal that animals have a breath of life just as human beings do. We could therefore say that animals have a spirit, yet only in the sense that they have a breath of life. They certainly don't have a spirit in the sense that they possess a godly nature. The human being, as God's highest order of living creature on earth was created in God's image. Our spiritual makeup therefore prompts a desire to connect and commune with God and drives us toward goodness and productivity. The human spirit is endowed with this "godly nature." This is a fact whether the spirit is born-again or not. All the passages we've looked at so far on the human spirit refer to this godly nature (e.g. Matthew 26:41). The passages we will now address refer to the breath of life.

Two words are used for 'breath' in the phrase "breath of life": The Hebrew word *ruwach,* which corresponds to the Greek *pneuma,* and the Hebrew word *neshamah (nesh-aw-MAW)*. *Neshamah,* like *ruwach/pneuma,* can refer to "breath," "wind" or "spirit."[32]

So *ruwach/pneuma* and *neshamah* are basically interchangeable words. Let's turn to Genesis 7 to observe biblical support for this:

---

[32] Although *neshamah* rarely refers to the human spirit's godly nature, it does so in Proverbs 20:27.

> **Pairs of all creatures that have the <u>breath</u>**
> *(ruwach)* **of life in them came to Noah and entered the**
> **ark.**
>
> > **Genesis 7:15**

> **Everything on dry land that had the <u>breath</u>**
> *(neshamah)* **of life in its nostrils died. (23) Every living**
> **thing on the face of the earth was wiped out; men and**
> **animals... Only Noah was left, and those with him in**
> **the ark.**
>
> > **Genesis 7:22-23**

The first text refers to the animals that accompanied Noah to his ark. They had "the breath of life." The second text refers to every living thing on earth that had "the breath of life"—human and animal—that died as a result of the flood. This is plain evidence that *ruwach* **and** *neshamah* **are used interchangeably in the Bible**.

These two passages clearly show that animals as well as humans have the breath of life. This proves that the breath of life cannot be a reference to the human spirit's "godly nature" because the animal spirit possesses no such nature. This is what distinguishes animalkind from humankind: The human spirit, which is created in the image of God, possesses a godly nature whereas the animal spirit is merely a breath of life, an animating life force from the Creator. Because the human spirit is endowed with a godly nature, people possess an inherent inclination toward goodness, productivity and godliness; which is contrasted by the carnal nature, the inclination toward destruction, negativity and evil.

Animals of course have neither a spirit (godly nature) nor flesh (sinful nature). Animals are instinctual creatures that live and act by instinct. Their actions are therefore neither good nor evil, unlike human beings. <u>Chapter Four</u> of *Hell Know* offers scriptural proof that the same Hebrew and Greek words for "soul" *(nephesh/psuche)* are used in reference to animals in the Bible. Biblical translators usually render *nephesh/psuche* as "creature(s)" or "thing" in such cases (see for example Genesis 1:20,24 and Revelation 8:9 & 16:3). In these contexts "soul" *(nephesh/psuche)* must be defined in its broadest sense as "a living being." Like humans, animals are living beings or living souls, but unlike humans they lack both a spiritual dimension and carnal dimension. In other words, animals are living souls but they do not have a spirit or flesh—a godly nature or sinful nature. Because they lack the higher spiritual dimension inherent to people, animals are unaware of the existence of God and lack the ability or desire to commune with Him.

In light of this, whenever the Hebrew word for "spirit"—*ruwach*—is used in reference to animals in the Scriptures we know it always refers to the breath of life, the animating life-force of the Almighty that enables them to live. This is the extent and limit of their spiritual dimension. Let's observe support for this:

> **"I [God] am going to bring floodwaters on the earth to destroy all life under the heavens, every <u>creature</u>** *(nephesh)* **that has the <u>breath</u>** *(ruwach)* **of life in it. Everything on earth will perish."**
>
> Genesis 6:17

This verse describes both animals and humans as **nephesh** ("creatures"), which is the Hebrew word for "soul;" and then goes on to state that these creatures (souls) have the "breath of life." "Breath" here is the Hebrew word for 'spirit,' *ruwach*. Since *ruwach* is used in reference to both animals and humans we know it refers to the breath of life, the animating life force from the Almighty that sustains all living creatures, and not to what we understand as the human spirit's godly nature, the human inclination toward goodness and godliness. Animals, once again, do not have a spirit as such. Keep in mind that "breath" in this passage simultaneously refers to physical breath, which we'll look at in a moment.

All this is made clear in this passage from Psalm 104, which contextually refers to animals of all kinds (see verses 17-25) and, in fact, includes human beings as well (verse 23):

> **Thou [God] dost take away their <u>spirit</u>** *(ruwach)*, **they expire. And return to their dust.**
>
> **(30) Thou dost send forth thy <u>spirit</u>** *(ruwach)*, **they are created;**
>
> Psalm 104:29b-30a (NASB)

This text plainly shows that all animals are created by a *ruwach* from God (verse 30) and **expire** when God takes this *ruwach* away.[33]

Animals do not have a spirit in the sense of a godly nature as humans do, but both animals and humans have a spirit in the sense of a breath of life that animates and sustains them; and that's what *ruwach* in this passage is referring to. This is why most other translations do not translate *ruwach* as "spirit" in verse 29, but as "breath" (see for example the NIV, KJV and NRSV).

Let's observe another passage:

> **Man's fate is like that of the animals; the same fate awaits them both: As one dies so dies the other. All have the same <u>breath</u>** *(ruwach);* **man has no advantage over the animal. Everything is meaningless.**
>
> **Ecclesiastes 3:19**

This is an enlightening verse. It says that both humans and animals have "the same *ruwach.*" While there is the possibility that *ruwach* in this verse is referring to mere physical breath, we will see momentarily why this conclusion must be ruled out. *Ruwach* here, again, refers to the breath of life—the animating spiritual life force from God— and not to what we understand as the human spirit's godly nature. This is obvious for two reasons: **1.** The text plainly states that both humans and animals have the same *ruwach.* Since animals don't have a spirit *(ruwach)* in the sense that humans have a spirit *(ruwach), ruwach* in this passage must refer to the breath *(ruwach)* of life because we know from other passages that both humans and animals are sustained by a "breath of life." **2.** Notice that the text says that both humans and animals have "the **same** *ruwach.*" All creatures have the same animating life force from the Almighty—the same spiritual breath *(ruwach)* of life. This

---

[33] Many translations translate *ruwach* in verse 30 as "Spirit" (capitalized) giving the impression that the verse refers to God's Spirit; but let's remember that there is no capitalization in the original Hebrew. With this understanding, it is clear that *ruwach* in verse 30 refers to the same *ruwach* referred to in verse 29, that is, the breath of life—the spiritual animating life force of the Almighty. See the NRSV rendition of this text and the accompanying footnote for support.

ruwach of life is a depersonalized life force. In other words, **it is the spiritual life force that gives life to the person, but is not itself the person; it gives consciousness to the being but is not the consciousness of the being**. It's comparable to electricity that lights up a lamp: The electricity enables the lamp to have light, but the electricity is not the lamp's light. Furthermore, when the lamp is unplugged and loses its source of electricity, its light expires. The same is true in regards to God's breath *(ruwach)* of life; as the aforementioned Psalm states, "Thou [God] dost take away their spirit *(ruwach)*, they expire" (104:29 NASB).

Two verses later, in Ecclesiastes 3:21, the writer of the book speculates on where the spirit of a person and the spirit of an animal go after death: "Who knows if the spirit *(ruwach)* of man rises upward and if the spirit *(ruwach)* of the animal goes down into the earth?" It's once again obvious that *ruwach* here refers to the breath of life and this is why the NASB translates *ruwach* as "breath" in this passage (even though most others translate it as "spirit"). This verse gives evidence that the writer was not referring to mere physical oxygen—in both this passage and verse 19 above—since it would be ludicrous to argue whether oxygen "rises upward" or "goes down into the earth." What then is the writer trying to express by this question? He's simply pointing out that, from a *purely natural viewpoint* ("under the sun"—the perspective of Ecclesiastes), human beings appear to be little different than the animals and both ultimately perish from this plane of existence. In reality, however, the human soul, unlike the animal soul, is created in the image of its Creator and thus possesses a higher spiritual dimension enabling us to be aware of our Creator and desire to commune with Him.

"The Breath of Life"—the Animating Spiritual Life Force from God

Continuing our study on the breath of life, let's turn to "the creation text" once again to observe how the breath of life figures into God's creation of human beings:

The LORD formed the man from the dust of the ground and breathed into his nostrils the <u>breath</u>

(neshamah) **of life, and the man became a living <u>being</u>**
(nephesh).

Genesis 2:7

We see here that God formed the body of man out of the essential chemical elements of the earth and breathed into his nostrils the breath of life and thus he became "a *living* soul." Earlier in this appendix we saw that *nephesh,* the Hebrew word for "being" or "soul," can refer more specifically to the body. You see, a body without the breath of life is a *dead* soul *(nephesh),* but, as seen above, a body with the breath of life is a *living* soul *(nephesh).* As such, it's obvious that it's the breath of life—God's spiritual life force—that animates the mind or soul and enables us to actually live (the body, once again, is merely the facet of human nature that enables us to function in the physical realm). Elihu makes this clear:

> **"If it were His intention and He withdrew His**
> **<u>spirit</u>** *(ruwach)* **and <u>breath</u>** *(neshamah),*
> **(15) all mankind would perish together and**
> **man would return to the dust."**[34]

Job 34:14-15

---

[34] Elihu's words are reliable, as he is either a type of Christ or possibly even a theophany, a visible manifestation of Christ (a good example of a theophany would be the commander of the LORD's army that appeared in Joshua 5:13-15). The biblical support for this is as follows: **1.** Elihu claimed to be "perfect in knowledge" (Job 36:4) whereas only the LORD is "perfect in knowledge" (37:16); the Lord, as well as Job and his three friends, would have certainly rebuked Elihu for this seemingly arrogant statement if, in fact, it were not true; **2.** Elihu's questioning rebuke to Job in 37:14-23 coincides perfectly with the LORD's questioning rebuke to Job in chapters 38-41; **3.** God rebuked Job because he "spoke words without knowledge" (38:1-2), as did Elihu (35:16); **4.** Job would not or could not respond to Elihu's rebuke (as he was sure to do with each of his three friends); **5.** God rebuked Job (38:1-3; 40:1-2 & chapters 38-41) and his three friends—Eliphaz, Zophar and Bildad (42:7-9)—for their error, but He never rebukes or even mentions Elihu. *Apparently* Elihu was right and just in God's eyes; **6.** Like Christ, Elihu acted as the mediator between God and man: Elihu spoke *after* Job and his three friends and *before* God (mediating between the two); **7.** Elihu righteously showed no partiality and refused to flatter (32:21).

We see here further proof that *ruwach* and *neshamah* are used interchangeably; although in this specific passage *ruwach* would refer to God's spiritual breath—his animating life force—and *neshamah* would refer to physical breath. God's spiritual breath of life animates the mind (disembodied soul) which in turn animates the body; and the body is physically sustained by physical breath. The *ruwach* breath of life could be viewed as the spiritual counterpart to the physical *neshamah* breath of life. Just as our physical body needs air to live and function, so our disembodied soul—our mind—needs spiritual breath to live and function. Just as physical breath is not a person; neither is spiritual breath a person.

Greek and Hebrew scholar, W.E. Vine, helps us to understand this relationship between the breath of life, the disembodied soul (mind) and the body: "**The spirit** may be recognized as the life principle bestowed on man by God, **the soul** as the resulting life constituted in the individual, **the body** being the material organism animated by **soul and spirit**" (Vine 589[68]). Keep in mind that when Vine refers to "spirit" he's referring to the breath of life and when he refers to "soul" he's referring to the mind.

Secondly, we see further proof that if God withdrew His breath of life all humanity would perish and our bodies would decay back to dust.

This is evident in this Psalm passage:

> **Do not put your trust in princes, in mortal men, who cannot save.**
> **(4) When their spirit** *(ruwach)* **departs, they return to the ground; on that very day their plans come to nothing.**
> **Psalm 146:3-4**

Ruwach ("spirit") here refers to the breath of life. When the breath of life departs, the human body merely decays into the ground.

At Death the Breath of Life Merely Goes Back to God

So what happens to the breath of life when a person (or animal) dies? It merely goes back to God from whence it came. As it is written:

> Remember Him [God]—before the silver cord is severed, or the golden bowl is broken; before the pitcher is shattered at the spring, or the wheel broken at the well, and the dust returns to the ground it came from, and the spirit *(ruwach)* returns to God who gave it.
>
> Ecclesiastes 12:6-7

Verse 6 uses various metaphors to encourage us to think of our Creator before death inevitably overtakes us. Verse 7 then simply explains what happens to the human body and the breath of life when we die. The breath of life, once again, is the spiritual life force from God that animates the human being and makes it a *living* soul. The breath of life gives life to the mind/spirit in the human body. When a person dies this depersonalized life force merely returns to the Creator who gave it. This is further proof that the breath of life is not just physical oxygen. When people die their physical breath simply returns to the atmosphere; there's no need for it to return to God. Yet when we understand that the breath of life is a spiritual breath—an animating life force from God—it then makes sense that it returns to its source, the Giver of Life from which all life flows (Psalm 36:9).

The fact that the breath of life returns to God is evident in Elihu's previously quoted statement: "If it were His intention and He withdrew His spirit and breath all mankind would perish together and man would return to the dust" (Job 34:14-15). The statement "If God withdrew His spirit and breath" implies that the breath of life will simply return to God who gave it.

Sheol/Hades: The Intermediate State between Death and Resurrection

If, at death, the body returns to the ground and the breath of life (spirit) returns to God, what happens to the mind, the disembodied soul? The Bible makes it clear that the soul of unregenerated people (*not* born-again believers) goes to *Sheol* at death. *Sheol* is the Hebrew equivalent to the Greek *Hades*.[35]

In the main part of this book we discovered that Sheol is the "assembly of the dead," according to Proverbs 21:16, which corresponds to the definition of popular Hebrew and Greek scholar, James Strong: "the world of the dead" (Strong 111). Sheol refers to the condition of the unregenerated soul between physical decease and resurrection and is therefore referred to as **"the intermediate state"** by theologians. Whatever the precise state of the disembodied soul is in Sheol/Hades, it should be emphasized that it is a *temporary* condition. Every soul will ultimately be resurrected to stand before God and be judged (Revelation 20:13). The nature of Sheol is of course the main topic of *Sheol Know* whereas *Hell Know* addresses the final, permanent state of the damned, i.e. the "second death," which is the result of being cast into the lake of fire.

Although we considered the two main views of the nature of Sheol in the main body of this study, let's briefly look at them again in relation to human nature. Before we do, it should be re-stressed that the Bible clearly shows that Sheol/Hades refers to the condition of *both* righteous and unrighteous souls intermediate between physical death and resurrection, but only *before* the ascension of Christ because such souls lacked redemption in Christ. Since the Lord's resurrection, however, believers are spiritually regenerated and therefore redeemed from death (Sheol); they therefore go straight to heaven when they die, as detailed in Chapter Ten.

The reason most Christians don't realize that Sheol/Hades refers to the condition of both righteous and unrighteous souls (the former from

---

[35] Acts 2:27 quotes Psalm 16:10 where the Greek *Hades* supplants the Hebrew *Sheol*.

Old Testament periods only) is because of an interesting translation "cover up," noted in Chapter One: The policy of the King James Version translators was to translate *Sheol* as "hell" only when the passage referred to unrighteous souls (e.g. Psalm 9:17); however, when the text referred to righteous souls, they translated *Sheol* as "grave" (e.g. Genesis 37:35). Needless to say, this gives the impression to the common English reader that Sheol/Hades only refers to the condition of wicked souls between death and resurrection. It should be added that subsequent versions have corrected this translation error; in fact, many adhere to the policy of leaving Sheol/Hades untranslated (e.g. NRSV, NASB and NEB).

Let's observe the two prominent views regarding the nature of Sheol/Hades:

1. **Sheol/Hades is a place where unrighteous souls go to immediately after death and consciously suffer constant torment until their resurrection on judgment day.** According to this view, the disembodied souls of pagans who died hundreds or thousands of years ago have been in a constant state of roasting torture ever since even though they haven't even been judged yet. The only proof text for this position is Jesus' tale of the rich man and beggar from Luke 16:19-31. This story is about a rich man and poor man, Lazarus, who die and go to Sheol/Hades ("hell") where they experience highly contrasting conscious states—the rich man suffers constant fiery torment hoping for a tiny bit o' water for relief, which isn't given him, while Lazarus enjoys comfort in "Abraham's Bosom." Adherents of this position insist that this story should be taken literally and, in some cases, that the rich man and Lazarus are actual historical figures. They insist that every other reference to Sheol/Hades in the Bible must be interpreted (or ignored) in light of this literal interpretation of Jesus' tale. Amazing, isn't it?

2. **Sheol/Hades is the graveyard of dead souls where souls "experience" the condition of death itself; in short, they're dead ("sleeping") and "awaiting" resurrection.** Those who adhere to this view contend that there are countless biblical texts that support it. As we've seen in the main body of this study, the Bible describes Sheol/Hades as a state where souls cannot remember or praise God

(Psalm 6:5 & Isaiah 38:18); it is a state of silence (Psalm 31:17-18, 115:17 & 94:17); it is a condition likened unto "sleep" (Psalm 13:3, Job 3:13 & Matthew 9:24); and it is a state where souls "know nothing" because there is "no work or thought or wisdom in Sheol" (Ecclesiastes 9:5,10 NRSV). Psalm 49:14-15 even says that sheep go to Sheol; sheep of course do not go to a place of fiery conscious torture when they die, but they do enter into non-existence, the state of death. This all agrees with Revelation 20:5, which plainly says that dead souls in Sheol/Hades "did not come to life" until their resurrection after the thousand-year reign of Christ on earth. If they "did not come to life" until Judgment Day (as shown in Revelation 20:11-15) this obviously means that they will be **dead** until then. This is in complete harmony with Jesus' simple proclamation that Martha's brother—the *real* Lazarus, not the fictitious one from the parable—was **dead**, which he referred to as sleep (John 11:11-14); Jesus didn't say anything about Martha's brother—the *real* Lazarus —consciously hanging out in some nether paradise with Abraham, which would've been the case if we take his tale about the rich man and fictitious Lazarus literally. Adherents of the view that Sheol/Hades is the condition of death contend that Jesus' story of the rich man and Lazarus is obviously a parable, a symbolic and fantastical tale, and not a literal account of the nature of Sheol. They contend that since Jesus "did not say anything to them without using a parable" (Matthew 13:34b) and the tale of the rich man and beggar comes in a long string of parables and, in fact, starts with *the very same words as the previous parable*, the tale must be a parable. This is clear from its usage of symbolic language like "Abraham's bosom" (KJV) and fantastical elements, like the rich man, in agony in flames, asking Abraham to have Lazarus dip the tip of his finger in water so he could cool his tongue—not even his hand or finger, the *tip* of his finger! Like that's going to help his roasting condition one iota. It's as if Jesus was shouting in a megaphone: "This isn't meant to be taken literally!"

This second view, that Sheol/Hades is the graveyard of dead souls where souls only experience the condition of death itself—non-existence—would make sense of the Psalmist's statement:

His breath goeth forth, he [his body] **returneth to**
his earth; in <u>that very day his thoughts perish</u>.
Psalm 146:4 (KJV)

This passage makes it clear that, at death, when the body of an unsaved person returns to the dust and the breath of life returns to God, his or her very thoughts perish, that is, the their consciousness ends. This agrees with Solomon's statement that there is "no thought" in Sheol/Hades because those who are dead "know nothing" (Ecclesiastes 9:5,10). This makes sense when we understand that it is God's breath of life that actually animates our being (i.e. soul); in other words, the spirit of life grants us consciousness and enables us to live. If this spiritual force that animates our being leaves us and returns to God then our being and consciousness will naturally die. The "remains" of the soul (mind) would go to Sheol/Hades, the "realm of **the dead**." Sheol/Hades could thus be viewed as a sort of mass graveyard for the remains of souls—the common grave of humankind, which we could refer to it as "gravedom." Notice, incidentally, that the above Psalm passage says absolutely nothing about the disembodied soul of the unrighteous going to a place of fiery conscious torment when they die. On the contrary, it plainly says that their "thoughts perish"—their very consciousness expires; this is the most literal and accurate English translation of the text.

One might understandably inquire: If the Bible doesn't really teach that Sheol/Hades is a place where souls are held in a state of conscious torment until their resurrection, how did this belief become the orthodox view of Christendom? Aside from the obvious reason that our forefathers failed to adhere to a thorough and honest examination of the Scriptures, I attribute this error to two influential factors: the influence of Greek mythology and the influence of Catholic mythology. According to pagan Greek mythology, Hades—later called Pluto—is the god of the underworld where most souls endure a lethargic and empty existence while some are tormented by hideous winged spirits called Erinyes (Scott 148). Greek mythology and philosophy slowly crept into the Judeo-Christian mindset and became intermixed with biblical truths. This was the foundation upon which Dante Alighieri's *Divine Comedy* was built in the early 14th century. This famous poem is an allegorical narration of Dante's imaginary journey through Hades, purgatory and Heaven.

Dante's detailed descriptions of Hades, although plainly unscriptural and fantastical in nature, were essentially accepted as truth by the medieval Roman church. Likewise, in our present era, Mary K. Baxter's unscriptural and fantastical "divine" visions of Hades are embraced by numerous people, even more so Bill Wiese's claims in his popular book *23 minutes in Hell*. Thus many sincere Christians today adhere to a mythological view of Sheol/Hades rather than a purely scriptural one. The problem with this is that God's Word provides a rule for Christians concerning all doctrinal matters: **"Do not go beyond what is written"** (1 Corinthians 4:6). In other words, when it comes to an important topic like the nature of Sheol, don't go beyond what is written in the God-breathed Scriptures! Enough said.

All this information about Sheol/Hades provokes many questions, which are addressed and answered in the main body of this book.

The Limitations of Human Language

Getting back to "the breath of life," some readers may feel that I've gone into this issue a little too deeply, but it's important for us to understand that the Hebrew and Greek words for "spirit" *(ruwach* and *pneuma)* can refer to either the human spirit or the breath of life in biblical passages pertaining to human nature. The passage and context will determine which of these *ruwach* and *pneuma* refer to. If we assume that *ruwach* and *pneuma* always refer to the human spirit, the part of human nature that is opposed to the flesh, then the Scriptures can become very confusing. For instance, we would have to conclude that animals have a spirit just like humans have a spirit. Yet, we must understand that when God inspired people to write the Scriptures by his Holy Spirit (2 Peter 1:20-21) he was limited to flawed human language. No human language is an exact science. Language is indeed a wondrous human creation, but it often makes little sense. We saw proof of this earlier in this appendix when we saw that the Hebrew word for "soul," *nephesh,* can refer to a dead body, a living whole person (spirit, mind and body), or the immaterial facet of human nature (mind or mind & spirit). To further confuse the issue *nephesh* most often refers to "life" in the Bible.

Needless to say, the definition of *nephesh* depends on the passage and its context. So it is with the Hebrew and Greek words for "spirit."

The Greek *Pneuma* in Reference to the Breath of Life

Let us now turn our attention to the New Testament and observe occasions where the Greek *pneuma* obviously refers to the breath of life and not to the human spirit.

The following verse from Revelation is talking about God's anointed two witnesses who were killed by "the beast" and laid dead in the street for three and a half days:

> **But after three and a half days a <u>breath</u> *(pneuma)* of life from God entered them, and they stood on their feet, and terror struck those who saw them.**
> **Revelation 11:11**

Pneuma, the Greek word translated as "breath" here, obviously refers to the breath of life—God's animating life force—and not to the human spirit as described earlier in this appendix. The breath of life animates the mind and spirit, the disembodied soul, which in turn animates the body. The way this verse describes how God resurrects these two people coincides with how he gave life to Adam (Genesis 2:7) and how he miraculously brought to life a bunch of dry bones and flesh in Ezekiel 37:1-14 (a vision that the LORD gave Ezekiel).

Pneuma likely refers to the breath of life in this popular passage as well:

> **As the body without the <u>spirit</u> *(pneuma)* is dead, so faith without works is dead.**
> **James 2:26**

In light of the above-cited texts, it makes sense to regard *pneuma* here as a reference to the breath of life—the animating life force from God. If it is not a reference to the breath of life then we would have to conclude that *pneuma* in this case refers to the entire immaterial facet of human nature, mind and spirit (this is W. E. Vine's interpretation [593]). It makes little difference however, as it is God's breath of life that animates this immaterial facet of human nature which, in turn, animates the body.

Conclusion: The Biblical Definition of Human Nature

In light of all the scriptural data we have examined, human nature could best be defined as such: **The human being is a <u>living soul</u> consisting of <u>spirit</u>, <u>mind</u> and <u>body</u> animated by a <u>breath of life</u> from God.**

Here's a diagram to illustrate this:

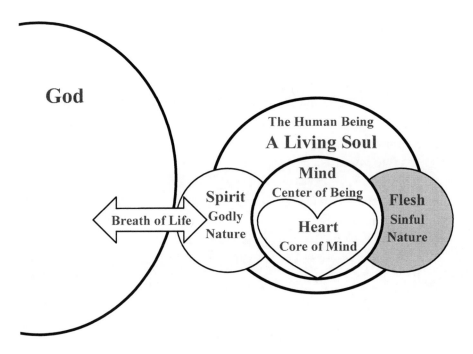

Closing Word

Sheol Know is Part II of a two-part series on human damnation. *Hell Know* is Part I and addresses the "second death," which is how the Bible describes the fate of unredeemed people cast into the lake of fire on Judgment Day. While both *Hell Know* and *Sheol Know* are stand-alone works they go hand-in-hand. If you haven't read *Hell Know*, be sure to pick up a copy.

Bibliography

Brown, Francis/Driver, S.R./Briggs, Charles A. *Brown-Driver-Briggs Lexicon.* Peabody: Hendrickson Publishers, 1994

Bullinger, Ethelbert W. *A Critical Lexicon and Concordance to the English and Greek New Testament.* Grand Rapids: Zondervan Publishing House, 1975

Dake, Finis. *Dake's Annotated Reference Bible.* Lawrenceville: Dake Bible Sales, Inc. 1961, 1963

Fackre, Gabriel/Nash, Ronald H./Sanders, John. *What About Those Who Have Never Heard?* Downers Grove: InterVarsity Press, 1995

Griesmeyer, Gary J. *The Myth of Everlasting Torment.* Gary Griesmeyer (www.wordonly.net), 2001-2003

Hagin, Kenneth E. *Man on Three Dimensions*. Tulsa: Faith Library Publications,1988

Hagin, Kenneth E. *Zoe: The God-Kind of Life.* Tulsa: Faith Library Publications, 1981

Lindsey, Hal. *The Liberation of Planet Earth.* Grand Rapids: Harper, 1974

Lindsey, Hal. *There's a New World Coming.* New York: Bantam Books, 1973

Kirkwood, David. *Your Best Year Yet!* Pittsburgh: Ethnos Press, 1996

LORD, The. *English Standard Version (ESV). Holy Bible.* Chicago: Crossway, 2001

LORD, The. *International Standard Version (ISV). Holy Bible.* Los Angeles: Davidson Press, 2013

LORD, The. *King James Version. Holy Bible.* Iowa Falls: World Bible Publishers

LORD, The. *New American Standard Bible. Holy Bible.* Nashville: Holman, 1977

LORD, The. *New English Translation (NET). Holy Bible.* Dallas: Biblical Studies Press, 2006

LORD, The. *New International Version. Holy Bible.* Nashville: Holman, 1986

LORD, The. *New International Version (Revised). Holy Bible.* Nashville: Holman, 2011

LORD, The. *New King James Version Study Bible: Second Edition.* Nashville: Thomas Nelson, 2012

LORD, The. *New Revised Standard Version. Holy Bible.* Nashville: Nelson, 1989

LORD, The. *The Amplified Bible.* Grand Rapids: Zondervan, 1987

LORD, The. *Quest Study Bible: New International Version.* Grand Rapids: Zondervan, 2003

LORD, The. *World English Bible (WEB).* Salt Lake City: Project Gutenberg, 2013

LORD, The. *Weymouth New Testament.* Ulan Press, 2012

LORD, The. *Young's Literal Translation (YLT).* Grand Rapids: Baker Books, 1989

MacArthur, John. *The MacArthur Study Bible: New King James Version.* Nashville: Word Bibles, 1997

Reagan, David. *God's Plan for the Ages: The Blueprint of Bible Prophecy.* McKinney: Lamb & Lion Ministries, 2005

Reagan, David. *Will Our Pets Be in Heaven?* Christ in Prophecy (television program).

Robertson, Pat. *Answers.* Nashville: Thomas Nelson Publishers, 1984

Scott, Miriam Van. *Encyclopedia of Hell.* New York: Martin's Press, 1998

Servant, David. *Heaven Word Daily.* Pittsburgh: Ethnos Press, 2009

Shannon, Michelle. *Do Pets Go to Heaven?* Retrieved from http://www.lamblion.com /articles/articles_religious20.php

Strandberg, Todd. *Defending the Pre-Trib Rapture.* Retrieved from https://www.raptureready.com/rr-pre-trib-rapture.html

Strong, James. *Strong's Exhaustive Concordance.* Grand Rapids: Baker, 1991

Vine, W.E. *Vine's Expository Dictionary of Biblical Words.* Cambridge: Nelson, 1985

Wright, N T. *New Heavens, New Earth: The Biblical Picture of Christian Hope.* Cambridge: Grove Books limited, 1999

Fountain of Life
Teaching Ministry
(Psalm 36:9)

The mission of Fountain of Life is to **set the captives FREE** by **reaching the world** with the **life-changing truths of God's Word,** the **power of the Holy Spirit** and the **Great News of the message of Jesus Christ.**

We're calling Warriors all over the earth to partner with us on this mission!

Other Books by Dirk Waren:

The Believer's Guide to Forgiveness & Warfare (2012)
Legalism Unmasked (2013)
HELL KNOW! (2014)

Printed in Great Britain
by Amazon.co.uk, Ltd.,
Marston Gate.